THE PETERBOROUGH BOOK OF DAYS

BRIAN JONES

First published 2014

The History Press
The Mill, Brimscombe Port
Stroud, Gloucestershire, GL5 2QG
www.thehistorypress.co.uk

British Library Cataloguing in Publication Data.
A catalogue record for this book is available from the British Library.

ISBN 978 0 7524 7932 3

Typesetting and origination by The History Press
Printed in India

– JANUARY 1ST –

1798: Until wider town roads allowed carriages to go where they wished, and increased cleanliness encouraged walking, the wealthier Peterboronians – and ladies in particular – rode or used sedan chairs. In 1790, Mr Henry Walker of Westgate had introduced a sedan chair service to the Peterborough well-to-do. These were the taxicabs of the day with set fare tables, prebooking and tipping. However, they were not regulated, so it was very much a case of 'user beware'. In late 1797, a committee was set up to organise the service and a letter of this date stated that: 'the Gentlemen of the Committee for the Management of Sedan Chairs beg leave to acquaint the Ladies of Peterborough that they may be always accommodated with Chairs by sending their orders to Mr Henry Walker in Westgate, who is appointed the Master, and is therefore answerable to provide upon due notice given'. (Tebbs, H.F., *Fenland Notes & Queries – Soke of Peterborough*, Peterborough: Oleander Press, 1979)

1904: The 1903 Motor Car Act required that all vehicles had to be registered and display the registration marks in a prominent position. Peterborough's prefix letters were 'FL'. The first one – FL1 – went to local dentist, Mr R.S. Parris, on his motorcycle. By the end of the first week, four cars and seventeen motorcycles had been registered. By 1909, Peterborough had thirty-four motor cars licenced. (Mitchell, Neil, *The Streets of Peterborough*, Neil Mitchell; 2007)

– JANUARY 2ND –

1154/5: Abbot Martin de Bec died on this day after a short illness, having taken to his bed the previous Sunday. Abbot since 1135, he can be described as the founder of modern Peterborough. He moved the 'vill' (town) and its market from the flood-prone east of the abbey to the west; leaving the old St John's church where it stood. He also built a new 'main entrance' to the monastery, still standing as the great West Gate to the cathedral and precincts, as well as repositioning the market. The latter lasted until 1968, and is now called Cathedral Square. He also laid out the roads of the town, and if he were to return today, he could safely find his way along all the town centre streets. He may, however, get a tad confused by the dancing fountains and Queensgate. (Mellows, W.T., *The Peterborough Chronicle of Hugh Candidus*, Peterborough Museum Society, 1980; Various, *People of Peterborough*, Peterborough Museum Publications, 2009)

1976: A major storm on this day did considerable damage to the cathedral; four pinnacles and half of the spire at the south-west corner were blown down. The repairs took two years, with four new pinnacles matching the damaged ones carved and placed into position and the damaged stonework at the base of the spire repaired. (Harper-Tee, John, 'The Peterborough Story', *Peterborough Evening Telegraph*, 1992)

– JANUARY 3RD –

1850: At this time Peterborough had two significant and long-established schools – The King's School and Deacon's School. The *Times of London* on this day carried the following advertisement with a box-number-style point of contact in Peterborough 'School Assistants': 'A young man about 18 is wanted who writes a good hand, is well versed in arithmetic and has been accustomed to tuition. Salary £10 per annum, with board and lodging in the family.' Which school was actually advertising was sadly not mentioned.

1928: On this day, a huge volume of water and broken ice swept into Peterborough from the upper reaches of the River Nene, swirling under the Town Bridge. The water depth gauge indicated that the river was 14ft 8in (4.5m) deep; nearly 6in (15cm) higher than the previous day and way above the norm. With the rush of water, the occupants of the cottages in the low-lying area near Bridge Street took refuge in their upper rooms. Notwithstanding the risks involved – no health and safety rules then – sightseers stood on the Town Bridge to view an immense expanse of water stretching across acres of meadowland, broken only by the treetops and hedges showing above the flood. (*Peterborough & Huntingdon Standard*)

‒ JANUARY 4TH ‒

1772: Mary Langton, in a will of this date, bequeathed the residue of her estates and effects – after payment of her debts, legacies and funeral expenses – to the minister and churchwardens of Peterborough, to be placed out on government or other securities. She directed that on the feast of the Annunciation (25 March) every year, they should distribute the interest thereof amongst the poor of the said parish not receiving alms, as they should think proper, so that no one person or family should receive more than 5s in one year. The clear residue of the testatrix's estate, which amounted to £740, was laid out in July 1777 in the purchase of £945 7s 4d. Three percent reduced annuities. By 1831, this was still held in the names of Messrs J.W. Clark, Benjamin Bull (both by then deceased), William Simpson and James Hayes, with ongoing discussions regarding a proposal to transfer the stock to new trustees. It was agreed that the dividends – then £28 7s 2d a year – would be distributed as required by the minister and church wardens among the poor persons belonging to the parish, and not receiving parochial relief, in the sum of 2s 6d each. (Parliamentary Papers, House of Commons and Command)

~ JANUARY 5TH ~

1928: On this Thursday the great flood that had hit Peterborough on Tuesday, and caused significant damage on Wednesday, showed signs of easing. There was an absence of the ice blocks that had been in evidence earlier in the week. The current was still exceptionally strong and the gauge at the bridge showed the water nearly 1ft higher than before, at 15ft 6in (4.75m) deep. A local waterman who 'knew about such things' suggested that, provided it didn't rain in the next twenty-four hours, the floods had reached their maximum, pointing out that with such a wide expanse of meadowland now taking the water, further rises in the water level were unlikely. However, the flow caused two untenanted houseboats to break from their moorings just above the Great Northern railway bridge and get swept downstream towards the Town Bridge. One became partially submerged and gradually sank, until it could pass under the bridge arches. However, as it passed under the bridge, the roof came off second best in the collision and was wrenched off. The other houseboat had swung round broadside to the bridge, and was eventually towed off and moored – thankfully, not too much worse for wear, it would seem. (*Peterborough & Huntingdon Standard*)

– JANUARY 6TH –

1928: 'Fox and Hounds Inn Gutted by Fire' was the *Peterborough & Huntingdon Standard*'s headline on 13 January. It contained a graphic description of the previous Friday's devastation in the village of Longthorpe – a day full of incident such as it had never experienced before. It described how, following the gale that had swept the countryside during the earlier part of the day and played havoc with trees, roofs and chimney pots and caused general uneasiness among many householders, the inhabitants of Longthorpe were preparing to settle down to a night of calm. That calmness was shattered when the alarm was raised. The Fox & Hounds Inn, an old and picturesque stone structure with a thatched roof standing on the main Peterborough to Wansford road, was completely gutted by fire. After many strenuous hours of fighting the flames by the Peterborough brigades, only the four walls, remnants of the ceiling and centre chimney stack were left standing. Happily, the wind had dropped to a considerable degree when the outbreak occurred, but despite this, the sparks flew in all directions, which created the danger of neighbouring thatched roofs being ignited. A careful watch was kept and a supply of water in readiness in case of such an emergency.

‒ January 7th ‒

1536: It was on this day that Katherine of Aragon, Henry VIII's first wife, died at Kimbolton Castle. Catherine always referred to herself as Henry's only lawful wedded wife and England's only rightful queen. In late December 1535 she penned one final letter to Henry, addressing him as her 'most dear lord and husband'. She is buried in Peterborough Cathedral and her resting place continues to attract many visitors from the world over. (Jones, B.R., *A Monumental & Memorial walk around central Peterborough*, TalkingHistory, 2004)

———

1897: Peterborough's late Victorian shopkeepers were tough traders: cutting prices and recycling was far from unusual. The following advertisement in the *Peterborough Advertiser* is quite typical:

BEDDING – quotations given for re-making all kinds of bedding. We are doing a large wholesale trade in this department, and defy competition for price, quality, make and wear. CASH CUSTOMERS should try us before buying elsewhere, as we never refuse a price for any of our goods if we have to SELL AT COST PRICE. Get your prices elsewhere and see if you don't save at least 3/- in the pound by offering us your READY MONEY. We shall never refuse cash so try us. We shall always be pleased with your offer even if you don't buy. Try the LONDON FURNISHING CO., Long Causeway, Peterborough.

— January 8th —

1941: One result of the defence and security measures put into place in the city during the Second World War was that they often caused different but equally dangerous situations. One such example occurred on this particular Wednesday. At 9.25 a.m. on this wet morning, Lance Corporal Dubock of the Military Police Corps was riding his motorcycle and sidecar along Lincoln Road, towards the junction with Alma Road, when he lost control on the wet road. He skidded into the path of an oncoming car, driven by a Mr Tucker. The impact threw him over the car's bonnet onto the end of a roadside air-raid shelter before he hit the ground between the shelter and a tree. Within fifteen minutes he was admitted to hospital, but died at 9.20 p.m. that evening. At the inquest the following day, Mr Tucker suggested that the air-raid shelter was in a rather dangerous position to both traffic and pedestrians. The coroner agreed, noting that most had been built on the roads due to the lack of space on the pavement, thus causing vehicles to pull out further than usual to see around bends and corners. A verdict of accidental death was returned. (Gray, David, *Peterborough at War 1939-45*, David Gray, 2011)

⁓ JANUARY 9TH ⁓

1892: During the summer of 1891, Mr and Mrs Rimes and their three boys moved into a house on Mayor's Walk. They were joined by Mr Want, her brother, and Mr Easy, her brother-in-law, as lodgers. Mr Rimes worked nights as a 'special labourer' on the railway. From late October 1891 to the early days of January 1892, Mrs Rimes, the boys and the lodgers rarely had a good night's sleep. The *Peterborough Advertiser* records that during the night-time hours, the family heard 'most unwelcome and unexpected rappings at the front door and against the partition wall of the building – noises most unmistakable and unwelcome'. The boys often experienced midnight intrusions and, on one occasion, both lodgers and the boys were all 'suddenly deprived of their bed coverings'. It came to a climax during the night of 29 December 1891, when those in the house heard something that they described as 'a huge sack of coals toppling pell-mell down the stairs'. The neighbours heard the noise as well and said it sounded like 'a cannon going off'. Several witnesses said that the 'troubles' were always preceded by a low humming sound, like that made by a rushing wind. The Rimes family moved out and nothing similar has been reported since.

— January 10th —

1797: During a spring clean in 1922, Mr G.C.W. Fitzwilliam of Milton Hall found a sixteen-page printed book, dated 1798. The book recorded the rules of the Peterborough Agricultural Society and a report of its first meeting on this day in 1797. Until the discovery of this book, the society only had records dating back to the 1830s, which had always been considered to be its founding. The book proved that wrong: it was in fact on Tuesday 10 January 1797, at a meeting held at the Angel Inn, Peterborough – under the chairmanship of Mr William Waller – that the Peterborough Agricultural Society was formed. The Earl Fitzwilliam had been elected the first President. At the first society show, the sum of 10 guineas was offered to any member of the public in general – most likely someone who worked the land for his livelihood – who would communicate to the society an effective method of destroying the wireworm in the land with perhaps an ulterior motive: two guineas were offered to the labourer in husbandry who had brought up the most numerous family without parochial assistance! (Tebbs, H.F., *Peterborough*, Oleander Press, 1979; Mellows, W.I., 'Peterborough's Municipal Jubilee', *Peterborough Standard*, 1924)

~ January 11th ~

1794: John Hinchliffe had been Bishop of Peterborough for almost twenty-five years when he died on this day after a long and paralysing illness. As bishop, he played an active role in the House of Lords during the American Revolutionary War. From 1789 until his death, he also fulfilled the role of Dean of Durham – a very long way to commute to fulfil his duties there! He was at university with Richard Cumberland – later a noted dramatist and civil servant – who had described John as 'an undergraduate below my station'. Much later he wrote that 'Hinchcliffe might well be called the child of fortune, for he was born in penury and obscurity, and was lifted into opulence and high station not by the elasticity of his own genius, but by that lucky combinations of opportunities, which merit has no share in making, and modesty no aptitude to seize'. I'd love to know what John's view of Richard was. (Carnell, Geoffrey, *The Bishops of Peterborough 1541–1991*, RJL Smith & Associates, 1993)

———

1977: Peterborough and its surroundings abound with ancient habitation; archaeology is everywhere. It was on this day that Peterborough's mayor, the Development Corporation chairman and many others gathered for the formal opening of the Archaeological Field Centre in Ham Lane, Orton Waterville – the first purpose-built archaeological field centre in the country. (Wild, J.P., *Durobrivae – a review of Nene Valley Archaeology 5*, Nene Valley Research, 1977)

— January 12th —

1850: Today's *London Daily News* raised a question with regard to the Game Act 1831 as it stood and the burden it placed on the County Rates. Major landowners bred animals for their table (or allowed natural breeding to take place). Many families, though, were perpetually short of food, especially meat. As a result, poaching in rural England was widespread. It was also a criminal offence – and getting caught usually meant prison. The bald facts presented by the *Daily News* ran as follows: 'We hear that no less than twenty-five men have been committed to Peterborough gaol within 13 days for committing trespasses in pursuit of game upon lands belonging to the Marquis of Exeter [the owner of Burghley House and its expansive estates].' Prison meant the family lost its breadwinner and frequently, therefore, became a cost on the Poor Law rates. The imprisoned poacher also cost the state money – and on his release would have a criminal record and therefore find it difficult to get work. It created a vicious downward spiral … but for what? The crime was for trespass with intent rather than theft. What was true here in Peterborough was true through most of the kingdom. Soon the laws would start changing – but too late for these Peterborians.

~ January 13th ~

1719: When Thomas Deacon died on 19 August 1721, his will – dated 13 January 1719 – changed the lives of many people, both at that time and to this day. Throughout his life he had been influential in the life of the town. He was a major landowner in and around the town, a feoffee (a trustee who holds an estate in land, for the use of a beneficial owner), a Governor of the Town Estates and a significant member of the woollen trade in the town. His will left the bulk of his land to St John's church and the town feoffees with the strict instructions that all the profits were to be used for charitable ends. One such end was that a school, with a schoolhouse, should be set up in Peterborough for the teaching and instructing of twenty poor boys whose parents had assets worth less than £50. The boys were to be taught to read, write and cast accounts and, in due time, should be placed as apprentices. The school closed and reopened in 2007 as the Thomas Deacon Academy, in buildings that OFSTED described as 'impressive and thoughtfully designed'. (Miller, Julie, *People of Peterborough*, Peterborough Museum Publications, 2009)

~ January 14th ~

1837: St Peter's Freemason's Lodge was founded in 1802, and over the next twenty years, they moved premises a number of times. In 1822 the lodge was located at the Windmill Inn (where Barclays' city centre branch is now) when, through lack of activity, the Grand Lodge erased it from membership. However, some of the members continued to meet as friends at the Windmill. Then, one evening in 1836, Thomas Ewart, a grocer new to Peterborough, joined them for a drink. Talk turned to Freemasonry and Thomas persuaded the group to re-form their lodge. Having been persuaded, they applied for a new warrant, were accepted and St Peter's Lodge was finally reconsecrated on this Saturday, with Thomas Ewart as their first master. All that was needed now was the formal evening meal – known as a Festive Board. Unfortunately, there was no food available at the Windmill, as the landlady had passed away just before the consecration ceremony took place. Undeterred, the group crossed the Market Place to The Talbot and dined well. They didn't desert the Windmill though – they just seem to have added to their rules that there was to be no eating or drinking at the Lodge meetings. (Peterborough Local History Society Magazine)

$-$ January 15th $-$

1889: The *Peterborough Advertiser* of 19 January carried a small article on a woman who went by the name of Alice McKenzie. It reported that at 10 a.m. on 15 of January, she had entered Mrs Popp's pork butcher's shop in Long Causeway and purchased a pennyworth of 'chitterlings' (the small intestines of a pig), which she immediately devoured in the shop, in such a hurried way that Mrs Popp formed the distinct impression that she was starving. Having eaten these she demanded more $-$ for free. Mrs Popp called for help from the police $-$ more, she said, to get Alice out of her shop than to have her arrested. When PC Smith arrived, he took Alice out of the shop and straight to the police station in Milton Street $-$ with Alice singing her head off. At the station she was charged with begging, but at the court hearing, the chairman of the bench stated that there was no basis for a conviction and Alice was free to go. Six months later, the national newspapers were reporting on Alice McKenzie again. She had been found dead in Castle Alley, Whitechapel. Could she have been the eighth and final victim of Jack the Ripper? (*Peterborough Local History Society Magazine*)

— January 16th —

1818: What was described as a numerous and highly respectable meeting, with the Rt Hon. Earl Fitzwilliam in the chair, was held at Peterborough Town Hall on this Friday for the purpose of 'taking into consideration the most efficient measures for the establishment of a Savings Bank in that city for the benefit of its industrious poor inhabitants and those of its neighbourhood'. The savings bank was to be formed for 'the purpose of providing a secure and profitable investment for the savings of the frugal and industrious of the community'. It would be achieved as follows:

> [by] establishing and maintaining an Institution to receive deposits of money for the benefit of the persons depositing the same and to accumulate the produce of so much thereof as shall not be required by the depositors, their executors or administrators, to be paid in the nature of compound interest; and to return the whole or any part thereof to the depositors, their executors or administrators deducting only out of such produce so much as shall be required to be retained for the purpose of paying and discharging the necessary expenses attending the management of such institution according to the regulations herewith specified.

(Huntingdon, Bedford and Peterborough Gazette)

~ JANUARY 17TH ~

1897: Two Salvation Army Officers, armed with the requisite brooms and suitably rigged, ragged and disguised, practised the art of 'faking' – the name given to crossing sweeping by professionals. Relating their experiences – extended over a considerable time and a wide area – the amateur sweepers arrived at the conclusion that unless one had a really good crossing, and that, too, on a very muddy day, pence were few. If the road was fairly clean the average man in the street was apt to treat the mournful 'faker' – although he simulated the most racking cough – with scorn by crossing beside, not on, the cleanly swept path. At the same time the investigating Salvationists brought the knowledge that there are crossing sweepers who manage to make a decent living, but by also working up a connection in window cleaning, running errands, and doing odd jobs in genteel neighbourhoods. However, the poor fellow who spends his last copper in the purchase of a penny second-hand broom, and sallies in search of a crossing to sweep, may well deem himself fortunate if at the end of the day he has gained enough to secure a shelter for the night and food for the morrow. (*Peterborough Advertiser*)

− January 18th −

1929: On this Friday, the *Peterborough & Huntingdon Standard* carried a report on a court case concerning bus proprietor Thomas Arthur Smith of Bourne, who pleaded not guilty to a summons for driving a motor bus at a speed exceeding 20mph at Werrington on 15 December 1928. PC Trundle stated that he had followed the bus on his motorcycle and found it to be travelling at 32mph. Under cross-examination, he said that he would not consider it excessive if the defendant allowed an hour to travel from Bourne to Peterborough. Smith responded that he had been warned that there was a speed trap being used and was careful not to exceed 20mph. Under oath, he said that he left Bourne a few minutes after 10 a.m., was stopped by the policeman for not quite ten minutes and arrived at Peterborough at 11.15 a.m. Mr Brompton Wadsley of Thurlby, an agent to the Central Sugar Beet Co., stated that he could see the speedometer all the way and the speed was never more than 20mph. He had an appointment in Peterborough and became rather anxious, because the bus was going slowly. The defendant was found guilty and fined £1.

1893: Following a proposal by Alderman Percival, the city obtained a Merryweather & Sons steam fire engine, 'for the better protection of life and property'. It arrived on this day. during the mayoralty of Joseph Clifton. In 1882, Clifton had moved from Stamford, where he had been landlord of the Crown Hotel, to Peterborough to take charge of the Angel Hotel on Narrow Bridge Street. In 1884, he joined the Peterborough Volunteer Fire Brigade and became its captain in 1890. He was also a great supporter of the city Fire Brigade. During this time, he kept the volunteers' firefighting equipment in the coach house attached to the Angel Hotel. To mark his long-standing support of the fire services in Peterborough, the 'Merryweather' ‒ Peterborough's first steam fire engine ‒ was named 'The Clifton'. (Mellows, W.I., 'Peterborough's Municipal Jubilee', *Peterborough Standard, 1924*)

1988: The *Peterborough Evening Telegraph* reported on this day that, despite city councillors having decided that extra security for city flats was needed to beat thieves, vandals, vagrants, and the like, their £475,000 scheme for entry phones and electric locks for every flat would not be completed until 2004, unless extra cash was found.

~ January 20th ~

1928: The rail yards of Peterborough were a dangerous place to work. On this Friday evening, a horse was killed and its attendants had a narrow escape when a number of shunting trucks crashed into a lorry at the wharf sidings at Peterborough East station. The lorry, loaded with three tree trunks weighing about 3 tons, belonged to Mr Charles Baker of Woodston, and was in charge of his son, Mr Alfred Baker, and Mr W. Stimson. Drawn by three horses in single file, it had cleared the shunting lines, but the end of one of the trees overhung the track. The foremost of six railway wagons crashed into the obstacle with such force that the lorry was pushed over, the trees rolling to the ground. The horse nearest the lorry fell, and was pinned down by one of the trunks, which lay across its hindquarters, although the two attendants jumped clear of the falling trees. The unfortunate animal died almost immediately, despite the timber being quickly dragged clear by willing assistants. The other two horses were not hurt, but the shafts were broken. The side of the lorry which came into contact with the truck was badly damaged. (*Peterborough & Huntingdon Standard*)

— JANUARY 21ST —

1898: The carriage works of Brainsby's in Cumbergate, along with two shops in Westgate, in the occupation of Messrs Baker & Cooper, were destroyed by a major fire. This area later became the rear access to the post office's parcel depot. The firm would rise again as Thomas Brainsby & Sons in 1905, building bodies for such cars as Crossley, Fiat and Hotchkiss, as well as a fair number for Rolls-Royce. The company faded away in the 1920s then re-appeared as Brainsby-Woolard, constructing coach-built bodies. This firm was a partnership between the original Brainsby family and a salesman by the name of Charles Harry Woolard. It ceased operation in 1936. (Mitchell, Neil, *Streets of Peterborough*, 2007; Mellows, W.I., 'Peterborough's Municipal Jubilee', *Peterborough Standard*, 1924)

1929: An outbreak of foot-and-mouth disease was discovered on this Monday morning among dairy cows at the farm of Mr William Heading at 210 Lincoln Road, Walton. The owner noticed that one or two of his cattle were not well and reported the matter to the police; later that day an inspector from the Ministry of Agriculture and Fisheries (now known as Defra) confirmed the disease. A restriction order covering a 15-mile radius from Walton was declared and a ministry official became resident in the city. This outbreak was nearer the city than had ever occurred before and all appropriate people were advised that 'too much precaution cannot be taken'. A total of thirty-four cattle and six pigs were destroyed. (*Peterborough & Huntingdon Standard*)

— January 22nd —

1991: This Tuesday was Princess Diana's first official visit to the city. Her prime reason for the visit was to attend the World Leprosy Day service at the cathedral. Afterwards, on her way to the Town Hall to see the Eurotunnel Exhibition, she flouted the formality of royalty and indulged in a walk down Bridge Street to chat to the crowds, many of whom had been waiting for three hours or more for her. She lunched at the Haycock at Wansford, where the guests had paid £100 or more each for the privilege, all the money going to help build a leprosy hospital in Thailand. Diana then returned to Peterborough to visit the Sue Ryder Home at Thorpe Hall, where she met Lady Ryder. She then spent some time talking to the staff as well as the people who were involved in getting the building into shape. The princess' day ended with a visit to the King's School as a part of its 450th anniversary commemoration. She made a return visit to the area in May of the same year, when she visited RAF Wittering with Prince Harry. The 7-year old was 'pleased as punch' to be allowed to sit in the cockpit of a Harrier jump-jet. (Harper-Tee, John, 'The Peterborough Story', *Peterborough Evening Telegraph*, 1992)

– January 23rd –

1903: It was on this Friday that the long-delayed Board of Trade inspection of Peterborough's new tram system took place – officialdom always takes its time, you know. Two trams left the depot for the Market Place to pick up the official parties. When everyone – including the inspectors – was on board the first car, the driver set off with a fearful jerk, throwing virtually all the officials off their feet! One wonders if this was a case of nerves, carelessness or intent – we'll never know that. However, the driver reversed the car, made a fresh start and moved off in an extremely smooth manner. The second car followed on, carrying several members of the council and members of the press. Despite this faulty start, the trams passed the test with flying colours. The Peterborough tram service was formally approved and trams from Long Causeway to Walton and Dogsthorpe were able to start carrying passengers. At this time, the Peterborough Electric Traction Co. had twelve open-top trams for the service. Why, you may ask, were the trams open top? It was because roofed trams would have been too high to pass under the Rhubarb Bridge! (Mitchell, Neil, *Streets of Peterborough*, 2007; *Peterborough Advertiser*)

— January 24th —

1798: At a previous meeting, the 'Gentlemen of the Committee for the Management of Sedan Chairs' had discovered that many of the sedan chairmen – the men who carried the passengers – had been underpaid. As a result, in a meeting held on this day, they issued a tariff of fixed rates. Notification of this tariff was to be in clear view of users. 'Taking a passenger to and from a dinner or tea visit would be charged at one shilling. If the passenger was to be taken to or from an Assembly or a Ball the charge would be one shilling and six pence. Furthermore – if the chairman was kept waiting beyond the usual time at which they are ordered to attend, they shall, after having given notice they are in waiting, be allowed additional payment at the rate of sixpence for every half hour waiting. However, the extra fare was not to be extended to the monthly assemblies.' A proviso also advised that the person to be carried must not exceed 20 stone in weight! The last sedan chair hired was for Miss Percival in 1864. (Tebbs, H.F., *Peterbrough*, Oleander Press, 1979; Mitchell, Neil, *Streets of Peterborough*, 2007)

– January 25th –

1913: At the monthly meeting of the Peterborough Rural District Council on this Saturday there was a deep debate recorded by the *Peterborough Citizen* the following Tuesday under the headline 'Castor invasion by Peterborough house hunters – What Castor Expects'. Peterborough was expanding and new houses were desperately needed, leading to what we now call 'Not in my backyard' syndrome rearing its head. Castor parish council did not think it was desirable to erect the proposed houses and suggested a different type of house, each having a rood of land and being more suitable for widows and retired men. Cllr Goodyer argued that the new houses should be for working men, as there were already more cottages for the elderly than workers in Castor. Cllr Kemp, however, commented that there were already plenty of cottages for widows and old men. It was workmen's cottages that were needed now. Cllr Lee responded that he did not think that, as agricultural people, they would not be able to pay the rent. The clerk, having heard these comments, concluded that it would be impossible for people to pay 4*s* 6*d* and rates. The meeting moved on with no decision recorded.

– January 26th –

1861: During a recent spell of very bad weather, the Guardians of the Peterborough Poor Law Union had granted temporary outdoor relief to some able-bodied agricultural labourers who had been unable to work through no fault of their own. As a result, the National Board had requested that they be furnished with a statement showing the number of persons relieved that were at variance to the General Prohibitory Order. They also requested particulars of the numbers of persons in each family and the amount of relief that had been afforded. At this Saturday's meeting of the Board of Governors of the Peterborough Poor Law Union, the clerk read a letter that had come from the National Poor Law Board. It stated that 'having regard to the accommodation afforded by the workhouse, and to the number of inmates therein, the Board thought it desirable that the Guardians should, in future, offer to relieve the necessities of this class of person in the workhouse. They should apply that test of destitution so long as the circumstances permitted with regards to each application.' In other words, 'rules is rules', and using common sense and compassion are not allowed. (*Lincoln, Rutland and Stamford Mercury*)

— January 27th —

1871: St Paul's church in New England – the Railwayman's church – faced many obstacles in its early days. The *Peterborough Standard* of 5 March carried the following plea that must have stemmed from some serious head scratching on this Tuesday back in late January:

> St. Paul's Church, New England: The Committee under whose superintendence the above Church has been erected ventures to appeal to the clergy, gentry, and the tradesmen of Peterborough and its neighbourhood, for subscriptions to enable them to provide for the liquidation of their remaining liabilities. The entire outlay on account of the building has amounted to £4761 4s 1d whilst the total subscriptions up to the 27th January were as follows:- Great Northern Railway Shareholders £3,369 6s 9d and General Subscribers £1,077 0s 11d = a total of £4,446 7s 8d leaving a deficiency of £314 16s 5d without taking into account the cost of lighting the Church, which is yet to be provided for.

There then followed a list of fifteen contributors who had collectively provided £99 18s 6d in sums ranging from 10s to £50, followed by: 'Further subscriptions will be thankfully received by the Treasurer, Henry Pearson Gates Esq, The Vineyard, Peterborough.'

- JANUARY 28TH -

1909: On this day, the American House of Representatives suspended business while Congressman Boutelle declared that 'everyone who has read of the collision between the *Republic* and the *Florida* must feel that there was one silent actor in the tragedy whose name should be immortalised, the Marconi operator on the *Republic*, Mr John R. Binns'. John Binns (who was also known as Jack) went to St Mark's school in Gladstone Street, and the Boys National School (both in Peterborough) before starting work aged 15 in the Great Eastern Station telegraph office. In 1901, he began work as senior operator in the Colchester telegraph office. Over the next eight years he built up a reputation of outstanding excellence while teaching himself how to fix broken lines, apparatus, and connections and completing a Marconi three-month Telegraphy & Shorthand course in just five weeks. In January 1909, as chief telegraph operator on the RMS *Republic*, he set sail from New York with passengers seeking Mediterranean warmth instead of a cold American winter. In thick fog on 24 January, the steamship *Florida* rammed the *Republic*. For the next eleven hours, Jack used all his skills to improvise repairs to his damaged transmitter and seek help. All passengers were saved. (jackbinns.org; *Peterborough Local History Society Magazine Millennium Edition*)

~ January 29th ~

1536: On this Wednesday, Katherine of Aragon, the first wife of King Henry VIII, was buried in Peterborough Abbey. Her funeral cortège had left Kimbolton on Monday, had stopped overnight at Sawtry and, after morning Mass there, her body was borne to Peterborough. There, at the door of the church, 'it was honourably received by the Bishops of Lincoln, Ely, and Rochester, the Abbot of Peterborough and the Abbots of Ramsey, Crowland, Thorney and others'. Each, wearing their mitres and hoods, accompanied it in procession to the Chapel of Rest, which had been prepared in anticipation of the queen's arrival. There the body was placed upon eight pillars of beautiful fashion and roundness, upon which were placed about 1,000 candles, while eighteen banners were hung around the chapel. Solemn vigils were said that day. On this, the following day, 29 January, three bishops each performed Mass. Afterwards, the body was buried in a grave at the lowest step of the high altar, over which they put a simple black cloth. 'In this manner was celebrated the funeral of her who for 27 years had been true queen of England.' Records show that 12*d* paid 'for drink for the bell ringers at the burial of Katherin of Aragonuriel'. (Jones, B.R., *A Monumental & Memorial walk around central Peterborough*, TalkingHistory, 2004)

~ January 30th ~

1897: On this Saturday, so the *Peterborough Citizen* tells us, the quarterly meeting of the Peterborough Local Government and Municipal Offices Association was held at the Bedford coffee house. The meeting is actually described as a continuation of a previously adjourned quarterly meeting. As the association is reported to have only been formed for three months, that doesn't seem to harbour a good future! However, it was reported that they already had a membership roll of twenty-one – a gratifying achievement – although just twelve members were recorded as present at this meeting. Described as being of a business character, they discussed the Superannuation Bill which, they said, was promised to be brought before Parliament during the present Session. It was pointed out that the bill was a scheme which had been formulated years ago – so there's nothing new there, then. A motion to support the bill was carried unanimously but, it was decided that they would not petition the local MP until the bill was brought before Parliament. Political procrastination is nothing new either. The journalist was probably bored by now because the report finishes with the comment 'this was all the business of public interest'!

— JANUARY 31ST —

1818: On this day the *Huntingdon, Bedford and Peterborough Gazette* carried the following notice: 'In the first page of this day's paper we present to our readers a detailed prospectus of Peterborough's creation on 16 January last of one of those most excellent institutions called Savings Banks. Much has already been said in favour of these establishments. In many humble families where the odd pence had formally been expended in libations at the ale house, they have been suffered to accumulate in the Savings Banks, till the pence have amounted to such sums as have enabled the humble cottager to introduce many article of domestic comfort to his family, that were hitherto strangers to his fireside. Cleanliness and contented cheerfulness have in many instances succeeded to penury and squalid misery. We would particularly draw the attention of the heads of families to the important subject; as by inducing their servants and dependents to invest their surplus monies in these institutions they will inculcate such a spirit of industrious frugality as will not only benefit their employers but ultimately improve the conditions of Society at large. This institution is open to the inhabitants of the surrounding villages in either county.'

1858: Over the years there have been a number of railway stations in Peterborough. Peterborough East was the first, opening in 1845 to serve the Eastern Counties Railway (ECR). The Great Northern Railway (GNR) first used the East station but soon realised that they needed their own – this opened in August 1850. By 1853, their railway heading north was operational, with the line running alongside the Midland Railway as far as Helpston with adjacent but separate level crossings at various places, including the Crescent level crossings in Peterborough city centre. The interchange between the two stations was inconvenient, so on this day the Midland Railway opened the Peterborough Crescent station – a short distance from the GNR station. This significantly simplified the passenger interchange. Bit by bit, the rail companies rationalised their operations. The Midland Railway trains began using the GNR station and, on 1 August 1866, the Crescent station closed after just eight years of operation. An often-asked question is 'Why Crescent station – and now Crescent Bridge?' The name comes from the beautiful crescent of houses – similar to those in Bath – that were swept away to make room for the railways in the first place. (Various sources)

— February 2nd —

1630/1: Children were a problem around Peterborough's wells. Every well had a winch and bucket, which were often misused. There are many references to the carpenter being paid to do repairs or inserting a pin to prevent them being overwound. Today's record says: 'To Clarke the carpenter for takeing out of the Towne Well the 2 buckettes and for making of pins to stay the wheel that the boys may not turn yt and so break the roape ... 6*d*'. (Tebbs, H.F., *Peterborough*, Oleander Press, 1979)

1928: At around 10 p.m. on this day, the city fire brigade was called to a fire on Padholm Road at the premises of Mr Leo Hammond, builder and undertaker. Two men had noticed flames and smoke billowing from a wooden shed at the end of the garden, and immediately raised the alarm. With help from a Mr Flatt, they had rescued some chickens from a nearby shed. The brigade were sadly unable to save Hammond's shed, which had contained several benches and a quantity of tools. The fowl house was slightly damaged but the brigade prevented a further spread of the flames. By 11 p.m., the fire was completely extinguished and the brigade left. The cause of the fire remained a mystery. (*Peterborough & Huntingdon Standard*)

— FEBRUARY 3RD —

1830: The earliest street lighting in Peterborough – using tallow candles – appears to have been in Westgate in the mid to late eighteenth century. By the end of the century, various oils, including whale oil and later colza oil (a non-drying oil obtained from rape seeds), were being used. As the nineteenth century progressed, some started to consider the use of coal gas for lighting purposes. The British Gas Light Co. was formed in 1824, but discussion between it and Peterborough broke down. It didn't stop the city getting gas lighting, though. John Malam had been trained by Matthew Boulton in the creation and use of gas for lighting. His equipment was in use at the Westminster Gas Works in London when he set up his own private company at the northern end of St John's Street with the aim of supplying gas lighting to Peterborough's streets. His first gas lamp came into use in City Road – the first lamp being lit on this day. By 1844, most of Boonfield had gas lamps as well. Malam's business was eventually taken over by Theo Sawyer, an ironmonger in Narrow Bridge Street. In 1868, the company would become the Peterborough Gas Co., with a £10,000 capitalisation. (Mitchell, Neil, *Streets of Peterborough*, 2007)

— FEBRUARY 4TH —

1808: When a number of French Napoleonic prisoners of war were scheduled to be taken under armed guard from the town to the Norman Cross prisoner of war camp, things didn't quite go to plan. Due to the lateness of the hour, the British soldiers of the 77th Regiment guarding them decided not to expose themselves to the risk of the prisoners escaping into the night and instead placed them in the backyard of the Angel Inn in Narrow Bridge Street. Guards were in place and all settled down for a quiet night. However, one of the prisoners decided to make a break for it and began to climb over the wall. He declined to stop when told – perhaps he spoke no English – and was shot as he climbed the wall. Dr T.J. Walker records him as 'dying in twenty minutes'. Some say that his dead body was left half over the wall as a deterrent to others. Certainly, no one else tried a similar escape that night – or during the march to Norman Cross in the morning. The subsequent inquest brought in a verdict of 'justifiable homicide'. In another incident, a prisoner jumped from Nene Bridge and was shot as he surfaced. (Walker, T.J., *The Depôt for Prisoners of War at Norman Cross, Huntingdonshire 1796 to 1816*, Constable & Co, 1913; Lloyd, Clive L., *A History of Napoleonic & American Prisoners of War 1756–1816*, Antique Collectors' Club, 2007)

– February 5th –

1872: At an inquest today, a Peterborough coroner was investigating the case of 'an unknown male infant whose body had been found in the cesspool of a privy at Marholm'. From the post-mortem, he deduced that the child had been dead some six weeks but that it was not possible to presume whether the child had been born alive or dead. At the following quarter session, Harriet Green, a servant girl in the employ of Mrs Mann of Helpston, was brought before the sessions accused of 'concealment of a baby at birth'. Harriet had complained of back trouble and retired to her room the previous September. Mrs Mann sent for a doctor but Harriet refused to let him into her room and left early one morning without giving any notice. When the baby was found Harriet denied that it was hers but, when the soiled apron was found in her room, she confessed and was promptly arrested. She stated that the baby was a fine child and did not cry. She admitted putting the child into a slop bucket and depositing it in the privy at the bottom of the garden. She was sentenced to three months' imprisonment. (*Peterborough Advertiser*)

~ February 6th ~

1686: A letter from Lieutenant Francis Tanckred to the Duke of Somerset records an incident on this day.

Pardon the boldness of a poor lieutenant's writing to you, but it is to desire justice so I do not fear it. Wednesday night last – February 6th – Mr Justice Hack came to beg my assistance to take some rogues that had slit a woman's nose, almost killed a child and threatened the death of a man that came to him for justice. They had set up their flag of defiance against the poor country people. I sent the quarter-master with 16 men to surprise them or fire on them if they incurred any opposition. He took them all napping by their mistresses and brought them before Mr Hack who has committed them to prison. No harm was done to the dragoons or them. They brought their arms and colours with them….. PS Our soldiers are happy here, for the townspeople love them and I am really happy in a good bishop, the clergy and all the gentry.

(Longden, H.I., *Harleian Society*, 1935)

— FEBRUARY 7TH —

1556: After fifteen years of what Symon Gunton described as 'new transformed government', John Chambers, the last abbot of Peterborough monastery and first Bishop of Peterborough, died. In modern parlance, John knew how to 'go with the flow' and 'not to ruffle too many feathers'. Gunton – the seventeenth-century author of *The History of the Church of Peterborough* – wrote 'but probable it is, that Abbot John loved to sleep in a whole skin and desired to die in his nest wherein he had lived so long, and perhaps might use such means, as might preserve (if not his means to his Church, yet) his Church to posterity'. Chambers was also living proof that it is who you know rather than what you know that can have most influence on career advancement. His contemporaries called him the 'luckiest of all', but surviving the machinations of Cardinal Wolsey and Thomas Cromwell, and the religious uncertainty of Tudor times needed skills as well. The support of John Russell, 1st Earl of Bedford – one of the most powerful men during this part of the sixteenth century – did no harm either! One could see John being just as successful in the modern world. (Dawes, Joan, *People of Peterborough*, 2009; Gunton, Symon, *The History of the Church of Peterborough* 1686/1990; Carnell, G.C., *The Bishops of Peterborough*, 1993)

- February 8th -

1653: On this day, John Ashley and Sampson Frisby contracted with Lord Chief Justice of the Commonwealth, Oliver St John, for thirty-eight windows for a mansion at Hill Close, Longthorpe. Later known as Thorpe Hall, it was one of the very few 'grand' houses built during the time of the Commonwealth. (Bunten, J. and McKenzie, R., *The Soke of Peterborough*, 1991)

1800: John Montague assaulted John Blake with intent to rob on this day. Blake had seen Montague in the Fox & Hounds public house at Longthorpe and later, as he went home, he was attacked by Montague, who pushed him off the road and demanded his money. A skirmish followed and they fell into a ditch together. Three witnesses stated that they had heard groans from the ditch and found the pair, with Montague lying on Blake, who accused Montague of attempted theft and murder. Montague claimed Blake had called him a 'wild ruffian' and that 'the old man attempted to murder him by striking him with a stick'. The reporter records that 'Montague is an American who broke out of Peterborough gaol some time ago, and conducted himself in a very impudent hardened manner during his trial'. He was found guilty and sentenced to 'deportation to the eastern coast of New South Wales, Australia for seven years'. (*Lincoln, Rutland and Stamford Mercury*)

— FEBRUARY 9TH —

1901: One thing that strikes me as I trawl through the stories of Peterborough's past is the frequency of charitable functions in the late Victorian and Edwardian eras. Organised by the great and the good of the city, these gatherings seem to have been consistently well supported by the working families of the city. On this day, the *Huntingdon Standard* carried a piece headlined 'Hospital Saturday Fund' which is very much a case in point. It is from the Infirmary, Peterborough, dated 25 January 1901, and it reads:

Sir: I am requested to send you as Chairman of the Hospital Saturday Committee a copy of a resolution passed unanimously at the annual meeting of the Governors held at the Infirmary on Tuesday last, January 22nd 1901, viz: 'That the Governors at this Meeting wish to record their thanks for the liberal contributions of the Working Classes of Peterborough and District, amounting this year to £380 (three hundred and eighty pounds) handed over by the Hospital Saturday Committee, and also that thanks be given to those ladies and gentlemen who collected on Hospital Saturday.' I am, sir, your obedient Servant, A.C. TAYLOR, Secretary. F. Rouse, Esq., Chairman, Hospital Saturday Committee.

— FEBRUARY 10TH —

1885: On this day, the *Peterborough Standard* announced that:

> A large piece of land, situated on the Park Road, at the rear of Willis's Auction Rooms, has been purchased for the purpose of erecting a Catholic church and presbytery. The plot of ground, 2,765 yards in extent, was purchased for £1,782 8s 4d. It has frontage to Park Road, Fitzwilliam Street and the road bounding Mr Little's property. It will be a handsome stone edifice, consisting of nave, north and south aisles, transepts, chancel, and probably a tower. Adjoining it will be a presbytery.

The church opened in October 1896. (*Peterborough Local History Society Magazine*)

1928: The high winds on this day had developed into a gale by the early hours of Saturday. During the night, the telephone call box by the side of the town clerk's office was blown from its base, while the glass front of the official noticeboard hanging on the wall of the office was smashed by the force of the wind. Policemen on night duty had a busy time finding and rousing the owners of properties where sun blinds were blown down and doors were forced open. Among the shops losing their blinds was Freeman, Hardy & Willis in Long Causeway, while the New Inn in New Road had its door wrenched off its hinges. (*Peterborough Standard*)

⁓ FEBRUARY 11TH ⁓

1823: Receiving rewards for casting your vote for the 'right' man – or bribery, as we call it now – at parliamentary elections was common at this time. Any 'scot and lot' voter (a person who paid a church or poor rate in Peterborough borough) who asked could have 10s a year off his rent and 5s for every vote he cast for the Fitzwilliam nominee. However, any tenant not voting 'correctly' was liable to have notice to quit at the end of the year. When Sir James Scarlett won his by-election on being appointed Attorney General in 1823, an unknown local diarist noted that: 'Feb 11 Election; Scarlett 523, Wells 31: April 10 – Scarlett paid his voters'. He made a similar entry following the 1857 election; simply recording 'Election: nothing but bribery.' (Tebbs, H.F., *Peterborough*, Oleander Press, 1979)

1871: Peterborough experienced an extended cold snap from Tuesday 8 February through to Friday 18, with this Friday being the coldest at just 19 degrees Fahrenheit. Though the river was only partially frozen, and not safe for skating, there was plenty of sound ice on the extensive area of flood waters. As a result, skaters and sliders of both sexes and all ages put on their 'pattens' (wooden soled sandals that fitted over normal shoes and boots) and had fun. (*Peterborough Standard*)

— February 12th —

1871: The previous day's fun turned to tragedy on this date when 20-year-old William Royce and his younger brother John went skating on the flood ice. Eyewitnesses reported that ice appeared to give way beneath William and that he shot into the river feet first. John and others rushed into the water to attempt to rescue him, but without effect, the only result being to put their lives at risk as well. The body was retrieved but, despite the efforts of two doctors, William died. A post mortem that evening returned a verdict of 'Accidentally drowned while skating'. (*Peterborough Standard*)

1901: At the Norman Cross Petty Sessions, Edward Abbott, labourer of Yaxley, was summoned by Superintendent Allen for committing an act on a public footpath at Yaxley on 2 February. Pleading guilty, Abbott was fined 5*s*. I just wonder what this act might have been! (*Peterborough Advertiser*)

1928: At 8 p.m. at the city picture house, a grand concert by Daisy Strickson in aid of the War Memorial Hospital was held. Pieces by Chopin, Bach, Monti, Sehira and Weber were followed by a five-minute interval. Pieces by Wagner, Liszt, Carey and Chopin were followed by a closing piano and organ duet of Wagner's 'Athemest du Nicht', performed by Daisy Strickson and Frank C. Olsen. (*Peterborough Advertiser*)

— February 13th —

1154/5: Following the death of Abbot Martin de Bec, 'all the congregation met together to choose a man among them who should be their father and shepherd, and guardian lest by reason of their delay some stranger should make his way in by payment of bribes'. They chose William de Waterville. All formalities and procedures were followed and on this first Sunday of Lent, 'with a great procession he was welcomed into his own home of Burch (the name of Peterborough at that time)'. (Mellows, W.T., *The Peterborough Chronicle of Hugh Candidus*, Peterborough Museum Society, 1980)

———

1901: The records of the Petty Sessions on this day give us a glimpse of a very different Peterborough to that of twelfth-century monastic life. John Chambers (horse keeper) and Arthur Frisby (engineman), both of Orton Longueville, were summoned for being drunk and disorderly on the highway at Castor and were fined 10s plus 3s cost each; the Bench dismissed a case of assault between Matthew Dawson and Edward Emblow when the two protagonists produced conflicting evidence; and 19-year-old domestic servant Annie Berridge was accused and found guilty of obtaining 4s from Martha Withers by false pretences. She pleaded guilty, but the chief constable stated she had never been in trouble before, so she was instead bound over for twelve months, to appear if called upon (*Peterborough Advertiser*)

~ February 14th ~

1824: John Thompson, son of builder John Thompson, 'arrived' today. Gwen Beatty suggests that the best way to start talking about John Jr is to ask, 'What was he NOT involved in?' John became famous across the country for building churches and cathedrals – two of which were in Peterborough. Between 1883 and 1887, he rebuilt the central tower of Peterborough Cathedral. He also built and partially financed St Mark's, where he worshipped, taught at Sunday school and served as churchwarden. He was elected a city councillor in 1874; made a city alderman in 1888; and served as city mayor four times between 1881 and 1897. Following his death in 1898, the *Peterborough Advertiser* noted that 'his whole life appeared to be concentrated on God and to the moral and spiritual welfare of his fellow men'.

1964: The *Peterborough Advertiser* carried an article with the headline 'A man with a job which is not due to finish before the year 2000!' That man was landscape consultant Arnold Weddle, who was to oversee a £1.5 million project reclaiming some 2,000 acres of derelict brick-pit fly ash around Fletton. For over 100 years it had been a key player in Peterborough's growth, and its replacement would be another significant element of our twenty-first century city – the new Southern Township of Hampton. (*Peterborough Advertiser*)

— FEBRUARY 15TH —

1871: As the extreme cold weather continued, a skating match was arranged for this Tuesday afternoon with a prize of a leg of mutton for the winner and a shoulder of mutton for second place. The race surface for amateurs was considered very good. The *Peterborough Standard* reported that, 'the floods near the north Bank where the trials came off, presented a very animated appearance'. There were ten entries for the races. The final was between Messrs C Richmond, R. Blades (both of Peterborough) and T. Payne (of Stanground). Richmond succeeded in carrying off the leg of mutton and Payne the shoulder, leaving Blades with nothing but the paper's comment that he finished 'with the satisfaction of having worked creditably and having been fairly vanquished'! At the end of the race the organiser, a Mr T. Blackman, raised 16*s* for prize money for a second day's racing. However, there was a change in the weather on the Wednesday and the racing did not take place. The *Standard* reported that Mr Blackman spent the 16s collected on forty quarter loaves, which were distributed to that number of working men who could prove that they were unable to gain employment.

— FEBRUARY 16TH —

1561: During the Catholic reign of Mary Tudor, Edmund Scambler was one of those who ministered – at considerable risk to himself – to the Protestant underground congregations that met in different places in London. Following the death of Mary in 1558, the recognition of this commitment led to an early appointment as Chaplain to Archbishop Parker of Canterbury. He was also granted a prebendary – a share of the revenue of a cathedral – at York and Westminster. In November 1560, Queen Elizabeth nominated him to the See of Peterborough – quite possibly as a result of 'suggestions' from William Cecil of Burghley. Edmund Scambler was consecrated Bishop of Peterborough at Lambeth Palace on 16 February 1561 and because of Peterborough's poor endowments at the time, he retained his prebends at York and Westminster. He moved on to become Bishop of Norwich in 1585. Over the centuries, Bishop Scambler has been vilified locally, as it was he who passed large areas of the Soke and the judication of them to the Queen. She very soon after granted them to William Cecil – who had supported Scambler's appointment as Bishop of Peterborough to the Queen! Another case of not what but who you know? (Carnell, Geoffrey, *The Bishops of Peterborough*, RJL Smith & Associates, 1993)

− FEBRUARY 17TH −

1866: Today saw the opening of the new Cattle Market. For centuries it had been held in the city centre market square and the roads around it! Shopkeepers and pedestrians were getting totally fed up with the mess and inconvenience of pens and were demanding that 'something should be done'. A solution was found on a field called Simpson's Place adjacent to the then recent developments along the New Road. The site was accessed via entrances from Midgate next to the newly completed Swan Place & Swanspool and off Midgate at its junction with Westgate − roughly where the two meet Broadway and Long Causeway now. At long last, the shopkeepers and their customers could go about their city centre business without the raucous calls and rumbling bellows of cattle and their masters. (Mitchell, Neil, *The Streets of Peterborough*, Neil Mitchell; 2007)

−−−

1940: Over 500 men between the ages of 20 and 23 registered for 'call-up' at the Peterborough Labour Exchange on this Saturday. Of these, only five raised a conscientious objection. In the end, 490 actually signed up, 64 with the Navy and 130 with the RAF. The rest offered no definite preference. Not surprisingly, bearing in mind the industrial landscape of Peterborough, there was more than usual number of recruits who were in reserved occupations − mainly engineering. (Gray, David, *Peterborough at War 1939–1945*, David Gray, 2011)

– February 18th –

1911: This Saturdays programme at the Electric Theatre included 'Special Graphicos' containing the latest events, including Tottenham Hotspur *v.* Middlesbrough; the Cambridge Boat Race crew in training; a collision between the steamships *Alemonia* and *Isleman*; a major railway smash in France and the capture of some bear cubs. They were also offering 'A Wife's Romance' and 'Rough Weather Courtship'! Looking ahead to the following week, they had a Grand Special on Tuesday, Wednesday and Thursday of 'The Air Pirates of 1920' and a 'wonderful' picture depicting 'A Battle of the Future'. How much would all this cost you? Well, for the 2.30 p.m. matinees and 6.30 p.m. performances there were seats at 3*d*, 6*d* and 1*s*. The Saturday afternoon children's screenings were twopence. In this same issue of the *Peterborough Standard* was a plea by the Peterborough Women's Unionist Association for the women of Peterborough to 'not fail to come and hear the celebrated Lantern Lecture on South Africa by Councillor A.R. Atkey of Nottingham at the Drill Hall on Thursday next, February 21st at 8 p.m.' Having clearly stated that 'All are welcome', the advertisement added the caveat that it was a 'Women Only' event!

~ February 19th ~

1871: The *Peterborough Standard* of 26 February carried a brief and to the point report on events of this day. Brought before the magistrates' court were Griffiths Everitt, a drover, and labourer William Seaton, both of whom were charged with being drunk and riotous in Peterborough on this Sunday. Mr A. Allen of the Black Boy and Trumpet at the Westgate end of Long Causeway reported that Everitt was committing a nuisance in front of their house and on being reproved, used very bad language. At the same time as this was happening outside, Seaton was abusing his mother, and making a great noise in the newsroom corner of the hostelry. The court was advised that Griffiths Everitt had not been charged on a similar matter before. He was, therefore, fined 1*s* with 14*s* costs and was advised that, should he default on either the fine or the costs, he would be imprisoned for seven days. The magistrates were advised that Seaton, however, had been previously convicted. As a result, he was fined 17*s* and 6*d*, with 12*s* and 6*d* costs. In his case, defaulting on either element would result in him having twenty-one days' hard labour!

– FEBRUARY 20TH –

1942: One of the major fears during the war was a gas attack. As a result, as well as being standard issue to Civil Defence and Service personnel, over 50,000 gas mask/respirators were in the hands of the general population of Peterborough. In the weeks leading up to this day, there had been some 500 information posters up around the city, along with advertisements and write-ups in the newspapers and loudspeaker reminders that there would be free checks, adjustments and repairs available for this most important piece of self-preservation. It had all fallen on deaf ears. On the first three days, only 230 respirators were taken in to the seven checking posts across town. Major R. de Gray, the deputy chief warden, was not impressed. He declared that 'the public can only blame themselves if the worst happens and they are unprepared. The Old Town Hall is open every day for the adjustment and repair of respirators, but this week has been one of the slackest we have known.' It appears that modern-day public apathy is nothing new. One also wonders who the residents of wartime Peterborough would have blamed if a gas attack had occurred and they had suffered as a result. (Gray, David, *Peterborough at War 1939–1945*, David Gray, 2011)

– February 21st –

1972: On this day, the new Barclays bank in Church Street opened. It was also the day that a footpath linking the Market Place with Priestgate became a reality. That had taken sixty-three years to materialise. In 1909, a petition had been served by twenty-two Narrow Street tradesmen against a proposed footpath adjacent to the Stamford, Spalding and Boston Bank, linking Church Street to Priestgate. They considered it to be wholly unnecessary, and inadequate for the purpose of relieving traffic in Narrow Bridge Street. They also considered it to be an expense and a nuisance. Cross Street, they stated, was only a few yards off and answered every purpose that a passage in the proposed position could possibly provide. That also had the additional advantage of being a roadway for vehicles. The petition also respectfully suggested that, for the safety of the public generally throughout the town, and more especially in Narrow Street, the Watch Committee should order the police to stop furious driving through all parts – whether of cars, trams or cycles – and to summon all such offenders before the Magistrates. A subcommittee was formed to consider the subject. The *Peterborough Express* of 3 November 1909 recorded that the subcommittee's decision was that the 'matter be adjourned for future discussion'! (*Peterborough Citizen and Advertiser*)

~ February 22nd ~

1927: Formed in London in 1924, the Ancient Order of Froth-Blowers (AOFB) was a humorous British charitable organisation 'to foster the noble Art and gentle and healthy Pastime of froth blowing amongst Gentlemen of leisure and ex-Soldiers'. Its byword was 'Lubrication in Moderation'. The initial aim was to raise £100 (around £5,000 today) for the children's charities of the surgeon Sir Alfred Fripp. In late 1925, the editor of *Sporting Life* started to publish articles on the order's gatherings, and the idea took hold of the public imagination. Each group formed was called 'a vat' and the Peterborough Vat was formed at the Campbell Hotel in 1926. Male members were 'Blowers', women 'Fairy Belles', and their children and their dogs 'Faithful Bow-Wows'. Those who enrolled others received titles. For recruiting twenty-five new members you became a 'Blaster'; 100 recruits made you a 'Tornado' and 1,000 made you a 'Grand Typhoon'. On this day in Peterborough, some 150 Blowers and Fairy Belles gathered at the Angel Hotel for supper and a dance. They would most certainly have joined in with the specially written Froth Blower's song 'The More We Are Together'. I wonder how many Blasters there were among the Peterborough Blowers. The charity as described closed on 8 December 1931. (frothblowers.co.uk; *Peterborough Local History Society Magazine*)

⁓ FEBRUARY 23RD ⁓

1891: At the Court at Windsor, the Queen's Most Excellent Majesty in Council, the Most Reverend William Connor Magee – technically still the Bishop of Peterborough, as he had been since 1868 – was, by Queen Victoria's command, sworn of Her Majesty's Most Honourable Privy Council and took his place at the Board of the Privy Council accordingly. He would be enthroned as Archbishop of York on St Patrick's Day – 17 March – but died seven weeks later, of influenza. (Carnell, Geoffrey, *The Bishops of Peterborough*, RJL Smith & Associates, 1993)

1892: Twenty-four years after they were first set, Councillor Joseph Batten raised the matter of the inequality of electoral representation in the three wards of the Borough of Peterborough and proposed that the borough be redivided into four wards. It was pointed out that, currently, the east ward elected nine councillors, the north ward six and the south ward but three. No one disagreed with the idea that redistribution was necessary but politics and vested interests were involved. Nothing changed and five years later, in 1897, the 3,076 electors in north ward still had 512 persons per councillor compared to south ward's 217 voters and east ward's 127. You'll find the next stage of this story reported in the entry for March 10th. (Mellows, W.T., 'Peterborough Municipal Jubilee', *Peterborough Standard*, 1924)

⁓ FEBRUARY 24TH ⁓

2000: In Peterborough's Bishop's Road Gardens stands one of the most telling and poignant memorials in the city. The memorial – made of Irish marble – recalls the life and death of two young men from Peterborough who gave their lives in the service of their country, protecting the wellbeing of residents in a conflict-ridden part of Ireland. Placed here on this day, it reminds us all that it is so often the young that suffer in conflict, and their families that carry the grief of their loss forever. Corporal Michael Boddy of the Royal Anglian Regiment was aged 24 when he was shot and killed by a sniper on 17 August 1972. He was on foot patrol along Selby Street, off the Grosvenor Road, in Belfast at the time and was the first Peterborough soldier to be killed in the Troubles. Lance Bombardier Stephen Restorick, aged 23, was the last British soldier of all to die at the hands of the IRA when he was shot by a sniper as he carried out a routine check on a car in Bessbrook, South Armagh on 12 February 1997. His death resulted in a public outcry, with Gerry Adams calling his death 'tragic'. His death brought peace a step nearer. (Jones, B.R., *A Monumental Tour of Peterborough City Centre*, TalkingHistory, 2009)

~ FEBRUARY 25TH ~

1882: The *Peterborough Advertiser* kept a close eye on the growth of the Great Northern railway station and the needs of staff and customers. In the paper of this day's date readers learnt that, in consequence of the lengthy trains that now stopped at the station, the company had decided to lengthen the arcading and to cover a larger portion of the platform than that covered at the time. Readers are also told that the arcading will be continued as far as the Lamp room, enclosing the Telegraph office in the process. This, it tells us, is all a very desirable improvement. (*Peterborough Local History Society Magazine*)

1976: On 28 May 1974, the *Peterborough Evening Telegraph* had reported the London Brick Co.'s chairman warning that 'a disastrous slide in house building will make 1974 an appalling year for home buyers, which could lead to substantial and damaging cuts in production'. Now Peterborough's world had brightened and the *Evening Telegraph* tells us that 'A building boom as Britain bottoms out of its economic crisis has brought a 200 job boost to the overworked brick industry in Peterborough. The all-systems-go news comes today from the mighty London Brick Co., which says it has a crowded order book and cannot make enough bricks without an extra 200 jobs in the Peterborough yards.'

~ FEBRUARY 26TH ~

1889: This day saw the birth of Francis (Frank) Arthur Perkins at Clifton Villa, Park Road, Peterborough. His name resonates still throughout twenty-first-century Peterborough – remembered and recognised as the founder and driving force of the company known throughout the world today as Perkins Engines. His father and grandfather were engineers manufacturing a wide range of agricultural machinery. In 1932 the business collapsed. The rest of the story begins on 7 June 1932 – and that's where you'll find it in this little book. (Warman, E., *People of Peterborough*, Peterborough Museum Publications, 2009)

1889: The *Yaxley Deanery Magazine* tells us that on this Tuesday a very successful concert was held in the girls' schoolroom in aid of the 'Fund for Lighting the Streets'. Nearly all the performers were residents in the parish and members of the Yaxley Glee Class, a fact that, it notes, speaks well for the musical talent of the parish. Five glees were sung, and both glees and songs were extremely well received and many encores were demanded. Altogether, it was considered one of the most successful concerts ever held in Yaxley. The room was well filled and about £4 was cleared for the Lighting Fund after paying expenses. (The National Archive, Ref HP102)

⁓ February 27th ⁓

1759: The constable's book of St Kyneburga's church at Castor shows a claim of 1s for the constable 'returning a warrant to prevent ye Cox being holled at on Shrove Tuesday'. This relates to him seeking to prevent a long-standing custom of throwing stones at a cockerel tied to a stake on Shrove Tuesday – something that continued in some parts of the country until the end of the eighteenth century. (Bunch, Allan and Liquorice, Mary, *Parish Churches in and around Peterborough*, Cambridgeshire Books, 1990)

1928: FLATS FOR BACHELOR LADIES – The *Peterborough and Huntingdonshire Standard* carried an 'artist's impression' of one of the three blocks of flats which were planned to be built and let to tenants whom a speaker at a promotion meeting described as 'Bachelor Ladies'. The scheme, launched by the Pantiles Housing Society, comprised twelve flats in three blocks, set round three sides of a courtyard facing All Saints church. In the centre of the courtyard would be an electric light standard with the light on all night, so that the entrance to each block would be 'well lighted'. The total cost of the scheme, including land, was estimated at around £5,500. The scheme appears to have sunk without trace, however.

⚊ FEBRUARY 28TH ⚊

1155/6: This was a disastrous Ash Wednesday for the monastery, the day 'the appointed allowance of corn for the abbey failed'. A poor harvest the previous year meant that there was no more in the barns. 'And from that time our lord the abbot – William de Waterville – began and continued to buy corn, malt, provender and beans, meat and cheese, wine and all things requisite' until the Feast of St Bartholomew (24 August 1156); but this could not be done save at great expense. (Mellows, W.T., *The Peterborough Chronicle of Hugh Candidus*, Peterborough Museum Society, 1980)

1795: A nationwide extreme cold spell thawed suddenly and unexpectedly on this Sunday. Thick, broken ice was washed down and formed a complete bank across the river at the bridge. It stopped the current, threatening major flooding in the town. One man attempted to resolve the situation by blowing up the ice with gunpowder wrapped in oilskins. However, he became stuck on an ice floe close to the explosive with his boat adrift. To save himself he plunged into the river and was eventually rescued by four men in a boat. Soon after, the gunpowder exploded, blowing ice everywhere and generating a massive flood which caused a great disaster for hundreds of families living on the banks of the Nene. What they did to the 'gunpowder man' is not recorded! (Currie, Ian, *Frost, Freezes and Fairs: Chronicles of the Frozen Thames and Harsh Winters in Britain from 1000AD*, Frosted Earth, 1996)

~ FEBRUARY 29TH ~

1984: 'London Brick – one of the Peterborough region's biggest employers – has finally lost its fight to remain independent', reported the *Evening Telegraph* on this date. After a bitter three-month battle for control, Lord Hanson and his vast Hanson Trust financial empire had won the day. Sir Jeremy Rowe had followed his father and grandfather as the chairman of London Brick but, in the end, money had won. Asked how he felt to have lost the battle, he replied 'I felt shock – and sheer fatigue. When one is the defender, not the predator, I don't think you realise the enormous pressure that you are working under.' In October 1983, the Hanson Trust announced that 'it had no intention of staging a takeover for London Brick – for the time being anyway'. In mid-December 1983 it made a formal bid of £170 million for the company. Jeremy Rowe described it as 'derisory'. The New Year saw a revised bid of £212 million also rejected but when the bidding went up to £247 million, the writing was on the wall. When Stock Exchange trading closed on this day, some 28 per cent of London Brick shareholders had accepted Hanson's offer. Hanson already held 29.9 per cent. The battle was lost (or won, depending on whose side you supported). (Harper-Tee, John, 'The Peterborough Story', *Peterborough Evening Telegraph*, 1992)

~ MARCH 1ST ~

1948: In dense fog at 7.00 a.m. at the Conington North signal box level crossing, a light engine travelling tender first at about 20mph collided with a Fordson 2-ton covered lorry crossing the line. Damage to the engine was negligible but the lorry, owned by the Huntingdon War Agricultural Executive Committee, was completely wrecked. The lorry was carrying ten German prisoners of war to their work at neighbouring farms. Its driver, also a German prisoner, knew the route well. As a result of the collision three of the prisoners were killed outright and three others, including the driver, died soon after admission to hospital or on their way there, despite immediate first aid being given by members of the railway staff and others at the site of the accident. The other five men were seriously injured. The later formal report commented that considering the density of the fog and the relatively isolated site, there was no unavoidable delay in obtaining medical assistance. A doctor and the medical officer of Sawtry prisoner-of-war camp, along with an ambulance from Peterborough, arrived at about 7.45 a.m. Six of the injured men left for hospital by about 8.00 a.m. and the remaining two at about 10.00 a.m. (Ministry of Transport report, 14 October 1948)

- MARCH 2ND -

1897: At the Peterborough County Court sitting of this day, a number of orders were made that give us a glimpse of the time. Charles Jenks, a labourer from Water Newton, had debts totalling £21 4s that had accrued due to his loss of work caused by illness. He offered to meet his debts to 8s 6d in the pound at the rate of 3s per month. An order was made allowing this situation. Daniel Monk, a labourer from Eye, was in deeper trouble with debts of £40 10s 4d. He was offering 9s in the pound on the debts – an offer accepted by the court and requiring him to pay at a rate of 6s per month. If my sums are right, that's five years of payments. Among the undefended cases we find that Charles Tebbs, butcher of Midgate, was seeking payment of £26 15s 6d from one W. Chapman of Robin Hood Chase in Nottingham. The claim was upheld and Chapman was required to settle the debt at 10s a month. Tebbs has to wait over four years for settlement of the debt – if he's lucky. (*Peterborough Citizen*)

— March 3rd —

1473: On this day one Robert Kirkton, a monk at Peterborough, received his commendatory letters from William Ramsey, Abbot of the monastery to Thomas, Bishop of Lincoln. These letters confirmed his status as a priest and, as protocol required, he moved on. Twenty-three years later he returned as the penultimate Abbot of Peterborough. (Gunton, Symon, *The history of the Church of Peterburgh*, ed. Symon Patrick, 1990)

———

1635: All Saints church, Paston, has a monument to Edmund Mountsteven, who died on this day aged 73. According to the monument:

> he gave an hundred pounds towards ye repare of ye Cathdral Church of St Paul, in London. His debts discharged & legacies payd the remainder He devised in good uses. He was a learned and religious Gent, a bountiful housekeeper to ye utmost of his abilitie & very Beneficial to very many Poore. His works praise him in ye Gates.

Edmund was the second son of John Mountsteven, MP for Peterborough from 1555 to 1558. John had obtained the Manor of Paston from Bishop Edmund Scambler – a man who appears elsewhere in this book. In 1929 the road that linked the Lincoln Road to Fulbridge Road was renamed Mountsteven Avenue in recognition of this family. (Bunch, Allan and Liquorice, Mary, *Parish Churches in and around Peterborough*, Cambridgeshire Books, 1990; Mitchell, Neil, *The Streets of Peterborough*, Neil Mitchell; 2007)

~ MARCH 4TH ~

1911: Speaking with evident gratification following last week's speech by Mrs Pankhurst, Miss Tebbutt, a local militant suffragette, felt that it had 'done the cause no end of good'. However, when asked about the local membership, she was less enthusiastic, saying simply that, 'members are coming in well, but you see, we have only been really started a short time, so you must give us a chance. There are some who are hesitating, but you see it is rather difficult to get the ladies of either Party to come out.' When asked if Peterborough would offer passive resistance to the census and Coronation fireworks in Peterborough, she felt that, as there were many business members in Peterborough, it would not be advisable for them to do this. Asked if any from Peterborough might go up to London to take part in the protest, she felt she could not say but personally, if she had not had business ties, she would join the demonstration. As to not filling in the census, Miss Tebbutt replied that to be in a position to make that protest one would have to be the head of the house, so it would be no use refusing as she was not the head. (*Peterborough Standard*)

— MARCH 5TH —

1892: This was the day that Arthur Holditch Mellows first saw the light of day. Between now and his premature death on 16 October 1948 (recorded elsewhere in this book), he would have a major impact on the life and development of Peterborough. On the outbreak of the First World War, he enrolled with the Hunts Cyclist Battalion and served with them for two years, watching over and protecting the North Yorkshire coast – rising to the rank of captain – before seeing action in Mesopotamia. Back home, he qualified as a solicitor and joined the family firm. He became East ward's city councillor in 1932 and in January 1935, was elected mayor of Peterborough. He became interested in the educational life of the city and was elected Vice Chairman of the Education Committee in November 1938, a position he held until November 1942 when he was voted to the Chair of the Committee. After the Second World War, his commitment increased further and he was appointed to the National Education Committee of the Municipal Corporations. The *Peterborough Standard* of 22 October 1948 summed up his life and character: 'He had three outstanding characteristics – tact, marked acumen and tenacity of purpose.' His memory is kept alive to this day by the 'Arthur Mellows Village College' in Glinton. (Miller, Julie, *People of Peterborough*, Peterborough Museum Publications, 2009)

~ March 6th ~

1854: The *London Standard* of this date carried a brief report of an action brought to the Northampton Civil Court by Mr Percival, the landlord of the Great Northern Hotel, Peterborough, against the defendant George Hammond Whalley, who 'at the last election was returned as member for that town, but was afterwards on petition unseated', to recover the amount of his bill for wine supplied at a dinner given to celebrate his return, and for the hire of post-horses and carriages during the election. The jury gave a verdict for the full amount claimed, deducting a sum of seven guineas, charged for posting and horses.

1915: A serious fire that occurred in Westgate this Saturday appeared to have been caused by the ignition of an engine on a motorcycle. Whatever the beginning, the result was major damage to the City Rubber Co.'s shop selling cycles, gramophones and assorted rubber goods. It was owned by Mr Woodman, who tried his hardest to put out the fire but only managed to get himself badly burnt and ended up in the Infirmary – the present museum building. Both the City and the Volunteer fire brigades attended the fire, with many of the local billeted soldiers helping as well. (Perry, Stephen, *Peterborough Vol. 2, a second portrait in old picture postcards*, S.B. Publications, 1989)

– MARCH 7TH –

1828: *The Times* newspaper recorded the story of 21-year old Elizabeth March, who appeared in court in Northampton having been indicted for having maliciously and feloniously set fire to the dwelling house of her husband John March, with intent to injure him. It appeared from the evidence that the prisoner had been living separately from her husband, who lived in Peterborough, for the past two or three years. A short time before the transaction in question took place she was heard to say, speaking of her husband, that she 'would not mind toasting the d....d old slip-shod to death'. The proven facts were that, on Sunday 11 November, she had thrust a lighted candle under the roof thatch of her husband's house and run away. A woman who lived opposite had seen the action and called out to the accused's husband. He 'jumped out of bed and pulled the still lighted candle and some burning straw out of the thatch, which he immediately extinguished by stamping his foot upon them'. The jury returned a verdict of guilty and the accused was sentenced to death. *The Times* commented that 'the prisoner, who was rather a good-looking woman, behaved with great levity in the dock'. (*Huntingdon, Bedford and Peterborough Gazette*)

~ MARCH 8TH ~

1118: The *Peterborough Chronicle* of Hugh Candidus tells the story of the monastic community at Peterborough from 655, when the very first one was established, to 1177 when he passed away. He is, understandably, in some doubt as to when the foundation stone of the third abbey church of the monastery – now the cathedral – at Peterborough was laid. The previous building had burned down on 4 August 1116 in the time of Abbot John de Sais/John of Salisbury. We are told that he promptly began the rebuild, laying the first stone on 12 March 1117. However, the formal 'foundation stone' of a building always waits for something firm to lie on. It needs to be seen by people present and future and it was on this date – 8 March 1118 – that the formal laying of the foundation stone appears to have taken place. The exact date of the church's completion – and its dedication by the Bishop of Lincoln – is equally confusing. One source says 4 October 1237 but the popular one is 28 September 1238. Whatever the dates may be, the abbey/cathedral church of Peterborough is a sight for sore eyes at any time. (Mellows, W.T., *The Peterborough Chronicle of Hugh Candidus*, Peterborough Museum Society, 1980; Gunton, Symon, *The history of the Church of Peterburgh*, ed. Symon Patrick, 1990)

— March 9th —

1934: CROSSING CRASH! Wansford Gates Demolished by a Lorry. REMARKABLE ESCAPE FROM GOODS EXPRESS. So read a story in the *Peterborough Citizen* of 13 March. It had happened in the early hours of this Friday when a lorry laden with fish demolished the Wansford level crossing gates just as a goods express was approaching. Lorry driver George Hoyland of North Shields thought quickly, revved up the lorry and charged the other gates. Signalman Charles Green down the line saw the incident and changed the signals to halt. George and the lorry were off the line just as the train passed. The unnamed engine driver had applied the brakes but the train didn't come to a halt until it reached Wansford station. Station Master F.W. Alton, who had been called from his bed at about 3.15 a.m., said he had been at Wansford for some ten years and that such crashes seemed to be almost a regular occurrence there. Four in a single period of twelve months, or upwards of eight or nine in his time, would be fair estimate, he claimed.

⁓ MARCH 10TH ⁓

1909: The *Peterborough Express* of this date reported a council discussion on the subject of stopping all football being played on the Stanley Recreation Ground. The matter was raised by the council surveyor, who advised the members present that if they didn't stop this activity, there would not be any grass left. He explained that the ground was in a very muddy condition because it was not used by those for whom it was initially intended. It was, in his view, used mainly during the winter by a set of fellows who were no credit to themselves or anyone else. Councillor Herbert replied that he had heard of the poor condition but suggested that the damage had been caused by the horse show. Mr Lamplaugh, meanwhile, thought it was all the better for the horses having been on it. Councillor Risely disagreed with Lamplaugh's statement, saying that it would be a long time before anyone would make him believe that men playing football would injure the ground as much as horses weighing a ton, with their shod feet. He just could not take that in. In the end it was proposed that football playing should be stopped – and the proposal was passed. (*Peterborough Local History Society Magazine*)

– MARCH 11TH –

1968: Since the mid-nineteenth century, Peterborough has been a railway city. The railways helped open up another major industry in the city: bricks. Both brought employment and overall prosperity to the city – particularly when they worked together. Peterborough bricks only reached across Britain thanks to the railway's ability to effortlessly move large and heavy consignments. A major by-product of the brick industry was fly ash – fine particles coming from brick firing – which can be used in the production of Portland cement. On this Monday there was a fatal accident when, at about 9.20 p.m., a train carrying many hundreds of tons of fly ash ran into the back of a similarly loaded stationary train, just south of Peacock Bridge. In the cab of the train were drivers John Theobald and Joseph Lee who both died at the scene, and guard Aubrey Dolman. Fifty police and firemen worked through the night under floodlight to free Mr Dolman from the tangled wreckage. Consultant surgeon Denis Bracey from the Memorial Hospital worked with the team from around 4 a.m. until 7 a.m. when, after ten hours, Mr Dolman was finally cut free and taken to the hospital suffering from a broken left leg. (*Peterborough Advertiser*; Harper-Tee, John, 'The Peterborough Story', *Peterborough Evening Telegraph*, 1992)

~ March 12th ~

1889: Following a long cold spell of weather, there was still some snow and ice around Stanground on this Tuesday afternoon, shortly before the mixed school broke up. Susannah Smith, 6, described as one of the brightest children in the infant school, returned home and begged her mother to let her go out for a few minutes to join five other children who were playing about outside. Soon they had all ventured out onto the snow-covered ice on the Lode. The ice gave way and all the children were tipped into the water, although two boys managed to scramble out. Charles Hill and George Baines heard the children cry and ran up to help. They went into the water and helped three children, all of one family, to the bank. They were joined by Mr W. Northcott and they searched but could find no trace of any others. It was not until the men had broken the ice and the water had been dragged that the body of Susannah Smith was recovered. The Deanery magazine later recorded that two days later, three boys were playing ball near the river at Water End and fell in and drowned. (The National Archive, ref. HP102)

~ MARCH 13TH ~

1497: Robert Kirkton, the 38th and penultimate Abbot of Peterborough monastery, was installed this day. His next thirty-two years as abbot were full of ups and downs, with people's views ranging from 'highly popular/great guy' to 'self-serving, thieving, conniving, cheating charlatan'! Whatever he was like in real life is now of little concern – but what he left is impressive. He was a builder (one writer describes him as 'Bob the Builder') and his legacy really highlights this. In the precincts, the great gateway and arch to the present Deans Lodgings is his work. Walk outside to the East end and admire the 'New Building', added by Robert to the original apsidal end. Visitors often ask me where the New Building is. When I point it out to them they often look askance at me – but it is new by Peterborough Cathedral standards, being only a little over 500 years old! Go in to the cathedral East end and you marvel at the vaulted ceiling of the New Building – it's Cambridge's King's College Chapel in miniature. With these legacies, perhaps we can forgive Robert's theft of land for his private enjoyment and his attempts to short-change Henry VIII on a debt that finally hastened his downfall on 9 March 1527. (Dawes, Joan, *People of Peterborough*, Peterborough Museum Publications, 2009)

– MARCH 14TH –

1908: 'Disgraceful scenes: Police hustled in the execution of their duty: Butcher's stall wrecked: Hostile demonstration against a city constable', read the headlines on this day. This trouble was caused by the arrest of George Dyer, a Fletton labourer, who was alleged to have been drunk in Long Causeway this Saturday night. When he threw a punch at PC Stevenson they ended up struggling on the ground – perhaps not unusual on a Saturday night. However, the crowd ganged up on the side of Dyer; a mob developed, market stalls were upended and the contents of a fresh meat stall vanished 'as if by magic'. Peterborough city centre came to a riotous standstill and trams into the 'suburbs' were being held up. PC Stevenson commandeered Mr Gaunt's shop – already the refuge of a number of ladies – got himself and Dyer inside and then bolted the door. With mob law continuing, more police arrived and managed to keep a space between the mob and the shop. After about an hour, a butcher's open cart was brought to the shop and Dyer bundled in. There was then a horse-drawn race through the crowds until they finally got to the police station. Dyer came up for trial on 25 August. You'll find the rest of the story there! (*Peterborough Express*; *Peterborough Local History Society Magazine*)

– MARCH 15TH –

1781: Matthew Wyldbore died on this day. In 1768 he was MP for Peterborough and, as the story goes, had been out near Flag Fen when a mist descended and he became lost. As he started to wander, he heard the church bells of St John's ringing behind him, turned and followed them safely back to his home. The story goes on to say that he retraced his footsteps the next day and discovered that if had had continued walking in the direction he was headed the previous night, he would have fallen into the fen and drowned. He was an active campanologist and, in his will, he left an annual legacy of £5 to pay for a peal of bells to celebrate his safe return. There was also £1 for a sermon to be read on the anniversary of his death and 10*s* to be given away yearly in the form of sixty twopenny loaves to the poor of Peterborough. From that day forth, in accordance with the will, 'Wyldbore's Day' has been kept as a festival at St John's church. In every particular, the ancient custom was fulfilled to the letter. (Bull, J. and V., *A History of Peterborough Parish Church of St John's*, 2007; Tebbs, H.F., *Peterborough*, Oleander Press, 1979)

~ MARCH 16TH ~

1897: In Peterborough the term 'Gate' does not mean a gate that opens and shuts. It is a derivation of the old Danish word 'gata', meaning street (Peterborough had been under Danish control in the tenth century). During the nineteenth century, the area for centuries known as Boongate underwent significant change. Boonfield Road, which had 'arrived' in the 1820s, was renamed Wellington Lane after the Duke of Wellington before becoming Wellington Street in 1890. The Henson family had lived for many years in a cul-de-sac off Wellington Street. In 1884 that cul-de-sac became a street, and was named Henson Street. Now, on this day, a 'valuable dwelling house' was to be sold by auction by Fox & Vergette at the Angel Hotel, at 6 for 7 p.m., viz:

> In Wellington Street: all that freehold dwelling house known as Welsh House, situated at the corner of Wellington Street and Henson Street, containing a front room with bay window; kitchen; pantry; wash-house; 3 bedrooms; large yard; out-house; stable; cart shed, cow hovel and open shed: now in the occupation of Mr Robert Harris at a gross annual rental of £15 18s 6d.

Boongate, like Peterborough, was changing. (*Peterborough Citizen*; Mitchell, Neil, *The Streets of Peterborough*, Neil Mitchell, 2007)

- MARCH 17TH -

1947: Heavy snowfall in early March had virtually isolated Peterborough and the surrounding villages. Over 1,000 lorries were stranded on the A1 between Wansford and Stamford. However, by this date, a rapid thaw had set in and the flow of the river at the Town Bridge had risen to some 200 million gallons an hour, compared with the normal winter flow of 12 million. The level had peaked about 8ft above normal, and between Castor station and Water Newton, the river was a quarter of a mile wide! Despite this, major flooding was avoided by pre-planning, by which the river levels had been lowered in anticipation of the results of a thaw. (*Peterborough Standard, Peterborough Citizen and Advertiser*)

1966: The *Evening Telegraph* told readers of the residential expansion plans, housing 172,000 people by 1981. The 'Londoner' incomers would be housed in 'urban villages' – mainly the Ortons, Sutton, Castor and Ailsworth – of between 5,000 and 10,000 people. Each would have its own shops, churches, public houses, community centres and other amenities. The fringe area to the east of the city would be reserved for 'noxious and low density industries'. Reading this, perhaps the achievement target date should have been 1984! Certainly Big Brother seemed to be flexing his muscles in this ancient rural city. (Harper-Tee, John, 'The Peterborough Story', Peterborough Evening Telegraph, 1992)

— MARCH 18TH —

1867: Thomas James Walker, Officer Commanding the 6th Northamptonshire Rifle Volunteers, published a poster from the Orderly Room this day announcing that the Annual General Meeting of the Peterborough Rifle Corps would be held in the Town Hall on Tuesday 26 March, at 8 p.m. The public were respectfully invited to be present. At the bottom of the poster was the following N.B.

> As it is impossible personally to canvass all the able-bodied young men of the town, Captain Walker earnestly appeals to them to avail themselves of the opportunity afforded by this meeting, to become acquainted with what is required from a Volunteer, in order that they may, if possible, join the ranks of the Corps, and thus discharge the duty incumbent on all Englishmen, of contributing to the maintenance of England's ARMY OF DEFENCE.

What was he worried about? Could it be the compulsory military conscription into the Prussian army initiated by Kaiser William I or was it the troubles closer to home caused by the Fenian Brotherhood? (Tebbs, H.F., *Peterborough*, Oleander Press, 1979)

1971: London 'overspill' families began arriving in Peterborough on this day. First to receive their keys were Michael Mulhern and family from Islington, followed by Patrick Riley and family from Maida Vale and Mr and Mrs John Rankin, from Islington. (*Peterborough Evening Telegraph*)

~ MARCH 19TH ~

1955: Having started life back in November 1937, the Embassy Theatre continued to pull in showtime audiences in March 1955. All this week – including this day, when there was a Saturday matinee at 2.30 p.m. – you could have watched 'RADIO'S BRIGHTEST FAMILY FEATURE' starting at 6.15 p.m. or 8.25 p.m. Who were they? They were Peter Brough & Archie Andrews supported by Graham Stark and Peter Madden, with Ronald Chesney and his 'Talking Harmonica'. The show also had 'full variety support'. Not your choice? Well, starting the following Monday, people could come and listen to the lovely Alma Cogan, who entranced many people the previous Christmas with 'I Can't Tell a Waltz from a Tango' and Record Round-up's Jack Jackson. Still not satisfied? Beginning Monday 21 March there was, in person, Mr Dickie Valentine, who was at the time riding high in the charts with 'A Blossom Fell'. The reader is informed that films are coming soon. In June 1954, the Embassy became the first to show CinemaScope in the East Midlands and one of the first outside London with 'Flight of the White Heron', the story of the royal tour of Australia. In September of this year it would show Fred Astaire and Leslie Caron in *Daddy Long Legs* with *The Dam Busters* the following week. (*Peterborough's Past, Journal of Peterborough Museum Society*)

1897: The *Swindon Advertiser* carried a *Peterborough Standard* report regarding Mr George Clarke of Alwalton, who claimed that 'some 4 years back I met with an accident; a year after that I had a stroke of paralysis. It left me without any nerve, I was like a child. I used to tremble like a leaf and I couldn't bear to hear the clock tick. But all that has passed away thanks to Dr Williams' Pink Pill for Pale People!' What a punch line – quackery at its best.

1919: Under the headline 'SHOP ASSISTANTS' PROTEST AGAINST LONGER HOURS', the *Times* reported on this day that the Early Closing Association had stated that considerable dissatisfaction was being felt among shop assistants in the grocery and provision trades, owing to the Maypole Dairy Co. giving instructions for hours of closing in their various branches to be made later. In Peterborough, the shop assistants picketed the company's premises as a protest, and threatened that, if a satisfactory answer was not received from the company, a public meeting of protest and demonstration would take place. Mr Larking, secretary of the Early Closing Association, had written to the Maypole Dairy Co. offering the association's services to bring about an amicable arrangement by convening a conference.

— MARCH 21ST —

1865: In 1859 Thomas Amies and William Barford had leased an iron works site on Queen Street. Today a deed of co-partnership was created as Amies, Barford & Company. The 'and Company' signified one Thomas Perkins of Hitchin. Thomas's son would continue the business and by the 1930s it would be manufacturing diesel engines, which are still known as 'Perkin's Diesels'. (*Northamptonshire Past & Present*, Vol. 6 1979)

1871: The *Peterborough Standard*'s 'Contracts' column on this date carried an advertisement that was a year out of date! The Guardians of the Peterborough Union are desirous to be provided with the following articles for the inmates of the Union Workhouse from 8 April 1870 to 8 April 1871. Patterns of the articles and tenders, with names of two sureties were to be sent to the workhouse, Peterborough on Wednesday 6 April before 10 a.m. For further particulars, readers were instructed to apply to the Master of the Workhouse. Obviously needs don't change. The list includes: aged men's clothes; disabled men's suits; able-bodied men's ditto; felt hats per dozen and braces at per dozen pair. For women they required trimmed bonnets per dozen; shirting linen; Lancashire House flannel; strong stays and various shoes and high boots – these were to be made of good kip leather with strong jean lining.

~ March 22nd ~

1929: This evening's meeting of the Peterborough Town Council saw the last stage in the preparations for the Narrow Street Improvement scheme when the council, 'with enthusiastic unanimity' accepted the lowest of twenty-one submitted tenders for the new Municipal Buildings and Shops – that of Messrs John Thompson and Sons Ltd, 'the famous ecclesiastical builders, of Peterborough'. Thompson's tender offered three choices – £189,639 for Portland Stone, £187,122 for Clipsham stone and £183,347 Weldon stone. The council announced the agreement, 'subject perhaps to a slight adjustment', as £186,300! (*Peterborough Advertiser*)

1978: On this day, Queen Elizabeth II, accompanied by Prince Phillip, attended three very different functions in Peterborough. The first was to open the new Magistrate's Court in Lower Bridge Street. The Courts of Petty Sessions had been held in the Sessions House, Thorpe Road since 1844. From August 1980 until 1987, the Crown Court would also be based here at the new building until it moved to its own new premises in Bishops Road. For their next duty, the Queen and Prince Philip moved on to open The Cressett, before ending the day with a visit to the National Shire Horse Centenary Show at Alwalton. Just a typical day for the Queen perhaps – but a very special day for Peterborough. (Harper-Tee, John, 'The Peterborough Story', *Peterborough Evening Telegraph*, 1992)

– MARCH 23RD –

1900: We often think that our twenty-first century hype about recycling is new. I can assure you, it's not. A frequent advertisement in the *Peterborough and Huntingdonshire Standard* around this time caught my eye.

> OLD FALSE TEETH BOUGHT – Many ladies and gentlemen have by them old or disused false teeth which might well be turned into money. Messrs R.D. & J.B. Fraser of Prince's Street, Ipswich (established since 1833) buy old false teeth. If you send your teeth to them they will remit you by return of post the utmost value; or, if preferred, they will make you the best offer, and hold the teeth over for your reply. If reference is necessary, apply to Messrs Bacon & Co., Bankers, Ipswich.

Now that really is recycling. I wonder how many Peterborians – and other readers – took part in this 'recycling for cash' offer?

1941: On this Sunday, churches across Great Britain held a second National Day of Prayer, as requested by King George VI. In Peterborough, the Home Guard formally escorted the mayor and corporation to the cathedral for the morning service. The first National Day of Prayer had been held on Sunday 26 May 1940, when the British Expeditionary Force was retreating toward Dunkirk. (Various sources)

~ MARCH 24TH ~

1690: The parish registers of St John the Baptist in Stanground record that, on this day, 'Hannah Sinke was then whipped according to law & sent away with a pass to Sunderland in the Bishopricke of Durham where she said she was born.' (Bunch, Allan and Liquorice, Mary, *Parish Churches in and around Peterborough*, Cambridgeshire Books, 1990)

1895: This day saw the death of Peterborough-born Edward Vergette – Mayor of Peterborough in 1885. Having completed his 'articles' with Alderman Percival, Edward had entered into a partnership, as solicitors, with Mr S.C.W. Buckle. Following the death of Mr Buckle in 1872, Edward became Clerk to the Guardians of the Poor of Peterborough, a post he held for twenty-three years. In the nineteenth century Peterborough had, in its centre adjacent to St John's church, one of the most significant and busy corn exchanges in the country, the secretary of which was Edward Vergette. When Alderman Percival resigned from his role as Coroner for the Liberty and Borough of Peterborough in 1876, guess who took up the reins – Edward Vergette! The family name Vergette – Edward and William, who was Chairman of the Peterborough Freehold Land Society – has been perpetuated to this day in the presence of Vergette Street which links Broadway to Eastfield Road. (Tebbs, H.F., *How the City has Changed*, Sharman & Co., 1975)

~ MARCH 25TH ~

1908: You may recall the kerfuffle of 14th March I mentioned earlier. Well … at the next meeting of the 'powers that be', Alderman Tebbutt mentioned that he had seen in a certain newspaper an illustration of the recent row in Long Causeway and, it would appear, considered what should be done about it. The mayor's response was that any response would 'only be giving the paper an advertisement' but not, it seems going as far as to suggest they ignored the whole thing. Alderman Tebbutt agreed with 'exactly so' before the mayor added: 'and I think that it will be advisable not to mention it'. Alderman Tebbutt 'closed' the exchange with: 'We don't want the town to be put under a stigma that there was a riot or anything of that kind', although Mr. Cliffe advised that the best course of action was to 'take no notice of it'. The newspaper in question was the *Peterborough Express*, considered by many councillors of the time as the lowest of the low, and so, a serious confrontation in which the police had been attacked and the press had come out very squarely on the side of law and order was neatly swept under the carpet by the officials of the corporation. Rather odd, one may think!
(*Peterborough Local History Society Magazine*)

1302: The Peterborough chronicler Walter of Whittlesey tells us that King Edward I and his wife Margaret of France were at the Abbey on this day. His records show that the visit cost the abbey over £235, including the cost of jewels and other gifts. At this time a labourer would be earning – in modern currency – 1p per day, with a craftsman earning 1½p per day. This means that the visit cost the abbey around £25,000 in modern terms! (Mellows, W.T., *The King's Lodging at Peterborough*, Peterborough Natural History Society, 1933)

———

1871: The *Peterborough Standard* carried the following in its 'Business Announcements': 'OLD WOMEN OF BOTH SEXES. A lecture on the above will be delivered at the Wentworth Room on Thursday evening next by the Rev. Arthur Mursell, of London – J.F.Bently Esq. will take the chair at Eight o'clock. Admission: Front Seats 1*s*, Second ditto 6*d*.' The following Saturday's *Standard* tells us that Mr Mursell's lecture on the above subject drew a large attendance at the Wentworth Room, Peterborough on the Thursday night. Arthur Mursell was a prolific Baptist minister and preacher of the late Victorian era who travelled the country delivering lectures on many facets of life. One wonders if he was in the city at the invitation of Peterborough's Baptist minister Thomas Barrass, known to Bishop Connor Magee as 'the Non-Conformist Bishop of Peterborough'.

~ March 27th ~

1857: It is very easy to forget how hard times could be at different stages of life in years gone by. The baptism records of St John the Baptist church in the heart of Peterborough give us a glimpse. Vincent, the son of Stephen and Emma Card, was born on 21 March this year. On this day, he was baptised at home 'on account of danger of death'. One can imagine the stress the parents were in. The record goes on to show that on 12 April 1857 'the aforesaid infant was carried to church and I, Thomas Seed, added sacred ceremonies and prayers'. Godparents present were Joseph and Helena Jinks (parents of the mother). Other records, sadly, show that Vincent died before the end of the month. (Bull, J. and V., *A History of Peterborough Parish Church of St John's*, 2007)

1975: Several thousand people lined the streets of Peterborough today when Elizabeth II, along with Prince Phillip, came to distribute Maundy money. They were greeted by the Rt Revd Douglas Feaver, Bishop of Peterborough. The royal procession, including the Yeoman of the Guard, then processed into the cathedral, where a further 3,000 were waiting to see ninety-eight recipients receive Maundy money. Among the recipients was Alderman Mrs Maud Swift, mayor of the city in 1959/60. (Harper-Tee, John, 'The Peterborough Story', *Peterborough Evening Telegraph*, 1992)

∼ MARCH 28TH ∼

1903: Today saw an extension to Peterborough's growing tram network when the service to Newark began, the trams travelling along the Eastfield Road. The driver – the motorman – had to stand in an open area to drive the tram and was exposed to all weathers. He worked a ten-hour shift, six days a week, at a rate of 5*d* an hour, which provided him with a weekly wage of 25*s*. (*Peterborough Advertiser*)

—

1916: On this Tuesday, a great storm inflicted itself upon Peterborough and the surrounding areas. Fierce winds were followed by a blizzard, which did enormous damage and disrupted many local services. Both tram and railway services were interrupted, with one goods train on the stretch between Walton and Werrington becoming totally entangled when telegraph poles and wires collapsed on top of it. Trees and telegraph poles were brought down, horse carts were blown over and structural damage was considerable. Many of the local tradesmen gave up their rounds and went home. Sadly, some people lost their lives. However, nowhere in the many column inches devoted to the subject were there any reports of blame or claim – people, it would seem, just got on with it! (*Peterborough Advertiser*)

− MARCH 29TH −

1787: At the assizes of this date, before Mr Justice Butler and a special jury, was a second hearing of a case whereas Joseph Hopkins was plaintiff and the right Honourable the Earl of Peterborough and Monmouth defendant. This case had been tried at the previous Lent assizes on an action brought by the plaintiff, who was trying to recover possession of an estate of about £100 per annum, held within the last few years by him and his predecessors on a lease for life granted by the late Earl of Peterborough in about the year 1728. This estate, on the lives becoming extinct, had fallen into the hands of the present earl, and due to the plaintiff not being able at that time to prove his further interest therein to the satisfaction of the court, a verdict was then given against him. In the present action the plaintiff claimed the estate, as before, by virtue of a lease for 500 years, said to have been granted by the late earl, under the title of Monmouth. After a trial of seven hours, a verdict was again given in favour of his lordship the Earl of Peterborough. (*Hereford Journal*)

~ March 30th ~

1851: In parallel with the decennial census, this day saw a unique survey carried out across the country: a census of religious worship. The returns were completed and submitted by the individual places of worship. In Peterborough, the cathedral return showed 130 at the morning congregation, with 90 at Sunday school. The afternoon congregation totalled 175. St John's church reported 900 persons at morning service, 500 in the afternoon and 1,100 in the evening! Can you imagine that now? There were also 300 at morning Sunday school and 40 in the afternoon. The newly established Roman Catholic chapel recorded 70 morning worshippers and 40 in the afternoon. The non-conformist returns, when added together, totalled 860 at morning services, 110 at afternoon and 950 in the evening. (*The 1851 Religious Census of Northamptonshire*; Northants Record Society)

1886: The City and Volunteer fire brigades attended a huge fire at English's timber yards. They could do little to stop a blaze that destroyed three saw mills, the engine and boiler house, three timber sheds; four cranes; eleven railway trucks and a multitude of other machinery and stock pieces across the near 2-acre site. The cost of the damage was estimated to be around £20,000 – a significant sum in 1886. (Mellows, W.T., 'Peterborough Municipal Jubilee', *Peterborough Standard*, 1924)

~ March 31st ~

1900: On this day, at last, Peterborough got electric street lighting. It had been procrastinating on the introduction of electricity to the city since 1879. On 6 April 1882, Hammond Electric was given permission to exhibit 'brush electric light' in Long Causeway. The Gas Committee was asked to report on this competitor to the established gas lighting. Surprise surprise; they were not in favour of electric lighting and the council turned the whole idea down! In 1894, they finally decided – in principle – to have electricity. In 1896, the council had an application to borrow £20,000 to finance the project turned down but challenged the decision and finally had the loan sanctioned on 1 April 1898. Nevertheless, almost two years to the day, Peterborough saw the works on Albert Place Meadow opened. It had taken the Council twenty-one years to bring electricity to the city. One wonders if they started it off this day rather than remind people of their foolish delays. However, the battery room was unfinished and for the first few weeks the supply was for less than twenty-four hours a day! Never mind – we had waited a long time, so what was a few more weeks' delay? (Tebbs, H.F., *Peterborough*, Oleander Press, 1979)

— APRIL 1ST —

1964: When, in 1963, the market moved from its centuries-old site in the middle of the city, the council set about realigning the road to ease traffic flow. This involved taking down the Gates Memorial, the drinking fountain monument to the city's first mayor, Henry Pearson Gates. It had been donated to the city by his wife and erected in 1898. The public were asked to suggest a new name for the site and 'Cathedral Square' was selected. However, the council had its own ideas about what should replace the memorial. It asked four sculptors to submit ideas and designs. In February, it had brought in three art experts to advise which was best. They unanimously selected one called 'The Seated Queen'. The council promptly put a model of 'The Queen' on display for public approval, despite one councillor saying: 'anything of a modern sort is going to create comment from those that don't understand it'. How right he was. Nobody wanted to 'understand' it, the 'locals' couldn't understand it and didn't want it anyway. It was on this rather appropriate day of 1 April that the council finally erased 'The Seated Queen' from their plans and cost estimates! (Harper-Tee, John, 'The Peterborough Story', *Peterborough Evening Telegraph*, 1992)

– APRIL 2ND –

1917: As the war continued in Europe, life in Britain got harder – although modern thinking might not agree on the following particular subject. Rising costs caused Paten & Co. – a significant wholesale 'Wine & Spirit Merchant and Beer Bottler' in the city – to write to all of their trade customers with the following letter:

> Dear Sir,
> We regret owing to the Government having further restricted the output of Ale and Stout we are compelled to again reduce your valued orders for Bass, Guinness and other Bottled Beers in the same proportion as the various Brewers curtail our supplies. Also to further increase our prices as shown below. Assuring you of our best services, we are, yours faithfully, PATEN & CO.

There then followed details of the new wholesale prices. Half-pints of India Pale Ales were now 4*s* a dozen, with pints at 7*s* 6*d* a dozen. Guinness' Extra Dublin Stout was the same price but Paten's Family Mild and Pale Ales was just 3*s* per dozen half pints and 5*s* 6*d* a dozen for full pints. Recycling was in place, with 1*s* per dozen being charged on all pint and half-pint bottles as a deposit, and allowed for on their return – and no exception could be made on this rule. 'So there!' (Padley, Priscilla, *Paten's Centenary – history of Paten & Co. Ltd 1898–1998*, Paton & Co, 2000)

~ APRIL 3RD ~

1935: In October 2010, the *Peterborough Evening Telegraph* and BBC Radio Cambridgeshire told their readers and listeners that Peterborough's All Souls Roman Catholic church had structural problems and was sinking! This may have frightened some, but it wasn't very new news. A letter of this date from architect Mr W.P. Hack provides a quite detailed report on the problems then confronting the church as regards settling – a problem that dated back to the original construction at the turn of the century. This is not the place to go into the whys and wherefores of the matter, but two fundamental lessons come to mind. Firstly, the builder was used to building Victorian villa houses for Peterborough's middle-class families, not large churches. Secondly, the land on which the church was to be built had once been the site of the medieval abbey's fishponds! I wouldn't worry too much though – the church should outlive all of us. (*Peterborough Local History Society Magazine*)

1946: 'A married couple wanted about the end of April, experienced as Cook and House – Parlourman, or an experienced Cook-General and House Parlourmaid; 2 in family; every convenience, very comfortable quarters including private sitting room; centre of East Midland city. Apply A J Paten, Mounds, Westwood Park, Peterborough.' (*Yorkshire Post and Leeds Intelligence*)

~ April 4th ~

1874: The *Peterborough Advertiser* on this day reflected on the success of a petition sent about twelve months previous to the Directors of the Great Northern Railway. The petitioners were concerned about the comparative lack of accommodation for the increased staff and passengers all – it would appear – being the result of the increased number of third class customers. The newspaper recognised that quite a lot of improvements were in place for the staff and – 'thank heavens', it said – the lavatory for the public use was being nicely fitted up with every convenience. At the north of this same platform, there was now a gentlemen's waiting room and first- and second-class ladies' waiting rooms. Not only that: the doors of all the waiting rooms and conveniences opened on to both the Midland platform and the down platform of the Great Northern line. We also learn that the porters' and guards' rooms were now large and commodious. These rooms were also fitted with lockers, and 'severally taken' by each of the men. The porters' and lamp rooms now had fires – these also heating a water tank that offered a constant supply of hot water for washing. It could also be used for replenishing foot warmers in cold weather! (*Peterborough Local History Society Magazine*)

~ APRIL 5TH ~

1564: Sixteenth-century Peterborough managed itself under a long-established procedure called 'Frankpledge' (peace pledge) where, essentially, groups of ten or so families were responsible for each other's behaviour. Fines – called 'amercements' – were levied for all agreed misdemeanours. At the 'Court of Frankpledge' on this day, the community in Highgate (Narrow Bridge Street in later life) gave us a good overview of the process. Three men were fined 1*s* each for having made 'encroachments upon the common street by throwing down blocks of wood to the nuisance of the inhabitants'. One – Robert Ardall – was also fined 1*s* for 'raising a heap of rubbish in the common street to the 'nuisance of tenants there'. There were also fencing problems with Laurence Robynson (2*s*) and John Browne (2*d*) being fined for not having made (built) the fences between themselves and their neighbours. Robynson had also failed to make his fence with Robert Drage by the date fixed at the last court and was fined 3*s* 4*d* for that. Ten individuals were each fined 4*d* for 'not having cleaned the common street but have allowed muck heaps to remain in the common street there to the nuisance of the tenants and inhabitants there'. (Mellows W.T. and Gifford, D.H., *Elizabethan Peterborough*, Northamptonshire Record Society, 1956)

~ APRIL 6TH ~

1870: In our modern, marketing-driven world of 'must have the latest at the lowest price' attitude it is perhaps reassuring that it is nothing new. The local papers of this day all carried Mrs and Miss Simms' advertisement, which 'begged to invite the Ladies of Peterborough to their show of Millinery of the greatest variety'. There were bonnets of the newest designs, which they had just received from London for the season. Also available were many other 'fancy articles' that were sure to please. They gratefully thanked the ladies of Peterborough for the favours they had received and hoped for a continuance of the same support. Mr and Mrs Simms also wished it to be known that they also had mantles, evening and other dresses – all made in the new styles. For taste and cheap prices, the ladies were asked to visit them at No. 2, Cobden Terrace, Cemetery Road, Peterborough. (*Peterborough Standard*)

1946: The Glasgow–Harwich boat train had a lucky escape today as it approached the Werrington Junction. Although the signals said clear, some 20ft of rail had been removed by the permanent way gang. Too close to stop, the engine 'jumped' the gap. A number of carriages derailed and some passengers were injured. No blame was placed on the driver. (*Peterborough Standard*)

~ April 7th ~

1871: At this Thursday's meeting of the Peterborough Improvement Commissioners, the chairman read a letter received from a Mr Burlingham, who had been contracted to wind the clock of St John's Parish church. He had also been asked to investigate the condition of the clock following complaints by many citizens of its irregularity. Burlington's letter stated that, in his opinion, 'the irregularity in the church clock was partly owing to the severe weather, and partly to the worn state of portions of the works'. To efficiently repair the clock would require it to be stopped for a fortnight. His estimated cost for the work was £3 10s, but if these repairs were executed, he was willing to reduce his charges for winding from £9 to £8. Mr Taylor and Mr Wyman, members of the committee, suggested that other tenders be sought for keeping the clock in repair and winding it for five years. Dr Walker and Mr Buckle, meanwhile, proposed that Mr Burlingham's offer be accepted. Referring to Mr Taylor's motion, Dr Walker stated that he did not wish the tender to be worded 'keep in repair' but 'repair' only. Dr Walker's resolution was carried by a majority of one. (*Peterborough Standard*)

~ April 8th ~

1847: For years, the people of Eye had worshipped in a small stone chapel dedicated to St Matthew. As the population of the village increased, it was decided that the village needed a new, larger church and commissioned George Basevi – an eminent architect and designer of the Fitzwilliam Museum in Cambridge – to draw up plans. Work had not even begun when he fell to his death while inspecting the bell tower at Ely Cathedral in late 1845. The work at Eye was taken over by F.T. Dollman and the new church, dedicated to St Matthew, was opened for worship on this day two years later. Despite its 'newness', some pieces from the past are incorporated in the present. One of the bells from the old church – made by Henry Penn of Peterborough in 1712 – remains; and the fourteenth-century font still welcomes newborns to the Christian faith. On the south side of the sanctuary is an old 'piscina' (used for washing sacred vessels after use) that was found in the vicarage garden in 1895, along with an unusual altar reredos memorial to the First World War, which not only remembers the fallen but the names of other villagers who served in the 'Great War'. (Bunch, Allan and Liquorice, Mary, *Parish Churches in and around Peterborough*, Cambridgeshire Books, 1990)

~ April 9th ~

1902: The foundation stones were laid on this day for the 'New England Club & Institute'. Forecast to cost £2,236 to complete, it was to be 'a hall for social purposes' to include a club, a 500-seat concert room, slipper baths, a smoking room and a reading room. It was finished and opened on 27 November 1902 but, despite all the best intentions, it would be, in many ways, a 'white elephant'. In the years that followed it would become insolvent; open as a cinema; be extended (1993/4) but, through it all, 'soldiered on' regardless. (*Peterborough Evening Telegraph*; Perrin, R., *The History of New England*, New England Residents Association, 1997)

1926: Charles Johnson told the *Peterborough Advertiser* how he had been walking along the lane from Dogsthorpe to Garton End at about 9.50 p.m. on this day when suddenly, right in front of him, about 20 to 30 yards away, appeared a black hooded figure about 5ft in height. The hood came right down to the ground, and the figure seemed to be gliding along 2 or 3ft above the footpath. Charles at once bolted forward and, as he did so, the figure glided rapidly away, and seemed to melt through the hedge. Johnson searched high and low after this but could find no sign of it. Spooky – or drunk? (Orme, Stuart, *Haunted Peterborough*, The History Press, 2012)

~ April 10th ~

1912: In 1910, a Peterborough man named John and his son George went to Canada, where they worked as waiters in the dining cars of the Canadian Pacific Railway. In 1911, the two were in Florida, where John put a deposit on a farm before returning to Peterborough to persuade his family to join them. Most were not sure but he insisted, and that was that. The family furniture was sent ahead, as goods took longer than people to make the trip. The family purchased their steerage class ticket for £69 11s. On 10 April 1912, the family boarded their ship moored in Southampton. They were the Sage family – and the vessel they boarded was named *Titanic*. (*People of Peterborough*, Peterborough Museum Publications, 2009)

1920: After the First World War, communities countrywide raised money to erect memorials in memory of those that had fallen. The majority were freestanding stone memorials, but Woodston chose to be different. On this day, the people of the town dedicated a lychgate on the north side of the church grounds to commemorate and remember their dead. It isn't just the lychgate itself that is different – the dates of the listed losses are between 1914 and 1919, rather than ending in 1918. Were the Woodston parishioners also remembering those who died from their wounds that following year? (*Peterborough Local History Society Magazine*, March 2009; robschurches.moonfruit.com; Bull, J. and V., Perry, S. and Sturgess, R., *Peterborough in Pictures Vol. 3*, S.B. Publications, 1990)

~ APRIL IITH ~

1857: John Whitwell was a very active – and popular – local politician in the mid-nineteenth century. The *Peterborough Advertiser* of this day described him as 'a man with a dry humour all his own who frequently said funny things that deserved a wider audience than they usually got'. One thing he promoted – in conjunction with the Peterborough Mechanics' Institute – was the taking of young people out of the city by train to view engineering works new to them. While applauding this, the *Advertiser* suggested that, as many people have yet to see a piece of artillery, would it not be beneficial and educational to have an artillery piece or two in the town centre. Venturing to say that the popular notion of 'a gun' would be more comical than correct, they suggested getting a couple of the Russian guns – 'the government have 100s of them' that were captured in the Crimean War – and mounting them properly in a public place. Apart from the rail bridge and the market lamp, there was not much decorative about the city, and plenty of room for additions. If not to foster the martial spirit, this would enlighten the youthful understanding of conflict and testify their respect for departed braves. Needless to say, no guns ever arrived! (*Peterborough Local History Society Magazine*)

~ APRIL 12TH ~

1904: It was on this day that Florence Saunders, the youngest daughter of Augustus Saunders, Dean of Peterborough, and a lady who deserves much more space than can be afforded in this book, died aged just 48. As a child she had accompanied her father on many hundreds of visits to the poor and sick of the Boongate area of the city. As soon as she was able, she joined the Evelina Hospital for Sick Children in London to learn nursing. On returning home, she committed herself to caring for the sick people she had experienced with her father, 'replacing their grandmother's remedies with treatments learned by a trained and caring person'. In 1884 she founded the Peterborough District Nursing Association and then went to Oxford's John Ratcliffe Infirmary for a while to learn hospital administration skills. The 'Black & White' building off Bishop's Road Gardens carries a plaque in her memory. Space limits us to just record her obituary as published in the *Peterborough Advertiser*: 'Notwithstanding the fact that her duties as Superintendent occupied much of her time, Miss Saunders never gave up her active work of visiting, soothing and healing, almost to the last she moved about in the much-loved uniform among her humble friends.' (*Peterborough Advertiser*; Liquorice, Mary, *Posh Folk: Notable Personalities (and a Donkey) Associated with Peterborough*, Cambridgeshire Libraries, 1991)

~ APRIL 13TH ~

1314: King Edward II 'called in' at the abbey on his way north to the disastrous Battle of Bannockburn. He stayed for three days in 'The King's Lodgings' – the rooms over the great entry arch – before moving on to Croyland Abbey at Crowland. We'll catch Edward again later on his way home. (Mellows, W.T., *The King's Lodging at Peterborough*, Peterborough Natural History Society, 1933)

1885: Two anniversary missionary meetings took place on this Monday. At the meeting of the 'Society for the Propagation of the Gospel', with Alderman Percival in the chair, the attendance was small. The secretary's statement showed that the local auxiliary had sent £66 4s 4d to the parent society. The 'Baptist Foreign Missionary Society' meeting, meanwhile, was chaired by Revd Thomas Barrass and is recorded as having a large attendance. The remittance to their parent society was £130. Why the difference between the two, you might ask? The answer lies, I believe, in the name of the person in the chair. Alderman Percival was a well respected and influential political man of Peterborough, while Thomas Barrass was a charismatic leader of the Baptist church in Peterborough. When he had been appointed pastor in 1852, the membership was thirty-six persons. By the date of this meeting, it had grown to 522! You will read more about this man elsewhere in this book. (*Stamford Mercury*; Jones, B.R., *Thomas Barrass – an Evangelical Individualist*, TalkingHistory, 2001)

~ APRIL 14TH ~

1870: The first Peterborough Bridge over the River Nene was a wooden one constructed by Abbot Godfrey in 1308, prior to a visit by King Edward II and his friend Piers Gaveston. Over the following centuries it had been washed away, fallen apart and repaired many times. Now, on this day, things began to alter. Peterborough had changed dramatically over the previous twenty-five years and a new, safe and reliable crossing was needed. An adjourned special meeting of the Improvements Commissioners was reconvened to consider the subject of the bridge. Some discussion took place as to the necessity or otherwise of first building a temporary bridge, but it was decided that would be a waste of time and money. It was also decided that the new bridge should be built in line with the street and that the present ramshackle wooden one should remain in place until the new structure was completed. This solution was finally achieved on 13 December 1872. (*Stamford Mercury*)

1909: The *Peterborough Citizen* of this day informs its readers that Mr & Mrs T. Osbourne and family, and Mr W. Rimes and Mrs F. Boon have left Farcet for Canada. It makes no mention of the relationship between the latter persons!

~ APRIL 15TH ~

1870: The *Stamford Mercury* tells us that there were, on Good Friday and Easter Monday, various entertainments provided for the public to suit the respective tastes of the Peterboronians, neighbours and visitors. I wondered what these may have been and tried to investigate. Well, on this day – Good Friday – in Peterborough town, the recreation ground was well filled while 'various sports were indulged in'. What these 'various sports' were is not recorded so I'll let your imagination bring these to life. There were also several large tea parties, one of which was held at the Grand Hotel in Wentworth Street – a significant establishment then vying for central Peterborough ascendancy with the Angel just round the corner – while another was at the Drill Hall. One I would like to have attended was the 'monster' tea party at New England. I'm not too sure, though, that I would have liked to have rounded off the day sitting through the lecture by Mr George Goodwin, which was 'remarkably well delivered and much appreciated, there being a fashionable platform and a very good audience in the body of the room'. The *Mercury* tells of the platform and the audience, but nothing about the lecture. Perhaps the journalist went to sleep!

~ APRIL 16TH ~

1913: For over sixty years, traffic and people wishing to enter or leave the city centre along Thorpe Road had to cross the Great Northern Railway lines via level crossings. The influx of motor vehicles into the growing city had made crossing even more challenging than before. On this day, that inconvenience came to an end. A new bridge – called the 'Crescent Bridge' in memory of the impressive crescent buildings that had been demolished to make way for it – was formally opened by the Mayoress of Peterborough, Mrs J.G. Barford, and Sir Frederick Fison, the chairman of the 'Bridges Committee of the Great Northern Railway'. The assembled crowd were told that the bridge was 360ft long and 43ft wide and weighed 800 tons. As well as causing the demolition of the crescent houses, the bridge had led to two hotels – the Commercial and the Milton – closing for business in piles of rubble. At the luncheon afterwards, Sir Frederick Fison pointed out that, but for the opposition of the Marquess of Exeter in 1847, the Great Northern line to Scotland would have passed through Stamford. As a result of that opposition, the town of Stamford had practically stood still while the city of Peterborough had increased its population more than three times. (*The Times*; *Peterborough Citizen*)

~ April 17th ~

1882: The charismatic and self-effacing Bishop of Peterborough, William Connor Magee, gave an after-luncheon speech on this day to nearly 200 guests at the opening of an 'Industrial and Fine Art Exhibition'. The chairman introduced him as 'an orator and divine whose name will live in the annals of nineteenth-century Peterborough'. The bishop began by acknowledging the references to the oratorical powers of the individual who was about to address them, and said that they would be glad to know that oratory on that occasion was limited, and that he was not about to forfeit his title to that praise by addressing to them a long speech. There were, he said, two facts connected with these proceedings agreeably present in his mind: one was there was no spare room in the exhibition; and the other was that there was no spare time at the luncheon. The result would be that they would have the pleasure of seeing a very interesting and very large exhibition of successful handicraft and a very limited exhibition of speechcraft. What the guests would enjoy that day would be the spectacle of a great deal of very good work and a very limited amount of very excellent speaking. (*Lincoln, Rutland and Stamford Mercury*)

~ APRIL 18TH ~

1643: Today's the day that Parliamentarian forces attacked and captured Royalist-supporting Peterborough – quite an easy job, one feels, as the city put up no known resistance! There is a story that Oliver Cromwell banged his head as he rode through the great Norman Gate, but he would have needed a rather tall horse and to be standing in the stirrups to get his head anywhere near the top of that arch. He is, however, thought to have taken over the house in the vineyard, so it is quite probable that the gateway he hit was actually the one linking the vineyard to the graveyard. As well as the bang on Cromwell's head, the take-over resulted in the cathedral itself suffering significant damage, along with the memorial to Sir Humphrey Orme in the New Building. Orme died five years later, his grandson – also named Humphrey – taking on his position in Peterborough life. The family line remained in Peterborough until the early nineteenth century but, as you will see when you visit the cathedral, they never got round to repairing or replacing the monument so damaged in the Civil War! (Tebbs, H.F., *Peterborough*, Oleander Press, 1979; *People of Peterborough*, Peterborough Museum Publications, 2009)

~ April 19th ~

1882: The records of the Petty Sessions held on this day provide a brief view of the down side of late Victorian life in Peterborough. Robert Downs and Benjamin Henson were summoned for damaging some paint in George Vergette's barn. Henson appeared but Downs had absconded, so the case was adjourned and a warrant issued against Downs. Other cases included Hilary Broom, aged 11, being fined £1 1s 6d for damaging shoe lasts and other articles by setting fire to them in the house of Maxey shoemaker Anthony Garford. Robert Mease was summoned for neglecting to maintain his family but discharged on payment of costs, while fishmonger Alfred Jakes was summoned by Polly Ann, his wife, for threatening her. He was bound over on a penalty of £25 to keep the peace for six months – and to pay the costs of the hearing! Being drunk and disorderly in city Road cost Charles Sewell 17s. (*Lincoln, Rutland and Stamford Mercury*)

1941: On this day, 814 20-year-old city girls responded to their call-up papers – although some forgot their registration cards! Many of the girls had come with their mothers, while others had their boyfriends for company. Some are described as arriving 'with an army escort on either side'. Quite a few perambulators are also recorded as being parked outside the building. (Gray, David, *Peterborough at War 1939–1945*, David Gray, 2011)

$-$ April 20th $-$

1913: On this Sunday, Edward Carr Glyn, Bishop of Peterborough, preached to members of the Royal Society of St George in Westminster Abbey. He made the point that there were encroaching opinions that threatened patriotism, menaced the love of country and implied the relaxation, if not the destruction, of all the bonds that held the Empire together. They had done something to oppose the atheistic socialists and Little Englanders, whose influence would weaken national fibre and debase the honour of our country and its throne. In reporting this, the newspaper, under the headline 'Episcopal Indiscretion' declares:

Vilification of the workers is not the special prerogative of employers – it is participated in by their accomplices in the State Church. The hysterical outbursts of certain Bishops pass unnoticed; we get accustomed to wordy exhibitions by ecclesiastical enemies of the people. But the blazing indiscretion of the Bishop of Peterborough within the precincts of Westminster Abbey brings the bigots into fuller notoriety. The sneer at the 'misnamed working classes' comes with poor grace from one whose stipend of £4,000 a year is guaranteed by public funds. Much of the income of prelates is drawn from rack-rented slums. Bishops should not be pedagogues promoted for party services – they should be the elect of democracy.

(*Cambridge Independent Press*)

~ APRIL 21ST ~

1934: In September 1933, PC Palmby of the Liberty of Peterborough Constabulary had arrested Frederick Parish, who had subsequently been charged with the theft of £50. On this Saturday afternoon in 1934, PC Palmby and PC Biggs were on patrol on the Great North Road near Wittering when, walking towards them, was that same man. Recognising him, PC Palmby stopped him and asked his name and where he lived. The individual said he was William Taylor of 'no fixed abode' and refused to provide any further information. Palmby did not believe this reply and, at a special court before Alderman Craig on that same evening, it was established that the individual was 20-year-old Frederick Parish, described as a private soldier. He was charged with being a deserter from the Regimental Depot of the Essex Regiment at Warley since 3 April 1934. He was also charged with stealing a complete set of clothes and 30s in cash. Parish stated these were the property of his father Fredrick Parish of 110 Harrow Road, Leytonstone, E10. He also stated that he was 'Fed up with the Army. They gave me hell down there.' He was remanded for a military escort to arrive and return him to his regiment. (*Peterborough Citizen*)

~ April 22nd ~

1643: As a Royalist town, Peterborough suffered heavily during the prolonged occupation by Parliamentarian troops. While many great treasures were lost or destroyed, some were saved by quick thinking. One thirteenth-century collection of charters that related to the ancient Peterborough Abbey, compiled by Robert of Swaffham, the Cellarer of the Abbey, had been hidden in the ceiling high above the choir by Humphrey Austin, described as one of the 'singing men' of the cathedral. He had put it there, together with twenty pieces of gold, in February 1642 thinking that it would be safe in those unsafe and dangerous times. However, it was on this April day in 1643 that Henry Topcliffe, one of Richard Cromwell's soldiers, found the collection during the destruction of the choir. Humphrey acted quickly and asked for the book, telling him it was an old Latin Bible. The deal was done for 10*s* – Topcliffe actually giving Austin a receipt saying 'I pray let this Scripture booke alone for he hath paid me for it; therefore I would desire you to let it alone: by me Henry Topclyffe, Soulder under Capt. Cromwell, Coll: Cromwell's sonn.' (Martin, Janet D., *The Cartularies and Registers of Peterborough Abbey*, Northamptonshire Record Society, 1978)

~ APRIL 23RD ~

1800: At the Quarter Sessions of the Peace for the Liberty of Peterborough one Samuel Letts of Borough Fen was convicted of stealing three sheepskins, the property of Mr John Whitwell of Werrington. He was alleged to have taken the skins from three trees in the parish of Peakirk. In his defence, the accused alleged that he had got himself lost on Borough Fen Common and, being very weary, he took the skins down for the purpose of resting on them. He was found guilty of theft and was sentenced to one months' imprisonment, and to be publicly whipped on two market days. Public whipping of miscreants was a great attraction to the community at large – but not so good for the sufferer. (*Lincoln, Rutland and Stamford Mercury*)

1876: John Ruskin writes of Peterborough:

Sunday – in comfortable room with horriblest outlook on waste garden and vile buildings Italian architraves in brick of coldest mud colour – cretinous imitation. A Bridewell or Clerkenwell with Genovese cornices travestied! The Cathedral here for a wonder, spared. Bitter black day yesterday so cold I could neither stand to look at it an instant, nor at the beautiful old inn at Stilton.

From this it would appear that Ruskin disliked the city! (Evans, J. and Whitehouse, J.H., *The Diaries of Ruskin, Clarendon Press, 1956–59*; Russell, John, *Fair Spot and Goodly – Visitors' impressions of Peterborough*, Peterborough Arts Council, 1984)

– April 24th –

1934: The *Peterborough Citizen* of this date shows us that some things don't change. It reports that the first day of 'summer time' brought out hundreds of cars. All the approaches to the city were uncommonly crowded with traffic entering and leaving. At the same time there seemed to be more pedestrians than ever and the need for wider footpaths along certain highways was never more strongly emphasised than at Norman Cross where, with only sufficient room for two lanes of vehicles, large parties were encountered strolling abreast in the cool of the evening. Their motoring contributor states that during the weekend he encountered fewer instances of 'road-hoggishness' and a greater tendency to carefulness, but the 'echelon driver' – 'he who follows a stream of traffic with his off-side wheels well over the crown of the road so that he can see down the line is – alas – still with us'. Having been eased of the necessity of learning to drive skilfully by the introduction of synchromesh gears and the like, he was equally unimpressed with the removal of the responsibility for good judgement with the double white lines laid down for overtaking.

— APRIL 25TH —

1891: On this, St Mark's Day, Revd Mandell Creighton was consecrated Bishop of Peterborough in Westminster Abbey. In his sermon at the consecration, Dr Butler, the Master of Trinity College Cambridge, made the point that 'it is never easy to inherit the chair of renowned predecessors'. This was pertinent to the new bishop as his predecessor was Bishop William Connor Magee, who had just been appointed Archbishop of York. Little was Bishop Creighton to know was that one of his first duties at Peterborough would be to bury William Connor Magee two weeks later, on 9 May. (Carnell, Geoffrey, *The Bishops of Peterborough*, RJL Smith & Associates, 1993)

1998: This day is celebrated all around the world as Anzac Day – the day Australian and New Zealand forces landed on the Gallipoli Peninsula in 1915. In Peterborough, this day is observed for ANZAC forces in general, but one – Sergeant Thomas Hunter – is commemorated in particular. Thomas died in the Peterborough Infirmary on 31 July 1916 as a result of serious injuries received in the Battle of the Somme earlier that summer. This day in 1998 saw a very special service at the Broadway Cemetery Memorial, when six of Thomas Hunter's relatives were in attendance for the very first time. (Harvey, John W., *The Lonely Anzac*, Birches Publishing, 2003)

– APRIL 26TH –

1601: Today saw the consecration of Bishop Thomas Dove – the 5th Bishop of Peterborough. His account book records that: 'I was consecrated at Lambeth by the L. Archbyshop. 4 other byshops vs. London, Winton [Winchester], Ely, Chichester laying on theyr hands'. He adds that '£13 9s was paid out for yr dinner'. Dove was a noted preacher and, at some date before this, sufficiently impressed Queen Elizabeth I for her to remark that she 'thought the Holy Ghost was descended again in this Dove'. (Carnell, Geoffrey, *The Bishops of Peterborough*, RJL Smith & Associates, 1993)

1966: The *Peterborough Evening Telegraph* on this day headlined the possibility that people of Peterborough in 1981 could travel about a city of 172,000 inhabitants by a light railway system running silently on wheels of rubber. Alternatively, they may choose to travel across the city by car on a broad highway of motorway standard. These potential options were 'unveiled' when Tom Hancock – described by the ET as 'Peterborough's master planner' – spoke to an open meeting at Castor Village Hall. He was optimistic that the light railway would be providing a two-minute service across the city. Ah, the dreams of a planner – and the later realities of life!

~ APRIL 27TH ~

1941: On this Sunday afternoon, Peterborough came under attack. There was no panic though, because Peterborough was being defended by the city's Battalion of the Home Guard. The attack was part of a military exercise, with the 'offensive' forces being members of an infantry battalion attempting to break through the defensive line. The whole exercise was watched over and checked by the Zone Commander of the Guard, his Staff Officer and others while the attackers were overseen by their Commanding Officer. Both sides were recorded as showing great ingenuity – perhaps some skills learned in civilian life? The line of defence was recorded as holding firm, with just some minor breakthroughs, which were then strongly rebuffed. The observing officers congratulated everyone on the keenness shown and on the significant levels of attendance. I suspect everyone secretly had a great afternoon out as well. These would become regular training bouts, as Peterborough made sure that any 'unwanted' visitors would receive a warm welcome. By early October, this training involved three Home Guard battalions attacking Peterborough railway station with attackers and defenders using rifles and tommy guns – all firing blanks – as combatants hid behind garden fences and walls and anything else available! The station remained unscathed. (Gray, David, *Peterborough at War 1939–1945*, David Gray, 2011)

— APRIL 28TH —

1886: The Petty Sessions on this day had some interesting cases but this one tops the lot. William Johnson, an insurance agent from Manchester, was charged with committing bigamy at Stamford on 31 October 1884 with Minnie Edmunds – his wife Adelaide Johnson then being alive – and again on 13 February 1886, marrying Alice Mary Bloomfield at Kingston upon Thames. It appeared that the prisoner married Adelaide, the daughter of John Bronbeck of Lynn, in 1883 and whilst living at Peterborough the following year, made acquaintance with Minnie Edmunds, the daughter of a railway fitter in Westwood Street. He courted her for two months, and then married her by special licence on 31 October 1884 at St Martin's Church in Stamford, in the name of William Roberts. They then went to Manchester for the honeymoon, and after being there for ten days, the accused stated that he must leave for Sheffield to keep an appointment. She had not seen him since that day, but hearing afterward that the marriage was void, she had married again. The third marriage with Miss Bloomfield was at Kingston Old Church on 13 February 1886. After evidence as to the marriages had been given, the accused was committed for trial at the next assizes. (*Stamford Mercury*)

~ APRIL 29TH ~

1908: It is amazing how widely across Britain Peterborough-related events were recorded. A short and to-the-point piece in the *Dundee Courier* of 30 April is typical:

> CANON'S TRAGIC DEATH: Alighting at St Albans from the 6.8 train from St Pancras yesterday, Canon Charles Hopkins fell dead. He had travelled down with his wife, and was in the act of giving directions to the 'busman, when he suddenly called out 'Oh, dear,' and fell back, apparently in a faint. Medical aid was at once summoned, and it was found that life was extinct.

The deceased was Honorary Canon of Peterborough. He was for many years (1871–1896) rural dean of Oundle, and during the last few years had helped at St Albans. Not recorded in the piece was that Charles had also been Domestic Chaplain to Peterborough's Bishop Jeune.

1941: Following a Ministry of Home Security circular on the carrying of gas masks, a Mrs Mellows organised four lectures, aimed principally at housewives of active servicemen, on how to handle a gas situation. The second talk was held on this day. Each lecture covered: latest information about gas attacks; first aid for gas casualties; how to protect yourself and dealing with incendiary bombs and fires. All lectures were very well attended. (Gray, David, Peterborough at War 1939–1945, David Gray, 2011)

– April 30th –

1859: In the nineteenth century, parliamentary elections were very different from those of today. Votes were 'bought' – a polite name for bribery and/or coercion. Despite three previous failures – you'll find the story on December 6th in this book – George Hammond Whalley was returned as Member of Parliament for Peterborough at this election. He was to remain a Member of Parliament for Peterborough until his death in October 1878. In 1900, in a review of the past century, the *Peterborough Advertiser* stated that he had 'unlocked the Borough from the Whig dominance'. (Liquorice, Mary, *Posh Folk: Notable Personalities (and a Donkey) Associated with Peterborough*, Cambridgeshire Libraries, 1991)

1945: At 7 a.m., a lorry carrying German prisoners of war from Glatton camp to work on nearby farms was travelling across the Conington railway crossing in thick fog. The visibility was down to 15 yards or so, according to an account in the *Peterborough Citizen*, when it was hit side-on by a railway engine. Six of the German prisoners died, while another five were injured. They were all being taken to Peterborough Infirmary by lorry when that was hit by a bus in the continuing fog. This collision badly injured two more persons. You will read about two more incidents at this crossing elsewhere in this book. (Orme, Stuart, *Haunted Peterborough*, The History Press, 2012)

~ MAY 1ST ~

1900: The May Day celebrations in this year were called the 'Khaki Carnival of Peterborough'. The whole ethos was support for the soldiers in the Boer War. The weather was kind – the *Advertiser* commented that 'there was just sufficient breeze to stir the flags which were hung in profusion in every part of the city'. People were amazed at just where all the flags and bunting had come from. The cavalcade was something few would forget with soldiers in uniform, clowns in costume and a tableau showing 'Looking after Tommy's Children'. 'Old timers' claimed that there had never been such a show in the city and the neighbourhood before. Equally impressive was the flow of visitors who poured into the city by road and rail, arriving long before noon and staying a long while afterwards. The accommodation in private houses, as well as in the hotels of the city, were strained to the limit but it was a telling testimony to the thoroughness of the committees who had arranged the carnival that everyone, visitor and townsman alike, seemed highly gratified, and indeed surprised at the greatness of the show. They were warmly congratulated on the perfect arrangements that characterised the proceedings from first to last.

~ MAY 2ND ~

1635: Described by Simon Gunton as 'a man of very pious life, and affable behaviour', Francis Dee was consecrated Bishop of Peterborough by Archbishop Laud at Lambeth Palace in May 1634. Laud's policy was to impose uniformity on the Church of England by enforcing a common style of worship across the country. Twelve months on, Sir Nathaniel Brent, the Vicar General of the Archbishop of Canterbury, visited Peterborough with instructions to provide a summary account of his activities and those of the cathedral for the archbishop. He records that he was 'met by the Bishop and his Prebendaries of the church; the Dean being absent on just causes'. He continues:

> The Bishop lodged me in his house and gave me very great entertainment during the time of my abode there. The cathedral church is very fair and strong, except in some places which are ordered to be repaired. The schoolmaster – one William Dickson – is very negligent by reason of his frequent preaching. He is admonished and promiseth amendment. The church has no statutes but is governed by orders of their own making. They are to send up answers to the articles and a copy of their orders to Lambeth before mid-summer day next.

(Gunton, Symon, *The history of the Church of Peterborough*, ed. Symon Patrick, 1990; Russell, John, *Fair Spot and Goodly – Visitors' impressions of Peterborough*, Peterborough Arts Council, 1984)

~ MAY 3RD ~

1661: For many centuries, 'petty crimes' were punished by putting the perpetrator into the stocks so that others could ridicule and abuse them. However, there is a record in the cathedral Dean & Chapter Accounts for 1661–62 for this day, for 'Item for two Stocks locks for the Lourell Yard 2*s* 4*d*'. 'Lourell Yard' is the cloisters. So who would have been locked in these stocks, and what sin/crime might they have committed? And why do they need new locks? Is it vandals; has someone escaped from them or has it been so frequently used that the locks are worn out? History so often leaves us with unanswered questions. The stocks were a favoured punishment for small offences committed by the lower classes – upper-class miscreants were put in the pillory. Resisting a constable or 'riotous behaviour' could see you end up in the stocks. At this time, the offender could be brought into the church at morning prayers to say publicly that he was sorry. He would then be placed in the stocks until the end of evening prayers. The punishment was generally repeated on the next market day. The eighteenth- and early nineteenth-century stocks were in the Market Place between the Guildhall and what is now Queensgate. (Mellows, W.T. and Gifford, Daphne H., *Elizabethan Peterborough*, Northampton Record Society, 1956)

~ MAY 4TH ~

1812: At the end of April 1812, Revd Mr Myers submitted a petition to the Prince Regent on behalf of his 'unfortunate nephew' D.T. Myers, then under sentence of death in Peterborough gaol. At the prince's command, a copy was sent to Peterborough magistrates requesting details of the circumstances of the case. The information was sent and a reply received stating that 'his Royal Highness would not reverse the decision'. As a result, Daniel Thomas Myers was hanged on this day, having been found guilty of committing an unnatural offence with another man in Burghley Park. The Revd Hinde accompanied the prisoner in the post-chaise to the gallows. That was preceded in the procession by a hearse and a coffin, and moved slowly amidst a concourse of 5,000 to 6,000 spectators to the usual place of execution on Peterborough Common. There a new drop had been erected under the gallows for the occasion. On the platform, Myers joined the clergymen in a prayer composed by the reverend gentleman, with whom the wretched man parted in a way that drew tears from the eyes of every beholder. Time will show that he was the last person to have this fate in Peterborough. (*Stamford Mercury*)

~ MAY 5TH ~

1891: It was on this day that William Connor Magee, Bishop of Peterborough from 1868 to 1891, passed away. In 1884, the editors of *Contemporary Pulpit* asked readers to send in lists of the 'greatest living English-speaking Protestant preachers'. Approximately 350 ballots were returned, and the results were printed in both *Contemporary Pulpit* and the 4 October issue of *The Spectator*. William Connor Magee was ranked seventh. He was a vibrant speaker who gave his oratory full rein; so much so that he was described by *Punch* in 1886 as the 'golden-tongued Magee'. He was also respectful of other Christian beliefs of the time, – referring to Revd Thomas Barrass, the leader of the Baptist congregations in Peterborough, as the 'non-conformist Bishop of Peterborough'. He once caused a national stir when, at the height of the temperance debate, he made a speech in the House of Lords stating that 'it would be better that England should be free than that England should be compulsorily sober'. For quite some time after this, however, he was frequently misquoted as the bishop who said that it was OK to get drunk! (Carnell, Geoffrey, *The Bishops of Peterborough*, RJL Smith & Associates, 1993)

~ MAY 6TH ~

1662: The cathedral's dean and chapter accounts provide many glimpses of happenings around Peterborough in years gone by. For instance, on this day, payments were made to the 'Slater about the Chapter House', along with a specific payment of *2s* for two loads of pargin mortar – a form of cement that was used on a building's surface to create a decorative effect. The Chapter House was second only in status to the church itself. I guess there's a 'makeover' in progress here! (Carnell, Geoffrey, *The Bishops of Peterborough*, RJL Smith & Associates, 1993)

———

1893: Henry Pearson Gates – elected the first Mayor of Peterborough in 1874 – died on this day in Jersey. In all he served four times as mayor of this city, the last being in 1887, when he oversaw the celebrations for Queen Victoria's Golden Jubilee. A permanent memorial to him – an impressive drinking fountain – was unveiled in the Market Place by his widow in 1898. It was hoped that the fountain would provide refreshment to the wayfarer and the weary, which it did for over sixty years before being removed, as new plans for the area were put in place. Later it was repositioned in the Bishop's Road gardens, minus its refreshing liquid, as a lasting memorial to one of the great men of Peterborough's long history. (*People of Peterborough*, Peterborough Museum Publications, 2009)

– MAY 7TH –

1857: Following a series of allegations by the editor of the *Peterborough Advertiser* that 'his Constabulary were becoming intoxicated whilst on duty', Chief Constable Bayly of the Liberty of Peterborough Constabulary responded today by sending the editor a copy of a letter dated 1 May, which had been sent to all 'Publicans, Beer-House Keepers &c' in the Liberty. That letter read:

Having given all the men at present employed in the Liberty Constabulary strict orders not to frequent Public Houses, I trust that you will assist me, as far as you possibly can, in carrying out such an order. I think it is also right to here quote the clause from the Act of Parliament relating to Victuallers &c harbouring or entertaining any Constable belonging to the Liberty Constabulary Force, or permitting such Constables to remain in his house, or on his premises, and for doing which such Victualler &c renders himself liable to a penalty of £5. After this caution, I shall feel myself compelled, for the good order of the Police, strictly to enforce the above penalty against any Victualler &c who may offend against the Act of Parliament as mentioned.

- MAY 8TH -

1839: Bishop Herbert Marsh was buried on this day in a prepared vault behind the altar in the 'New Building' part of the cathedral – the last bishop to be buried there. His wife Marianne was buried alongside him eight years later. He had died on May Day, after twenty years as bishop. Referred to by some as an 'enfant terrible', and others as 'the Peterborough Theological Laboratory' – the latter due to his deep knowledge and firmly held beliefs as an 'old-fashioned High Churchman'. He had been the centre of a controversy a few weeks before his death for taking up a political position in Peterborough – but that was nothing new. His obituary in *The Gentleman's Magazine* referred to his unpopularity: 'His attempts to repress Calvinism in his diocese soon rendered him obnoxious to the evangelical portion of the clergy, and several publications appeared on the subject that were ultimately brought before the House of Lords – but without material result.' Balancing this is a comment in the *Stamford Mercury* of 24 May 1839, attributed to the cathedral sexton, who supposedly said that 'the Bishop liked his pipe and many hours of the day were spent inhaling Greek and tobacco'. (Carnell, Geoffrey, *The Bishops of Peterborough, RJL Smith & Associates*, 1993; Jenkins, Eric, *Victorian Northamptonshire: The Early Years*, Cordelia, 1993)

‒ MAY 9TH ‒

1857: To the Editor, *Peterborough Advertiser*:

Sir ‒ The accident of Wednesday evening (6 May) having terminated fatally will, it is hoped, open the eyes of all parties connected with the direction and repairing of roads in this city. Broad Bridge Street has been newly paved; if Narrow Bridge Street had been served ditto, in all probability this lamentable accident would not have happened; but we need not be surprised to hear of accidents where roads are made as in Peterborough. Why not imitate the examples of large towns where, if granite blocks are to be laid, the ground for the intended road is first covered with a layer of concrete which makes a firm and durable foundation? Upon this the stones are placed, not straight across but in diagonal rows, thus affording safe foothold for horses. One would suppose that at Peterborough they are ignorant of the existence of such a material as concrete, and of the manner of arranging stones in road making, for the bottoming used in Broad Bridge Street was only sand, and the stones placed as in London 16 years ago. The word improvement can hardly be applied to the Commissioners of a town where no such thing ever takes place. I am, Sir, yours in sincerity, CORVUS

~ May 10th ~

1941: At 3.35 a.m. on this Saturday morning, four high-explosive bombs fell on the Priestgate/Cowgate area, damaging more than twenty houses and a dozen or so business premises. Two fire watchers were killed when one bomb demolished the part of the building they were in. Five other fire watchers were injured, three from one family. More bombs fell along Thorpe Road with minor damage and no injuries. (Gray, David, *Peterborough at War 1939–1945*, David Gray, 2011)

1943: This day saw the death of a very unusual hero – Jimmy the Donkey. Jimmy was a pack donkey born behind German lines in June 1916 at the Somme in France. During the Battle of the Somme, the 1st Scottish Rifles overran a German position and found young Jimmy alongside his mother's body. The Rifles took him back with them and adopted him as their mascot, weaning him on tinned milk and biscuits. Jimmy was wounded a number of times during the conflict but lived on. When he was demobbed in 1919, he was bought, through public subscription, by the Peterborough branch of the RSPCA. Jimmy lived in a paddock in Burghley Square and at his death was buried on the north-eastern boundary of Central Park. His memorial stone is there to this day. (Gray, David, *Peterborough at War 1939–1945*, David Gray, 2011)

— MAY 11TH —

1871: Mr J.F. Bentley, as Treasurer of the Peterborough Literary Institute, invited a number of his acquaintances to meet him in the committee room of the institute in Wentworth Street on this day to form a Natural History Society. It was decided that this society be called 'The Peterborough Natural History Society and Field Club' and that meetings would be held on the first Monday of every month. At this inaugural meeting, Mr Ellis had brought his microscope and Mr Henry English — elected Honorary Secretary of the new society on this day — some exhibits of caterpillars feeding on horehound. From this small beginning grew the Peterborough Museum Society, which underpinned the creation and development of the museum we have today. (*The Museum Society in Victorian Peterborough*, Peterborough Museum Society Summary of Proceedings 1976–80 review)

1884: Peterborough was still in shock following the dramatic fire at the infirmary two days previous, but it proved to be a catalyst for the expansion and development of its facilities. An appeal for restoration funds soon got underway. It stated that there had been 3,725 patients treated in 1883 and a total of 29,352 in the previous ten years. The appeal raised £3,000 for the hospital — and provoked a review of the fire service facilities, which were in place before the end of the year. (Tebbs, H.F., *Peterborough*, Oleander Press, 1979)

‐ May 12th ‐

1800–1900: On this day in Werrington during the nineteenth century – and either side as well no doubt – there would be a grand rook shoot. Behind Werrington Hall was an avenue of elm trees that was home to a large rookery. Today the birds would be culled to protect the new crops. When all was done, there would be rook pies made from the breasts of the young Rooks, with hard-boiled eggs and streaky bacon – all under a golden crust. (*Werrington Past, c.* 1970)

1910: On the day Londoners could watch the actual proclamation of King George V, following the death of his father King Edward VII, Peterborough ensured the great day did not pass the good people of the city by. The Market Place – now Cathedral Square - became the focal point. An impressive podium was set up in front of the Guildhall for the dignitaries of the city. In front of them formed a military guard of honour, accompanied by choristers to sing the praises of the new king. They were supported by three buglers. The rest of the Market Place and the upper floors of the Greyhound and Bell & Oak public houses were packed with loyal members of the Peterborough public. (Bull, J. and V., *Peterborough – a portrait in old picture postcards*, S.B. Publications, 1988)

– MAY 13TH –

1893: The *Northampton Mercury* of Friday 19 May tells us of a fire on the premises of a Mr Hunter of Woodston the previous Saturday when, in the afternoon, a stack of straw was discovered to be on fire. The Volunteer Fire Brigade was first on the scene with plenty of hose. Unfortunately, they had forgotten to bring a nozzle! However, the fire had already got too much of a hold on the stack for it to be saved. The brigade was, however, successful in preventing the fire spreading to other stacks in the yard.

1898: The *Stamford Mercury* of this date tells of seven youths who'd been summoned at the previous Wednesday's court by gardener George Tate of Dogsthorpe for damaging cabbages and rhubarb of the value of 3*s* 6*d* on 5 May. The seven were also summoned for 'cruelly ill-treating' a horse belonging to Tate. He said they all had either briars, stones or paling pulled off the park fence with which they thrashed the horse, causing it to tear round the field. They then played football with his cabbages and rhubarb (how do you play football with rhubarb?). The boys were each fined 1*s* with 1*s* costs on the first offence and 2*s* each with 1*s* costs on the second.

~ MAY 14TH ~

1915: Nine months after earlier anti-German troubles, Frank's Butchers in Westgate – a long-established family in Peterborough, but of German extraction – were again targeted by troublemakers. Just after 9 p.m. a crowd, mainly of soldiers, gathered outside their shop; more people soon joined them and before long, a volley of stones shattered the windows. The police and military arrived; the mayor appealed to the crowd to act with traditional justice and by 11 p.m. the streets were quiet, the crowds having dispersed and the soldiers returned to their billets. The damage was valued at £30 and was charged to the Peterborough Ratepayers' account. (Gray, David, *Peterborough at War 1914–1918*, David Gray, 2014)

———

1974: This day marked the culmination of many months of work on either side of the river, when city workmen would finally bridge the gap over the River Nene at Orton. All they had to do now was lower some concrete spans – each one weighing about 12 tons and nearly 60ft in length – with inch-perfect precision. By the end of the day, all was in place. However, through this whole process, one of the contractors' employees had been rowing about in a boat just in case of emergency. One wonders what he would have done if one span had slipped. Was he there to catch it? (*Peterborough Evening Telegraph*; Harper-Tee, John, 'The Peterborough Story', *Peterborough Evening Telegraph*, 1992)

~ MAY 15TH ~

1961: The people of Peterborough saw a subtle change in their newspaper today. As part of an EMAP reorganisation, the *Peterborough Evening Telegraph* – previously produced at Kettering as an edition of the *Northamptonshire Evening Telegraph* – was launched as an independent newspaper from the *Peterborough Advertiser*'s offices in Cumbergate. Over the next 50 years it would become an integral part of city life, with a much more impressive home facing Bourges Boulevard (Newton D. and Smith, M., *Stamford Mercury – three centuries of newspaper publishing*, Shaun Tyas, 1999)

1987: This was a final all-change day for the legal centres of the town. A new building on Rivergate was officially opened by HRH Prince Richard, the Duke of Gloucester. In days gone by, this land was within the grounds of the abbot's palace – a man who held the same responsibilities and powers as the new court complex! Now, after their seven-year 'temporary' occupation of parts of the magistrates' court in Bridge Street, the Crown court had again a place to call its own. Also on this day, the county court moved from its premises opposite Peterscourt on the corner of the Cattle Market to join them. At long last, Peterborough had all three of its court centres within a couple of minutes' walk of each other. Would justice now be quicker? (Bunten J. and McKenzie, E., *The Soke of Peterborough – a portrait in old photographs & picture postcards*, S.B. Publications, 1991)

~ MAY 16TH ~

1584: Richard Howland finally fulfilled his ambition of becoming a bishop when he was appointed Bishop of Peterborough. However, he soon discovered how poverty-stricken the diocese was, thanks to the acts of his predecessor Bishop Scambler. He had sold large tracts of the cathedral's estates and all its judicial rights to Queen Elizabeth, pleading the cause of his diocese and in particular trying to ease the excessive tax liability it carried for furnishing light horse for the army. Scambler was chaplain to William Cecil, Lord Burghley – the man to whom the Queen had given virtually everything she had received from Scambler! As bishop, Howland took first place at the funeral of Mary, Queen of Scots. She was committed to her burial place without any service although, it is claimed, he was prepared to take one. Howland aimed higher than Peterborough so, on the death of its archbishop in 1594, Howland was strongly recommended for the see of York by the lord president Henry Hastings, 3rd Earl of Huntingdon, as well as many others. The post, unfortunately, went to another. Howland died unmarried at Castor, near Peterborough, on 23 June 1600, and was buried in his cathedral, without any memorial or epitaph. (Carnell, Geoffrey, *The Bishops of Peterborough*, RJL Smith & Associates, 1993)

― MAY 17TH ―

1934: Football had been well established in Peterborough for many years, but times had become hard and, in 1932, both Peterborough City and Fletton United football clubs had ceased to exist. At a crowded meeting at the Angel Hotel on this Thursday, Peterborough United Football Club was officially voted into existence. As the previous clubs had failed due to debts, one of the first steps of the meeting – after agreeing the formation of the new club – was to cover the evening's expenses! The cost of the advertising and room hire was £2 4s 6d. A collection raised £4 2s 8d. The meeting agreed on the club being formed as a limited company, with shares of 5s each, and between fifty and sixty shares were taken up that evening. A suggestion that the new club joined a local league for the coming season was not popular, however, as it was thought that it did not show confidence in the future of the club. A subsequent application to join the Midland League for the coming season was successful and over 4,000 supporters turned up to watch the first home match. A reserve side was formed by the beginning of the 1934/5 season, and this played in the Peterborough and District League. The present day 'Posh' had been born. (*Peterborough Citizen*)

– MAY 18TH –

1877: Today's *Stamford Mercury* has the following two 'news' stories. Under the heading 'Reconciliation' we learn the following:

> A few mornings back the London correspondent of the *Nottingham Daily Journal* bore witness to the astounding and fearful fact that Mr Whalley [Peterborough's MP, of whom more elsewhere in this book] and Dr Kenealy had been warmly 'liquoring up' together at the bar of the House of Commons. Can this be true? If so, the nations of the earth may well tremble in the face of such a reunion of irrepressible dual power. 'To your tents ye children of Tichbornia: for the rulers of the strong hosts have become as one through the inspired fumes of B and S.' The man of melody and many sorrows has found once again his loving counterpart in the burley Chartist of dew drop moistened mane, and a rattle as of dry bones is heard as a sign of battle in the valley of despair.

Immediately below this we learn that there had been a considerable attendance of district agriculturists at the annual sheep-shearing and engine drivers' competition held at Boroughbury Barn. We are also informed that the contest in both the departments was well sustained. We don't get news like this now!

– MAY 19TH –

1877: It is easy to forget how critical overall sanitation control was – especially in growing communities such as Peterborough – in the nineteenth century, and the responsibilities of the Poor Law Unions. This notice in the *Stamford Mercury* reminds us:

LINCOLNSHIRE AND RUTLANDSHIRE AUDIT DISTRICT: PETERBOROUGH UNION and the RURAL SANITARY DISTRICT in the said Union. As Auditor of the above-named Audit District, I hereby give notice that I have appointed the Audit of the Accounts of the PETERBOROUGH UNION, and the RURAL SANITARY DISTRICT in the said Union, and of the several Parishes and Contributory Places contained in the said Union and District, or in the said Union solely, for the Half-year ended Lady-day, 1877, to commence on TUESDAY the 5th day of JUNE next, at 9.30 o'clock in the Forenoon, at the UNION BOARD-ROOM in PETERBOROUGH, when and where all persons who by law are bound to account at such Audit are required to attend, and to submit all Books, Documents, Bills, and Vouchers containing or relating to the accounts or to moneys assessed for and applicable to the relief of the poor or to sanitary purposes. Dated the 19th day of May 1877. (Signed) ROBERT AZLACK WHITE, District Auditor.

~ MAY 20TH ~

1975: Several thousand people lined the streets and 3,000 were inside the cathedral this Maundy Thursday when Elizabeth II, accompanied by Prince Phillip, made the first royal visit by a reigning monarch to the cathedral for over 100 years. She was there to distribute the traditional Maundy money. Historically, the recipients were chosen for their poverty and were entitled to remain as Maundy recipients for life; today, new recipients are chosen every year for service to their churches or communities, on the recommendation of clergymen of various Christian denominations. One man and one woman are chosen for each year the queen has lived (including the year she is currently living), and they receive Maundy money in denominations of one penny, two pence, three pence, and four pence, equivalent in pence to that number of years. On this day there were 98 recipients – 49 men and 49 women – including Alderman Mrs Maud Swift, a previous city mayor. A set of Maundy money can be seen in the cathedral and Mrs Swift's Maundy money is displayed in the Mayor's Parlour at the Town Hall. The queen and Duke of Edinburgh would return on the same date in 1988 to attend the 750th anniversary service of the consecration of the cathedral building. (Harper-Tee, John, 'The Peterborough Story', *Peterborough Evening Telegraph*, 1992)

– MAY 21ST –

1914: This Ascension Day was very hot and celebrated by a procession of clergy, choirs and members of the Church of England Missionary Society to an evening service at the cathedral. The service had started at St John's church, directed by Revd A.F. Maskew with Mr B. Manders as musical director. The sermon there was given by Canon P.H. Bowers, Rector of Market Bosworth. They then moved on to the cathedral and during the service there, the intense heat caused two of the choristers to faint and be relieved of their duties! (Bull, J. and V., *Peterborough – a portrait in old picture postcards*, S.B. Publications, 1988)

1934: It is recorded that over 4,000 people gathered at the London Road ground on this holiday Monday to watch the annual competitions held by the North Eastern District of the National Fire Brigades' Association. For nearly fifty years, Peterborough had benefitted from two fire brigades – the Volunteer and City forces. Rivalry was intense as regards emergency calls, and it was raised a notch or two more in this challenging environment. The Trailer Pump competition trophy had been held by the City force for the past two years but this time, in a very close-run thing, they had to bow to the Volunteers, who beat them into second place. (*Peterborough Advertiser*)

~ MAY 22ND ~

1906: It was on this day that a coroner's inquest took place in the Blue Bell Inn in Werrington. The inquest was regarding the death of an unknown woman aged about 25, who had been discovered drowned in a sheep dip. She had been found by 11-year-old William Lenton as he made his way to school. She was recorded as wearing a black dress with an underskirt and a hand-marked petticoat. She also had a white straw hat and scarf, black stockings and new shoes. They found £1 and some keys in her purse. Also recovered were two cheap brooches and a necklace of pearl beads. Dr Harold Clapham, the house surgeon at the Infirmary, reported that the death was caused by suffocation by drowning. Photographs were taken of the body and distributed to police and the newspapers. A few days later, she was identified as being the 21-year-old daughter of Frederick Arnold, a plate-layer living in Lakenheath, who came to Peterborough to confirm identification. He stated that he had received a letter from his daughter stating that she had left her employ in Nottingham and had sent her boxes on. She would not be returning home herself. (*Family History Magazine*)

~ MAY 23RD ~

1934: Following on from this month's re-establishment of football in Peterborough, today's *Advertiser* carried a letter from one Frederick C. Holmes of 'The Laurels', Ruckinge, Ashford, Kent, remembering a day sixty years previous, when a remarkable football match took place here and a London team brought their goalposts to Peterborough.

Football enthusiasts in Peterborough may be surprised to know that a remarkable Association Football match was played in their town about 60 years ago. The teams were Clapham Rovers (one of the leading clubs of the time) and, I believe, Sheffield Wednesday, but I am not quite sure about the latter. I suppose there were no football clubs in Peterborough at that time, consequently Clapham Rovers brought the necessary paraphernalia (goal posts, etc.) on the top of the railway carriage from London! The two teams had previously played a drawn game, and were ordered to play on a neutral ground. Admission was free and there were only a few spectators. What difference between then and now. Nothing better exemplifies the Latin quotation 'Tempora multantur nos et mutantur in illis' (The times are changing, and we with them). Whether this was an English Cup-tie, I don't know. The English Cup was first played in October 1871.

~ MAY 24TH ~

1870: The new Baptist Chapel in Queen Street was formally opened on this day. After a second afternoon service, a tea meeting in the adjacent Drill Hall was attended by so many people that the schoolroom and Drill Hall could not accommodate them, so tables in the schoolroom had to be spread a second time. In all, 1,530 people were entertained. Following the evening service, the Revd Thomas Barrass gave the assembled congregation an informative and amusing update on the whole project. He noted that the total cost would be in excess of £4,000, but that he could not say exactly how much beyond. He had already obtained, including conditional promises, something like £2,600. It was a handsome amount, and he was very thankful for it, but it had not been without some tugging! (Jones, B.R., *Thomas Barrass – an Evangelical Individualist*, TalkingHistory, 2001)

1941: This Saturday morning saw a mixture of incendiary and high-explosive bombs dropped around the Broadway and Lincoln Road area. Some 100 houses were damaged and three destroyed. One house was saved from destruction when PC Richardson climbed onto the roof and threw a burning bomb down into the road. Controversially, however, the siren had not been sounded until after the attacker had left. (Gray, David, *Peterborough at War 1939–1945*, David Gray, 2011)

1840: Monsieur J.M. Mallan, a surgeon-dentist from London's Ludgate Hill, 'begs to inform the nobility, gentry and inhabitants of this town and their vicinities that he may be consulted on Mondays at Mrs Swift's, Market Place'. He offers the following:

> … to fill the cavities of decayed teeth, however large, with Mineral Saccedaneum, the great advantage of which is that it is placed in the tooth in an almost liquid state, without heat or pressure, and immediately hardens into an enamel which by a recent improvement will not discolour. It allays pain, arrests further progress of decay, thus preventing the necessity of extraction. By this means, a mere shell is converted into a sound and useful tooth, and the unpleasant taint of the breath arising from it entirely removed.

What he doesn't say is that 'Mineral Saccedaneum' is almost pure mercury and is most definitely not a nice thing to have in your mouth! (*Lincoln, Rutland and Stamford Mercury*)

1853: At auction, William Prockter Stanley paid £1,800 for Lot 2 – a brewery, together with stables and a few other buildings. Plans show a new road – to be called Queen Street –cutting through to some new building plots. This was the beginning of the Queen Street Iron Works. Eighty years later, Messrs Stanley & Perkins leased the site to build their diesel engines. (Hillier, Richard, *Northants Past & Present*, Northamptonshire Record Society, 1979)

‒ MAY 26TH ‒

1657: Following his visit to Peterborough, Elias Ashmole, antiquarian, Windsor Herald and founder of Oxford's Ashmolean Museum, writes:

> Alfricus founded ye Chappell in ye middle of the Front of Peterborough Church and dedicated it to St. Thomas a Becket. It is 120 steps up to ye high leades and thence to the lanthorne 69 more. The monument that was made for the Monks that were martyred by the Danes, stands still in ye Church yar, over against the high altar on ye South side, where they were buried. Doctor Pothington lyes buried eastward of it.

The 'chappell' is the front porch, which has a secondary job of helping keep the glorious West Front standing. (Russell, John, *Fair Spot and Goodly ‒ Visitors' impressions of Peterborough*, Peterborough Arts Council, 1984)

‒‒‒

1855: The following notice appeared in the *Peterborough Advertiser* on this day:

> To Brewers, Inkeepers etc. ‒ To be Sold by Auction, by J Chamberlain, on Saturday, May 26th 1855; over the Corn Exchange, at 2 o'clock AN excellent BREWING PLANT, the property of Mr G WATTS, Kate's Cabin, CHESTERTON, who is declining the public business. The whole has been new within the last 4 years, Comprising Couler, two Mash Tubs, Underbeck Pump, quantity of Pipes and Sweet Ale Casks, together with other requisites for Brewing. Also to be Sold by PRIVATE CONTRACT, 120 gallon Copper, now standing upon the premises of Mr G Watts, Kate's Cabin.

‒ MAY 27TH ‒

1857: American writer Nathaniel Hawthorne, while US Consul in Liverpool, 'visited historical scenes in the spirit of the conscious tourist'. He spent two days in Peterborough and on this, his first day, he 'put up at the Railway Hotel and after dinner walked into town to see the cathedral'. He was struck by the West Front, declaring it 'unlike any other I have seen', but was not too keen on the painted ceiling. 'This adornment has the merit, I believe, of being veritably ancient; but certainly I should prefer the oak of its native hue, for the effect of the paint is to make it appear as if the ceiling were covered with imitation mosaic work or an oil cloth carpet.' (Russell, John, *Fair Spot and Goodly ‒ Visitors' impressions of Peterborough*, Peterborough Arts Council, 1984)

1930: The wards of Peterborough were expected to contribute toward the £100,000 needed for the New Hospital. East ward was £1,711 short of its target and, to bridge the gap, held a three-day 'Olde English Fayre' beginning on this date. The 'Cream of the Gentlewomen of the city' supported and ran over twenty events, all dressed in period costume. Their slogan was 'So buy our things, and see our shows, and bring our labours to a close. Then thanks to us, and thanks to you, the Hospital will have its due.' (Bull, J. and V., Perry, S. and Sturgess, R., *Peterborough in Pictures Vol. 3*, S.B. Publications, 1990)

~ MAY 28TH ~

1857: On this, his second day in Peterborough, Nathanial Hawthorne again 'walked up into the town and again visited the cathedral. On the way I observed the Falcon Inn, a very old fashioned hostelry with a thatched roof and what looked like the barn door or stable door in a side front. Very likely it may have been an inn ever since Queen Elizabeth's time.' He also records that 'we left Peterborough this afternoon and, however reluctant to leave the cathedral, we were glad to get away from the hotel: for, though outwardly pretentious, it is a wretched and uncomfortable place, with scanty table, poor attendance and enormous charges'. (Russell, John, *Fair Spot and Goodly – Visitors' impressions of Peterborough*, Peterborough Arts Council, 1984)

1869: St Paul's church – often called the Railwaymen's church – was consecrated at midday on this Friday by William Connor Magee, the Bishop of Peterborough. Built on land given by the Ecclesiastical Commissioners, the church cost £4,600, of which £3,500 was given by the directors of the Great Northern Railway. The first vicar was the Revd Charles Ball, who stayed for seventeen years, during which time Peterborough continued its rapid growth. He then moved on to the new parish of All Saints, which had been formed out of pieces of the parishes of St Marks, St Mary's and St Paul's. (Perry, Stephen, *Peterborough Vol. 2 – a second portrait in old picture postcards*, S.B. Publications, 1989)

‒ MAY 29TH ‒

1723: Henry Penn was a Peterborough bell founder, who cast more than 240 bells between 1703 and 1729. On this day he contracted with St Ives parish church to remove the six existing old bells and recast them. One Henry Norris was given a bond by the St Ives churchwardens to oversee the work and give an opinion on the quality of the new bells. Weighing near 69cwt, they were taken down in July and brought to the Peterborough foundry, where they were melted down and half a ton of new bronze bell metal added. This was now recast into eight new bells, the largest of these ‒ the tenor bell ‒ weighing almost 1 ton. By the beginning of September, the new bells were rehung in the tower of St Ives' church. On their first ringing, Norris and the churchwardens claimed the bells were not in tune and suggested that the bronze metal had not been new. Penn recast some but Norris remained dissatisfied. The matter eventually ended up before the Lord Chancellor on 20 June 1729, with the verdict being given to Henry Penn. It had all broken him, though, and he died and was buried in Huntingdon on 23 July 1729. (Lee, Michael, *Northamptonshire Past & Present*, Northamptonshire Record Society, 2004)

~ MAY 30TH ~

1859: From the early times of Danish occupation and the great Benedictine monastery, the area known as Boongate had a bad reputation. It was the street of the bondsmen and, with the Viking/Danish word for 'street' being 'Gata', it is easy to see how its name developed. As Peterborough expanded in Victorian times, things started to change and the area began to lose its bad name. The New Road was in place and 'modern' houses were being built along Brook Street and Chapel Street. Then, on 1 September 1857, the new parish of St Mary was created by Order of Council and, technically, Boongate was no more. On this day, eighteen months after its creation, William Connor Magee formally laid the first stone for the new – and first – church of the new parish. It was built on land given to the city by the Hon. George Wentworth Fitzwilliam – a member of the Fitzwilliam family of Milton, who were major Peterborough landowners and had owned the land on which Boongate stood since the late sixteenth century. At much the same time, the street through old Boongate that had been called Pig Lane since time immemorial was renamed St Mary's Street. (Bull, J. and V., *Peterborough – a portrait in old picture postcards*, S.B. Publications, 1988)

‑ MAY 31ST ‑

1941: As the conflict of the Second World War continued, more and more men were required to register for service. By now the threshold had been raised and all 40-year-old men were now 'eligible'. As a result, 737 men of Peterborough who had been born in 1901 went to the Employment Exchange to register, with more registrations arriving by post over the following few days. Of these, 55 asked to join the Navy; 251 the Air Force and 66 asked to join the Civil Defence. All others, except for three conscientious objectors, left it up to the powers that be to decide for them. (Gray, David, *Peterborough at War 1939–1945*, David Gray, 2011)

1963: Prince Philip, the Duke of Edinburgh, flew in by helicopter – which he piloted himself – when making his first major visit to Peterborough to promote his Award Scheme. He was greeted by the mayor, Councillor Carl Hall and given a tremendous welcome by all. A large exhibition and display was held on the Embankment, with all the schools in the region taking part. Later, at the invitation of Sir Peter Scott, he flew on to make a private visit to the Wildfowl Trust, now known as the Peakirk Waterfowl Gardens – Prince Philip was president of the trust at the time. The gardens have sadly long since gone. (Harper-Tee, John, 'The Peterborough Story', *Peterborough Evening Telegraph*, 1992)

~ JUNE 1ST ~

1646: This tale relates to St Matthew's church in Eye, where it is recorded that on this day was buried one John Hans, a pauper, who was 'above a hundred years old'. (Bunch, Allan and Liquorice, Mary, *Parish Churches in and around Peterborough*, Cambridgeshire Books, 1990)

1754: In Yaxley, the church register for today tells us of the death of Henry Jordan. 'He cut his throat with a Razor, and was brought in by ye Jury a Lunatick; and Orders were given by ye Coroner for him to have a Christian Burial.' At this time the law differentiated between cases of 'felo de se' (a felon on himself) – a self-murderer who had the will and intention of taking his own life, and suicides, who were considered to be of 'unsound mind'. The 'self-murderer' would be denied a Christian burial, as it was seen to be against God's law. (Bunch, Allan and Liquorice, Mary, *Parish Churches in and around Peterborough*, Cambridgeshire Books, 1990)

1912: On this day, a Post Office official instruction announced that Woodstone had to drop the letter 'e' from its name. As far as the postal service was concerned, the parish was now 'Woodston'. I wonder what happened to the mail if you left the 'e' on the address. (Mitchell, Neil, *The Streets of Peterborough*, Neil Mitchell, 2007)

‒ June 2nd ‒

1713: The *Post Boy* newspaper of this day carried a report on Peterborough celebrating the Peace of Utrecht, which concluded the War of the Spanish Succession, with a procession through the town. Attributing the description to Peterborough's Bishop White Kennett, it says that:

> There was a famous procession of woolcombers, the principle manufacture of the place: viz., the Masters on horseback, handsomely clad and adorned with a pretty variety of coloured wool, hats cockaded and laurel leaves in them who led a great number of journeymen in their Holland shirts of Dutch fine plain-woven linen and white wands tufted, with sashes and scarves of combed wool.

These skilled craftsmen had first come to Peterborough in the thirteenth century. After the Glorious Revolution in 1688, their prosperity increased and 1713 was probably a high point in their presence in Peterborough. By the end of the century their trade had ceased in the city, but it is still remembered in the name of 'their' street – Cumbergate. (Tebbs, H.F., *Peterborough*, Oleander Press, 1979)

1845: This day saw the opening of Peterborough's first railway station – built by the Eastern Counties Railway. In 1862, the company became part of the Great Eastern Railway and the station appeared on timetables as 'Peterborough (GE)'. From 1 July 1923 until its closure, it would be known as Peterborough East. (Various sources)

~ JUNE 3RD ~

1845: I mentioned the opening of Peterborough's first railway station in the previous entry. What was its impact? Well up to this time, to get to Northampton from Peterborough by road involved starting from Peterborough at 6 a.m. and travelling by gig to Thrapston. There you could join the Cambridge to Northampton coach, at a cost of around £4 return. Now, as from today, there is an alternative – a regular service of three trains a day each way on the Blisworth–Northampton–Peterborough railway line. A first-class return ticket on the railway would cost you just 7s 6d – comfortably within the pocket of the gentry and their ladies – and provided comfort comparable to that of the stagecoach. The second-class fare was 5s 6d. An open wagon, third class was 3s 6d – a not insignificant sum for most but a worthwhile option for a trader with customers further down the line. The platform at Peterborough's first station is described in Wheelan's 1849 *Directory of Northamptonshire* as 'something to behold with trains running on one or another of six sidings under a spacious iron roof supported by iron pillars, so forming six wide avenues. On both sides there are large stone platforms. Impressively grand.' (Tebbs, H.F., *Peterborough*, Oleander Press, 1979)

— JUNE 4TH —

1842: Following the Poor Law Amendment Act of 1834, the Peterborough Board of Guardians' first plan was to modify the existing 'houses'. However, these could not meet the new rules so, in 1836, they began the building of a new Union Workhouse on Thorpe Road. The details of the weekly meeting held on this day in 1842 by the Guardians of the Peterborough Union provide us with an insight into this still new way of coping with the poor of Peterborough. Edward Gibbons was in the chair, with twenty-three guardians present. The amount of out relief given in the past week as reported by the relieving officer was £69 18s 4½d in the Peterborough district, and £42 8d in the Crowland district – a total of £111 19s 0½d. Sixteen paupers had been admitted into the workhouse, while nine had been discharged. The total number remaining was given as 169. Also recorded were fifty-two vagrants comprising forty-five males, four females and three children. The total cost of workhouse maintenance for 1,243 days – almost three and a half years – was reported as £21 17s 3¼d. There was also a letter from the Poor Law Commissioners, recommending a division of the Peterborough medical district. This had previously been arranged by the Board and the suggestion adopted. (*Cambridge Independent Press*)

~ JUNE 5TH ~

1858: By an indenture of this date, the Guardians of the Poor of Peterborough Union conveyed the old Werrington Workhouse to the Trustees of the Werrington School Charity. It was then converted into two cottages, to be used as schoolhouses by the master and mistress of the new school built on the other side of Church Street. (*Werrington Past*, *c.* 1970)

1881: A robbery committed at Peterborough was a bit different to the average theft. John Hardy, who gave his address as London, went into the Bull Inn the previous evening, where his 'demeanour' was considered 'rather suspicious', although nothing happened. Before 8 a.m. the next day he returned, asking for a glass of ale, but was told that he could not be served until after 8 a.m. He loitered, then left. It was later discovered that the cash box – containing £9 – was missing. There was an obvious suspect and the police were called. Hardy had left town, so telegrams were dispatched in all directions. One was shown to a Spalding publican, who later saw someone matching Hardy's description. He told the police and the suspect was arrested. It was Hardy who, it appears, had gone to Stamford after stealing the cash box, bought various items of clothing, and then moved on to Spalding. (*Grantham Journal*)

– JUNE 6TH –

1834: We think modern advertising is pushy and – perhaps – misleading. This is a typical advert among many in the *Stamford Mercury* of the day.

A wonderful discovery for the tooth-ache: Knight's Vegetable Absorbent – a certain cure, however much decayed. This valuable medicine far exceeds all other remedies for speedily allaying pains in the teeth, nerves of the face and head, and in many cases of tic douloureux [still around today] has given ease and comfort where medical skill has been completely baffled. The Absorbent is perfectly harmless, and will totally subdue pain so as never to have a return in the same tooth, without injuring the enamel, or causing any other inconvenience to the patient than a slight momentary irritation in the nose and throat; this, with a knowledge that it will prove a grateful and soothing comforter to thousands who are daily suffering under excruciating pains in the teeth and nerves of the face and head, induces the Proprietor to bring this infallible remedy particularly before the notice of every individual by means of the public press. Sold wholesale by Dicey and Co, 10 Bow Churchyard, London; and retail by most druggists, at 1*s* 9*d*.

~ June 7th ~

1816: The new burial ground at the top of Cowgate had been in use for some time and discussions began in vestry meetings as to how the old burial ground on the north side of the cathedral should now be managed. One matter was resolved today, when agreement was reached that a footpath should be allowed through it via gates on the north and south sides. It was also agreed that the gates would be of a style that the churchwardens might think proper. (Mellows, W.T., *The Old Churchyards of Peterborough*, Northamptonshire Records Society, 1947)

1932: It was on this day that Francis (Frank) Perkins and his close friend Charles Chapman recovered from the collapse of the AGE group – see 26 February for this story – and formed F. Perkins Ltd. Their business was to develop further the high-speed diesel engine they had been working on. While this happened, the company was kept afloat by cash injections by Captain Chamberlain, Frank's brother-in-law. That faith was rewarded when the engines became vital power sources through the Second World War and beyond. For many businesses and people, Perkins Engines and Peterborough became one and the same. In 1998, Caterpillar acquired the Perkins Engines Co for $1.3 billion! (*People of Peterborough*, Peterborough Museum Publication, 2009)

– JUNE 8TH –

1688: Thomas White, Bishop of Peterborough, was one of seven bishops of the kingdom who challenged King James II's restatement of his 'Declaration of Indulgence' in this year. The Declaration declared that existing laws against Catholics and dissenters was 'hereby suspended' and bishops were required to 'cause the said declaration to be sent and distributed throughout their several and respective dioceses, to be read accordingly'. White, five other bishops and the Archbishop of Canterbury signed a protest to the king and were granted an audience on 18 May. They got nowhere and were – effectively – thrown out. Summoned to appear before the Privy Council on 8 June 1688, they refused to back down. The result was that all six bishops were committed to the Tower of London – White was the only Bishop of Peterborough to have experienced this. They came to trial in front of judge and jury in Westminster Hall on 29 June. On the following day, the jury returned a verdict of 'not guilty' and all the bishops were acquitted of any crime. By the end of the year, King James had left these shores and the Glorious Revolution was coming to fruition – and our Bishop of Peterborough had played an important part in that change. (Carnell, Geoffrey, *The Bishops of Peterborough*, RJL Smith & Associates, 1993)

– JUNE 9TH –

1929: Britain's Railway Queen, Miss Edna Best – described as a charming young Manchester lady, visited Peterborough over this weekend. Staying with Mrs Cullup of Gladstone Street, she was 'engaged on a mission of helping to promote peace in industry and co-operation among railwaymen of all countries'. A tall order for a young lady in what was still a man's world! This Sunday afternoon meeting attracted a large crowd to watch the entrance of the Railway Queen, making a stately figure in her robes and crown, with her charming bevy of attendants. Lieutenant-Colonel V.M. Barrington-Ward Superintendent of the LNER Southern Area, wondered:

> … what would have happened twenty years ago if the superintendent had come among his men like he was doing that day! (laughter) But, during the last 20 years there had been a different spirit abroad: instead of being master and man in the railway service, to-day they were brothers working for one common end (applause). The officers of the railway companies were out to work with the men, and wanted the men to work with them.

By this time the following year, the Great Depression was with us and this bright new world had changed. (*Peterborough Advertiser*)

– JUNE 10TH –

1334: King Edward III arrived in Peterborough on this day to stay at the monastery on a visit. He had crossed the, by now, dilapidated wooden bridge over the Nene and had obviously made some comments about it. When he discovered that no one seemed to take responsibility for the upkeep of this link with the wider world, he granted a licence to four local men to take tolls from merchants carrying goods across the bridge and, with that money, to maintain the bridge. Two of these are recorded as being the Rector of St Mary's church, Orton Waterville, and Richard of Lincoln, of Lincoln's Place in Midgate. (Bull, J. and V., *Scene Magazine*, 2012)

1931: Times had been hard and this was the day when the shareholders of the Peterborough Electric Traction Co. finally approved the merger of the old company into a new organisation, to be called the 'Eastern Counties Omnibus Co. Ltd'. Also under that umbrella were the 'Eastern Counties Road Car Co.', the 'Ortona Motor Co.' and the East Anglian part of the 'United Automobile Services'. Transportation in Peterborough had changed one last time. The final nail in the coffin arrived on 5 November, when the shareholders agreed a resolution to formally and finally wind up the old company. (*Peterborough Local History Society Magazine*)

— JUNE 11TH —

1855: This day saw the death at Paston Hall of one Fenwick Skrimshire, an English physician and naturalist who'd published a number of works of popular science and medicine. It was he who'd certified the poet John Clare as mad and was instrumental in committing him to the Northampton Asylum in 1841, having known him since 1820. He completed Clare's admission papers by answering the question 'Was the insanity preceded by any severe or long-continued mental emotion or exertion?' with 'After years of poetical prosing'. A medical graduate from Edinburgh University, Skrimshire had been active much earlier here in Peterborough. It is recorded that on 4 May 1816, he began giving out medicine to the general populace of Peterborough. Very few Peterborians were able to stay at the dispensary so, in 1819, a lodging house with a nurse who acted as matron, nurse and servant was established for them. Patients could stay after obtaining medicine, but their family had to bring them their food. Records for 1830 show 1,238 people being admitted during that time, with 916 being discharged as cured; thirty-four died and twelve left of their own accord. Sixty were recorded as being supplied with trusses. (National *Review*; Stedman Family Tree)

– JUNE 12TH –

1924: A cloudburst today resulted in a flood, which affected virtually all the city's streets. Two houses in Fitzwilliam Street used their basements as living rooms. Unfortunately, that particular road was flooded and the drains could not cope with the amount of water. The water pressure forced the basement windows open and totally flooded the rooms to a depth of around 5ft, with chairs and other items floating about. There was a child in one of the rooms and, just in time, a young girl ran from another room and carried the child to safety. Midgate was also badly affected. The fire brigade pumped the water away but many shops and businesses suffered. Perhaps worst hit was John Walker Watts – a costumier and milliner from Old Fletton, who carried on his business in the Midgate Buildings. As a result of the floods he filed a debtor's petition for bankruptcy on 13 December 1924 and attended the first hearing at the Official Receiver's Office in Petty Cury Cambridge on 30 December 1924. It was not until his case was heard at the Peterborough Law Courts on 6 November 1928 that his bankruptcy was formally recorded. (Bull, J & V., Perry, S. and Sturgess, R., *Peterborough – a third portrait in old picture postcards*, S.B. Publications, 1990; *London Gazette*; *Grantham Journal*)

— JUNE 13TH —

1700: Lord Fitzwilliam was the dominant landowner around Peterborough but spent most of his time elsewhere. The 'home' estate was managed, in the main, by Francis Guybon, his steward – who often had to prepare for visits that never happened. This letter to him from London is typical:

> Get all things ready speedily for some of us will come down if not all together. Get your brewing vessels ready and brew 4 hogsheads of small beer and two of ale. Allow 20 bushels of malt, 16 for the ale and 4 for the beer. Hop them so they can be drunk within a month from today. Don't let the drink want hops, yet not too bitter. I hope you have hired a man for the gates, etc., ready to come at three days warning. Likewise; two maids, one for the kitchen as good as possible, the other a good working servant. Send money speedily for I am in want on such an expensive occasion. (P.S.) Thoroughly air all the beds and clean the rooms at the great end, at the matted end, and at our end of the house.

I wonder what happened to the beer and ale if they did not come – surely Guybon would not let it go to waste. (Hainsworth, D.R. and Walker, Cherry, *The Correspondence of Lord Fitzwilliam of Milton & Francis Guybon his Steward*, Northamptonshire Record Society, 1990)

– JUNE 14TH –

1823: The *Lincoln, Rutland and Stamford Mercury* was the first widely available local newspaper. A system of newsmen, carts and coaches collected stories and advertisements from across the catchment area during the week then distributed the printed copies each week. Honesty and reliability of the newsmen was a high priority; failure to meet the required standards brought instant dismissal and frequent referral to the forces of law. On this Saturday John Booth, drum major of the South Lincoln Militia, was committed to Peterborough Gaol for trial at the Quarter Sessions, charged with embezzling money received on account of Messrs Newcomb of Stamford by whom he was employed as a newsman to Peterborough. In due time, Booth was sentenced to three months' imprisonment. (Newton, D. and Smith, M., *Stamford Mercury – three centuries of newspaper publishing*, Shaun Tyas, 1999)

1844: Built in the early 1700s on the west side of the Car Dyke, the Fengate Postmill was at this time owned and operated by James Holditch. On this Friday afternoon, Ann Rands visited the mill to buy barley meal. As she was leaving, she was struck on the head by the revolving sail and died. The coroner's report confirmed that she had received a mortal bruise on her neck and shoulder and had died instantly. James Holditch later claimed that the damage to the sail amounted to 1*s*! (*Family History Magazine*)

~ June 15th ~

1813: Matthew Wyldbore's name has solid resonances to this day among Peterborians. An enthusiastic campanologist, he is remembered for being saved by the bells of St John's when, one night, he was lost in a thick fog in Eye (*see* March 15th). He remembered that in his will when, in addition to many other bequests, he charged his estate in Peterborough to make an annual payment of £5 to be annually disposed of, on the day of his death, to the ringers of the parish church of St. John the Baptist, part in money and part in an entertainment, as the minister should think best, on condition they should ring one peal or more on the said day. His heirs inherited the estates and, on this day in 1813, in order to secure and perpetuate the above payments, Sir John Wyldbore-Smith conveyed, by a codicil to the will, a farmhouse in Newark, and several parcels of land totalling 11 acres in the Peterborough open fields to William Strong, William Simpson, and their heirs. The buck had been passed and the bells continue to ring out on Matthew Wyldbore's Day. (Parliamentary Papers, House of Commons and Command; Bull, J & V., *A history of Peterborough Parish Church – St John the Baptist 1407–2007*)

− JUNE 16TH −

1936: It was on this day that Itter Park, just off the Fulbridge Road, actually opened for the pleasures of the community. Arthur W. Itter was born in London in 1856 and had his life changed forever in 1878, when he became involved in the Peterborough's brick industry. In December 1901, the Stone Trades Journal described him as one of the largest single-handed brick manufacturers under the British flag. His son Arthur was born in 1899 and, in due time, became deeply involved in many aspects of Peterborough life − King's Dyke and Whittlesea brickyards being just two of them. His involved interests also encompassed religion − he was also actively involved with the Park Road Baptist church, where he held positions of both secretary and deacon. This element of his life is recorded in a 1936 book published by the Religious Tract Society, 'God's Errant Knight', written by Marguerite Williams. In 1933 he became mayor elect for the city, and in late 1934, he became the youngest mayor to hold office. Less than two months later he passed away, setting a new record for Peterborough's shortest mayoralty. (*Peterborough Local History Society Magazine*)

~ June 17th ~

1381: On 15 June, a mob started to gather in the centre of Peterborough to complain about a new tax – a 'poll tax'. Their focus was the local landlord and tax collector, the institution that effectively owned and ran the city – Peterborough Abbey. One can imagine the monks' nervousness as they sensed trouble from the mob gathered on the market square! The abbot knew that Henry Despenser, 'the Fighting Bishop of Norwich', was in the area and sent to him for help. Henry headed in with his eight knights, a number of archers and others he gathered from local gentry along the way. At his arrival, protesters fled in all directions. Henry gave orders to his troops to give no quarter. A contemporary account describes: 'Some fell by sword or lance without the church, some within, some even close to the altar. So those who had come to destroy the church and its ministers perished by the hand of a churchman. For the Bishop's sword gave them their absolution…' The church is likely to have been Beckett's chapel, which still stood at this time. Because of the spilling of human blood it was deconsecrated. Sometime later it was reconsecrated, then demolished to build the new parish church of St John. (Allington-Smith, Richard, *Henry Despenser: The Fighting Bishop*, Larks Press)

– JUNE 18TH –

1850: In 1786, the Whittlesea Mere had been surveyed and was adjudged to be about 3.5 miles long by 2.5 miles wide, giving a total area of some 1,570 acres of water. It was, on average, 5-6ft deep. By 1835, the Fen drainage had caused a reduction in water levels – in some place now no more than 2ft deep – and a significant growth of weeds. Nonetheless, it was still a great place for wildfowling. The Holme Decoy caught anything up to 600 birds a day during the season. In the summer, there was pleasure boating and fishing, followed by leisure and high-speed competitive skating in the winter. Fifteen years later, the face of Peterborough and the surrounding area was changing and the Mere was in the way. With the water depth now down to between 9 and 18in, this day saw the beginning of the final drainage. By the middle of November, the water was gone – channelled off into multiple rivers and streams – and by March 1851, the cutting of dykes had begun and the age-old Mere from time immemorial was no more. (*Stamford Mercury, Peterborough Advertiser, Peterborough Times*)

− June 19th −

1671: To celebrate the Restoration of the Monarchy following the collapse of the Commonwealth of Oliver Cromwell, the gentry − and others − of the town had subscribed to a fund 'for the building of a public cross or Town House'. John Lovin, the leading builder in the town, was given the contract and by this time it was almost complete. Behind the scenes, though, things were not going well and, on this day, the Feoffees met and realised that 'the accounts and differences between John Lovin and the inhabitants about the building of the Cross' did not balance. They were £56 in arrears! Now we know that there's nothing new to agreeing to put off a decision. It took until January 1672 to pay Lovin what was due to him. (Tebbs, H.F., *Peterborough*, Oleander Press, 1979)

—–—

1917: Before the Norman Cross magistrates on this Tuesday were Harry Brummitt, Frank Wray, Roland Charles Crisp and Cyril Bridgefoot, all of Woodston, and Thomas Brummitt of Wellingborough, all of whom were summoned by Thomas Goole of Rugby, inspector of the railway police, for trespassing on the London and North Western Railway at Orton Longueville on 27 May. They were each fined 25*s*. One wonders just what they were doing to deserve this. (*Peterborough & Huntingdon Standard*)

— June 20th —

1838: At about 2 a.m. on this quiet Wednesday, a passing policeman was wished a pleasant 'good night' by a man walking past. The policeman acknowledged the greeting and the man walked away. Not too many paces later, the policeman saw a man's head briefly protruding from the ground before vanishing. Now suspicious, he raised the alarm and woke the gaoler. On checking the cells, he found one of two brothers that had been committed for pig stealing seemingly asleep in the cell. There was no sign of the other. What was to be seen, though, was the debris from an excavated tunnel under the wall that led to the Minster Yard surface. There, a large stone slab carefully covered the opening. There is no record of the escapee ever being caught. (*Northamptonshire Herald*; Percival, Andrew, *Notes on Old Peterborough*, Peterborough Archaeological Society, 1905)

1917: At Peterborough magistrates' court, Mrs Susan Johnson of No. 26 Chapel Street was summoned for keeping a dog without licence. She said that the dog belonged to her son, who was at the war, and that she was keeping it for him. She was fined 7*s* 6*d*, but allowed to retain the dog until her son returned. One wonders how many families were in the same situation. (*Peterborough & Huntingdon Standard*)

‒ June 21st ‒

1887: Great celebrations were organised for Queen Victoria's Golden Jubilee. The proceedings opened with a service at the parish church of St John's. Elsewhere, 1,200 poor people were entertained at lunch in the Midland Railway wagon sheds in Thorpe Road. At 2 p.m. there was a great gathering of children on the Market Place, and between 10,000 and 12,000 people joined in singing the Jubilee Anthem. A vast company, headed by the mayor Alderman H.P. Gates and corporation followed by 5,000 children and many illuminated cars, then proceeded to the old Agricultural Show Ground in Lincoln Road, where tea, sports and entertainment were provided for the children. The Boat Club organised a regatta on the river, and in the evening the principal streets of the city were brilliantly illuminated. (Mellows, W.I., 'Peterborough's Municipal Jubilee', *Peterborough Standard*, 1924)

1887: Today's *York Herald* declared that:

> Perhaps one of the most interesting forms of midnight illumination will be the exhibition of a 'magnesium' (flare) on the west tower of Ely Cathedral. From that lofty elevation over the flat fenlands it is anticipated that it will be easily visible over an area of at least twenty miles ‒ as far as Downham Market to the north, Peterborough to the west, Cambridge to the south and Newmarket, the Gogmagogs and Brandon to the east.

— June 22nd —

1897: Suggestions as to a permanent memorial for Queen Victoria's Diamond Jubilee had been invited. Those recorded by Mr Mellows included the erection of public baths and wash-houses; a museum on a central site; a covered market; the restoration of the navigation between Peterborough and Wisbech and the erection of municipal buildings – this last suggestion came from the Mayor Alderman J. Thompson, a major local builder! The decision, however, was soon made to build a Jubilee wing at the infirmary. The foundation stone was laid on Jubilee Day by the mayor, in the presence of a large assembly of citizens. Elsewhere in the city, celebrations included a pageant of decorated cars through the city, and lunch for 400 aged poor at the Corn Exchange. In the afternoon, the Market Square was given over to some 6,000 children, who sang the national anthem and were afterwards entertained to tea in the different schools. (Mellows, W.I., 'Peterborough's Municipal Jubilee', *Peterborough Standard*, 1924)

1938: When Werrington's new Parish Hall was opened by Mr C.M. Everard, the architect, Mr G. Warwick, handed him an ordinary key wrapped in a treasury note which Mr Everard immediately handed over to the treasurer. The committee had thought this to be more useful than spending money on a silver key. (A past & present stroll around Werrington; *Peterborough Standard*)

— JUNE 23RD —

1863: Lord Palmerston was considered by some of his contemporaries to be a womaniser. During his second term as prime minister (1859–65), *The Times* named him Lord Cupid. Aged 79, he was cited as co-respondent in an 1863 divorce case, although it emerged that the case was nothing more than an attempted blackmail. It is easy to see, therefore, how many other stories appeared – often as 'Original Anecdotes' under the name of Mr Punch. One such anecdote in the *Stamford Mercury* caught my eye:

> The prettiest of all young ladies in the refreshment place in the station at Peterborough made a clever remark to Mr Punch the other night. He was affably taking a Bath Bun or two, and waiting for the bell to ring, and of course was in improving conversation with the fair attendants. 'My friend Lord Palmerston has had a good time of it in Scotland?' said Mr Punch. 'Yes Sir,' said the young lady, and 'he has praised the people there so much that I think he should in future be called Lord Butter-Scotch'. She pointed her words by handing to Mr Punch a packet of the delicate confectionary so named, and he was so overcome by his feelings that he went off without paying!

− June 24th −

1834: We tend to think of our era as the first to have wall-to-wall advertising with products good, bad and indifferent being pushed at us twenty-four hours a day. Summer boot sales help us dispose of things we don't want and seek out bargains that we would like. The nineteenth century, though, was just as pushy and adept. This one, in the *Stamford Mercury*, is typical of Peterborough sales of the time.

Household furniture, Grates, Coppers, Books, Glass, China and Earthenware, and other Effects, removed to the REPOSITORY, PETERBOROUGH, for Convenience of Sale, To be SOLD by Auction by Wm Edwards on Tuesday the 24th day of June 1834; COMPRISING four-post and tent bedsteads with chintz, moreen, and cheek hangings, feather-beds, mattresses, and other bedding, set of mahogany dining tables on patent principle, mahogany and other chairs, sofa, chests of drawers, press bed, pier and swing glasses, Brussels and Kidderminster carpets, china, dinner service, glass, and various earthenware, brewing and washing copper, register stoves, kitchen range, and useful articles, 50 lots of books, and various effects; also a light Cart on springs. Catalogues may be had at the usual places in the neighbourhood and the auctioneer's office, Peterborough, a week before the sale. Sale to begin at 11 o'clock.

‒ June 25th ‒

1937: On this Saturday, the traffic lights at the corner of Bridge Street and Bishops Road were switched on. They incorporated a pedestrian button, which lit up with a 'Cross Now' message! (Mitchell, Neil, *The Streets of Peterborough*, Neil Mitchell, 2007)

‒‒‒

1964: Many years before Queensgate opened and dominated city-centre shopping in Peterborough, the Oddenino Property and Investment Co.'s development project produced Peterborough's first 'prestige' indoor shopping centre. It was on this day that the building reached its highest point, and 100 workers downed tools! They did so with the blessing of the developers to attend the traditional topping out ceremony on the roof. Approximately 100 guests, headed by the mayor and mayoress of Peterborough (Councillor and Mrs George Bradley), were greeted by board representatives. The mayor, wearing a white coat, levelled off a specially prepared section and declared the building well and truly open. Named the Hereward Centre, the project prospered and within two years it was doing so well that traders asked the developers for extra floor space. A spokesman for the company said that trade was so good that extensions to the property would be profitable. Predictably, Queensgate changed the trading patterns of the city and in July 1989, the new owners of the Hereward site set about spending £1.5 million on giving the arcade a major facelift. (*Peterborough Evening Telegraph*; *Peterborough Advertiser*)

— JUNE 26TH —

1407: There were some controversial points behind the consecration of, and the first Mass at, St John's church by Peterborough's mitred Abbot Genge. Philip Repington, the Bishop of Lincoln, should have attended but, it was claimed, he had more pressing engagements. Bishop Repington was chaplain and confessor to King Henry VI and it was 'suggested' that he was too busy chasing promotion to come to Peterborough. Was it a coincidence that he became a cardinal in 1408? (Bull, J & V., *A history of Peterborough Parish Church – St John the Baptist 1407–2007*; Mackreth, Donald, *Peterborough – History & Guide*, Sutton, 1994)

1929: On this first day of four, Greater Peterborough celebrated 'Civic Week'. The mayor, corporation and guests first attended Divine Service at the cathedral, followed by a 'beating the bounds' ceremony. A 'very imposing and veteran private coach' transported the mayor, dean and aldermen as 'outside' passengers to visit the furthest boundaries of the enlarged city. These were on Thorpe Road, close to the Milton Park entrance; Marholm Road near Mucklands Wood; near the railway bridge on Lincoln Road, Werrington; at the bridge over the Car Dyke; on Newborough Road at Gunthorpe and at the boundary between Newark and Eye on the Eye Road. At each stop, the representatives of the old parishes were welcomed as citizens of Greater Peterborough. The Mayor, corporation and guests finished with luncheon at the Angel Hotel. (*Peterborough Advertiser*)

~ JUNE 27TH ~

1744: On this day, Edward Wortley Montague conveyed to the Feoffees of Peterborough 'Out of his free good will and charitable disposition, and for the better keeping and maintenance of the poor of the parish of St John the Baptist in a more decent, clean and wholesome manner than what they are now kept', two houses in Westgate and a 4-acre piece of grassland he had purchased from William and Mary Smith. He then built Peterborough's second workhouse on the site. (Mellows, W.I., 'Peterborough's Municipal Jubilee', *Peterborough Standard*, 1924)

1895: This Thursday evening's road race by the New England Bicycle Club landed thirteen members in the police court, charged with 'riding bicycles furiously on the highway at Werrington so as to endanger the lives and limbs of passengers'! Mr Batten for the defence pleaded not guilty, saying that he thought if the authorities wished to put a stop to road riding, they should issue a public notice. He drew attention to the fact that big races, with pacemakers, were run over the same ground without interference. It was stated that the police were bound to put a stop to the road racing, and record breakers would be dealt with the same way – if the police could get hold of them! The bench fined the defendants 2*s* 6*d* and costs each. (*Lincoln, Rutland and Stamford Mercury*)

‒ JUNE 28TH ‒

1787: Born on this day in Whittlesey, Harry Smith served in the local yeomanry at Norman Cross. In 1805, he was offered a commission in the army. He joined the 95th Rifles as a lieutenant, serving in Buenos Aires, South America in 1806 and Spain and Portugal from 1808. In April 1812, he married Juana María de los Dolores de León – a Spanish girl of well-born lineage. She followed him on virtually all of his later travels. In America he was at the battle of New Orleans, and saw Washington burn before returning to Europe for the Battle of Waterloo. In 1828 he was sent to South Africa, then known as the Cape of Good Hope. He became a provincial governor there, before being moved to India as deputy-adjutant-general of the forces there. He was made Knight Commander of the Order of the Bath, before returning to Africa as High Commissioner and Governor of Cape Colony. He and his wife are remembered there in the names of the towns of Harrismith and Ladysmith. They returned to England in 1852, where he retired, dying in 1860. The Sir Harry Smith Community School (now College) in Whittlesey is named after him. Quite an interesting life for a Whittlesey lad, don't you think? (*People of Peterborough*, Peterborough Museum Publications, 2009)

~ JUNE 29TH ~

1912: On this Saturday, the arrival of one of our early aviators, Mr William H. Ewen, piloting his Caudron biplane, caused great excitement in the city. When he touched down on a field at Walton, he became the first airman to land in Peterborough. He had flown up from St Neots as part of a major towns and cities circuit of Britain. During the day, the ex-mayor, Councillor C.E. Crawley, presented him with a silver rose bowl and a lucky silver horseshoe as a memento of his visit. Throughout the rest of this day and Sunday, Ewen gave many flying displays to the watching crowds. When he took off to fly on to Lincoln on the Monday morning, however, he failed to gain sufficient height and crashed. Ewen and his mechanic were thankfully unhurt – that horseshoe had obviously been lucky! Now, as well as having the kudos of being the first airman to land at Peterborough, he could claim to be the first pilot to crash here too! The plane was repaired over the next two days and they finally, successfully, took off for Lincoln on 4 July. He could now also claim to be the first to repair an airplane at Peterborough. (Perry, Stephen, *Peterborough Vol. 2 – a second portrait in old picture postcards*, S.B. Publications, 1989)

– June 30th –

1855: The *Peterborough Advertiser* carried this advertisement for the Bull Hotel:

WILLIAM PHILLIPS tenders his grateful thanks to the clergy, gentry, and inhabitants of PETERBOROUGH and Neighbourhood for the very kind support he has hitherto received in all the branches connected with his Establishment, and begs to inform them that he has recently purchased a neat Clarence Carriage for the convenience of his friends, which can be used with one or a pair of horses, and he will be happy to accommodate any Ladies or Gentlemen who may honor (sic) him with their patronage. Steady and careful drivers. He begs to remind Commercial Gentlemen that his Hotel has lately undergone great alteration and improvement: it is now replete with every convenience, and every attention will be paid to merit their support.

1888: George Carter, who had ridden to hounds with the Fitzwilliam Hounds for forty-three years, the last twenty-seven as 'Huntsman', retired on this day. He had seen good times and bad, ranging from an altercation with the gate keeper at the Thorpe station level crossing when he was riding with Edward, Prince of Wales, later King Edward VII, to having a dinner in his honour in 1872, where he was presented with a silver cup along with £763 in sovereigns collected from friends and well-wishers. (Liquorice, Mary, *Posh Folk: Notable Personalities (and a Donkey) Associated with Peterborough*, Cambridgeshire Libraries, 1991)

1897: The Clerk to the Council entered the following advertisement in the *Peterborough Citizen*.

> The Rural District Council of Peterborough: Inspector of Nuisances. Applications are invited for the Appointment of INSPECTORS OF NUISANCES for the Rural District Council of Peterborough. The appointment will be made subject to the approval of the Local Government Board. The person appointed will be required to perform the duties defined by the General Orders of the Local Government Board and the Public Health Acts, and to obey the Orders of the Council. The Salary will be £40 a year, inclusive of travelling expenses within the district.

Applying was no easy task, as there was not much time to do it. The order was issued on this day, appeared in the paper on 2 July and had to be received by the council on or before 6 July! The application, it was stated, should be in the candidates' own handwriting and must state age, qualifications and present occupation. Applicants were to provide copies of two recent testimonials, and that was all to be sent to J.W. Buckle, Clerk to the Council, Broadway, Peterborough. Selected candidates would have notice to attend the council, and reasonable travelling expenses would be allowed. Canvassing, directly or indirectly, would result in a disqualification.

~ July 2nd ~

1594: There are many things unique about Peterborough's cathedral – and one of the most unusual of these is the portrait of a sixteenth-century gravedigger over the front door! It is of Robert Scarlett – 'Old Scarlett' – who died on this day, at the age of 98. He is probably the only man of his profession to have an entry in the Dictionary of National Biography. As well as spending much of his life as the sexton at Peterborough Cathedral, he was also the parish clerk and sexton for St John's parish church. Three parish vicars came and went during his tenure. His duties included keeping the churchyard clean, tolling the bell at the death of a parishioner, and burying the dead in the cemetery to the north of the cathedral. His main claim to fame is that during his long career he buried two queens in the cathedral: Katherine of Aragon and Mary, Queen of Scots. He always said he buried three queens – the other was his first wife. She died in July 1584 and Robert remarried on 5 December 1585 aged 89! Legend also suggests that he may have been the inspiration for the gravedigger in Shakespeare's *Hamlet* – but to date, no proof has been found. *(Mellows, W.T., The Old Churchyards of Peterborough,* Northamptonshire Records Society, 1947; Dixon, George, *Old Scarlett,* Paul Bush, 1997)

- JULY 3RD -

1894: During this week, the Midland Railway Co. introduced an important improvement that, the *Peterborough Standard* claimed, 'may hereafter turn out to have been the starting point of a railway revolution'. On their new morning express from St Pancras, which did the journey to Glasgow almost in the same time as the West Coast express, the Midland Railway Co. were running a dining car for the use of the first and third class passengers alike, with meat at precisely the same price.

———

1970: As the face of Peterborough changed, many long-established businesses suffered. This Friday's *Peterborough Advertiser* highlighted three such businesses, all of which had received compulsory purchase orders to make way for the new Western Primary Road. Kenneth Henson's cycle shop at No. 917 Lincoln Road had been trading there since his father had founded the business some fifty years previous. At No. 909 Lincoln Road, the ladies' hairdressing salon had been started by Mrs Eva Wilson just before the Second World War. The Dandridge brothers' greengrocers' shop and nursery dated back even further; that had been founded by their father in the 1920s. All three of these personal, long-standing and successful businesses were given until the end of March 1971 to say farewell to their customers, close up shop and vacate their business home as the 'new' Peterborough advanced.

– July 4th –

1886: At the Peterborough Petty Sessions on 7 July Henry Jackson, a moulder from Rotherham, was charged with being drunk and disorderly on this Sunday. Mrs Emma Rollings of Midland Road claimed that on Sunday evening, at about 10.30 p.m., she – along with her little child – was coming through the subway on Thorpe Road to meet her husband when she met the defendant in the middle of it. The defendant was very drunk and used very bad language, promising to murder the child, at which point the witness snatched it up and ran away as fast as she could. Her husband afterwards lodged a complaint at the police station and the defendant was brought to her home, where she identified him as the man who had stopped her. She had never seen him before. PC Ellisten said that at around midnight on Sunday, he had found the defendant lying asleep near Mr English's gates on the Thorpe Road. He roused the defendant and found he was very drunk, although the defendant said he had not the slightest recollection of the matter. He was fined 10s with 12s costs; in default, a month's hard labour. The chairman expressed the court's gratitude to Mrs Rollings for bringing the case forward. (*Peterborough Express*)

~ July 5th ~

1894: Under the headline 'Caution to Emigrants', this week's *Peterborough Standard* provided information from the Emigrants' Information Office. We learn that the best season for going to Canada is far advanced and emigrants intending to go there this year should not delay. The principal demand is for experienced farm labourers; there is little demand for mechanics. In New South Wales, the number of unemployed around Sydney is said to be decreasing, with many men being employed in road making and prospecting on the gold fields; domestic staff are wanted. There is no demand for more hands in South Australia and in the north there is no demand for emigrants without capital; but as land is now very cheap, a man with a capital of £600 would find a good opening.

———

1919: Deputy Mayor Alderman Whitsed read the Proclamation of Peace after the Great War at the West Front of the cathedral. Later the Mayor, Alderman C.T. Vergette, led the Peace celebrations. In the morning, there was a review of ex-servicemen and afterwards a great united thanksgiving service at the Stanley Recreation Ground. In the afternoon, the citizens and their children were entertained at a gala in the new showground of the Agricultural Society at Eastfield. (Mellows, W.I., 'Peterborough's Municipal Jubilee', *Peterborough Standard*, 1924)

~ July 6th ~

1894: Victorian newspaper content is not always what you think. This week's *Peterborough Standard* tells us:

> A COLD TEAPOT SPOILS THE TEA. A little care is required to make a good cup of Tea, but it is well worth the trouble. Never make Tea without rinsing the pot with boiling water, and never use water that has been simmering a long time. Tea should be infused about seven minutes and kept hot all the time.

All good, sound advice – perhaps it is aimed at the July newlyweds. But reading on we learn that:

> In addition it is necessary to choose the right blend of tea. If you follow all our instructions and use Johnson, Johnson & Co's Pure Tea, which is sold in packets by grocers and dealers in Tea, you will find the evening meal promptly revives exhausted strength. As a test you may obtain a sample of tea, also a refined nickel silver spoon, by sending two penny stamps for postage to JOHNSON, JOHNSON & Co, 50 Southwark Bridge Road, London. We have the pleasure also to inform you that Johnson, Johnson & Co's pure Tea is sold in this town by T R Waite, Grocer etc, 39 Westgate, Peterborough.

It's an advert posing as news and advice.

– July 7th –

1784: Sometimes the crime and the punishment do not seem to balance. On this day, James Burley and George Barland were charged at the Old Bailey with stealing one cloth great coat, the property of the Right Reverend Father in God, Lord Bishop of Peterborough. Thomas Lord, giving witness under sworn oath, stated:

> I am coachman to the Bishop of Peterborough, he lost his great coat, value twenty shillings, on the 9th of June last, about twenty minutes before one. The two prisoners took it. I caught the coat on the prisoner Burly; it was upon the coach box at the Bishop's door in Conduit-street, I was just got off my box, and when I came out my coat was gone, and a man told me them two boys had taken it: one of the prisoners said nothing, and the other said he knew nothing of the matter, they were both running away, I believe they were sensible that I was pursuing them. Prisoner Burley claimed that a man run and dropped the coat, and I picked it up.

Both were found guilty of the theft, although the stolen item was valued at just 10*d*. Each was to be transported for seven years. (*Proceedings of the Old Bailey*, ref. t17840707-15)

~ July 8th ~

1515: The abbacy of Robert Kirkton was a time of extremes for both the monastery and the town. His great building projects have left us the New Building on the church and the Great Gate that now leads to the dean's offices. However, beyond this gate, he had allowed thirty tenements to fall into utter decay before turning the ground into a park for his deer! Running side by side with his grand projects was lax management and slipping morals. Kirkton himself 'wriggled and squirmed' when it came to repaying a debt to Henry VIII. When William Atwater, Bishop of Lincoln, visited the monastery on this day, he found many things 'out of order'. He reported that monk, John Walpole, was being seditious amongst his brethren. He also reported that he had stolen certain jewels from St Oswald's shrine, and what he could lay his hands on elsewhere, and given them to women in the town. So much for his vow of celibacy! It was also recorded that certain monks haunted a tavern near the monastery – probably in the Boongate area – and gave themselves up to singing and dancing in the dormitory until 10 or 11 p.m., to the consternation of the rest of their brethren. (Gunton, Symon, *The history of the Church of Peterborough*, ed. Symon Patrick, 1990)

⁓ JULY 9TH ⁓

1407: Following an agreement between the abbot and the parishioners of St John's, the great cemetery on the north of the church became the town burial ground. Previously this had been monastery's monks' burial place, but from this day onwards, monks would be buried in the ground between the Apsidal End of the abbey church and the old vineyard. Lettice Goodbody was the first 'ordinary' person to be buried in this ground. (Mackreth, Donald, *Peterborough – History & Guide*, Sutton, 1994)

⁓

1913: 'TWO POUNDS REWARD': so read a poster, signed J.W. Buckle, Clerk, on behalf of the Peterborough Joint Cemetery Board. It stated:

> Whereas some evil disposed person or persons have maliciously and wilfully taken away flowers from a Grave in this Cemetery: whoever will give such information as may lead to the conviction of the offender or offenders or any accomplice impeaching, whereby a conviction may be had in this or a time within one month from this date, will be entitled to the above reward. A free pardon will be allowed to any accomplice who may be admitted by the Justice to give evidence for the Crown. If the reward be claimed by more than one person, the Joint Board reserve the right of deciding when and in what proportion it shall be paid.

(Peterborough Museum)

– July 10th –

1901: The annual Peterborough Show was at its height when the *Northampton Mercury* reported on this year's three-day exhibition on its usual site. The weather was very suitable and the attendance a good one, whilst the exhibition was one of which the Peterborough Committee had every reason to be proud. This great show of the Midlands is noted for the grand collection of hunters and shires it yearly attracts, and on no previous occasion had a better lot of animals been drawn together. Judges were loud in their praise of the animals placed before them whilst those at the ringside – and these included many well versed in horse breeding – declared they had never seen a better show. The Royal 'was a mere county exhibition from a quality point of view compared with this,' exclaimed one well-known Yorkshire breeder who, presumably, knew what he was talking about. 'The Peterborough show deserves all the success it obtains, for there is no better managed exhibition in the country. The committee, with their excellent secretary, Mr J.E. Little, are experienced and capable, and do their best to make everyone comfortable and everything pass off without a hitch. They offered about £1,400 in prizes, and the satisfaction of obtaining a good entry.'

– July 11th –

1891: It was the practice during cold winters for the heating apparatus in the Congregational chapel in Westgate to be started on a Saturday, so as to heat the building ready for the Sunday service. The procedure was then to check the place at midnight on the Saturday. In the early hours of this Sunday morning, a fire broke out. A passing police officer raised the alarm and, with the city fire station close by, the brigade was quickly to work. It was connected to three hydrants before word was passed to the Peterborough Volunteer Fire Brigade. Their home truck was brought to the fire and soon got to work from a fourth hydrant. However, the fire had gained a strong hold on the building and, despite the efforts of both brigades, it spread into the roof and woodwork of the chapel. There was little that could be done, except to stop the fire spreading to adjoining buildings. When the roof fell in, molten lead ran from the windows and large quantities of bricks and heavy stonework fell, narrowly missing several firemen. By daybreak, the fire had virtually burnt itself out and all that remained were the four walls. (Mellows, W.T., 'Peterborough Municipal Jubilee', *Peterborough Standard*, 1924; Baker, Eddy A., *A History of Firefighting in Cambridgeshire*, Jeremy Mills Publishing, 2006)

– July 12th –

1796: A Peterborough Playbill gives us another glimpse of life in Georgian Peterborough. It tells us that:

> This present TUESDAY Evening JULY the 12th, 1796, will be presented A COMEDY called 'The SCHOOL for SCANDAL' To which will be added A FARCE 'The ENCHANTED ISLAND Or Free-born ENGLISHWOMAN. The whole concludes with an ELEGANT, GRAND, TRANSPARENT PAINTING, of THE TEMPLE OF LOVE, Designed and Painted by an eminent Artist.

It tells interested parties that this week's schedule is for performances on Tuesday, Wednesday, Friday and Saturday. I just wonder what was planned to happen on the Thursday. (Tebbs, H.F., *Peterborough*, Oleander Press, 1979)

———

1974: There was a big cheer in the pouring rain when a car was allowed to cross a new bridge that, we are told in this article from the *Peterborough Evening Telegraph*, could solve Peterborough's traffic problems! However, the job was not yet finished. The river bridge that spanned the Nene valley and would be carrying the Nene Parkway from the A47 towards the A1 still had to be surfaced. It was the works superintendent, Mr Peter Wardle, who took his own car over just to show it could be done. However, the official opening would not be until the autumn so, just in case anyone tried to copy Peter Wardle's drive, both ends of the bridge were firmly barricaded to keep joyriders away!

– July 13th –

1895: Two incidents of this day came before the police court. The first concerned Frederick Annis, an errand boy for Westgate chemist Mr Knight, who had been assaulted by Edward Quincey, a small schoolboy who threw a stone, half a brick and a piece of slate at him. It was claimed that Quincey exclaimed 'I've hit him in the back every time yet.' Costs were paid and Quincey's father promised to prevent a recurrence of the assault. At the same court hearing, labourer Harry Baldock was summoned for doing damage to a wooden beetle – a small, heavy-headed hammer – to the amount of 1s. We are not told just what kind of damage he did to the hammer! The case was dismissed. (*Lincoln, Rutland and Stamford Mercury*)

1968: Speaking to the Dogsthorpe Road Ukrainian Club, city alderman Walter Setchfield said that, for the sake of immigrants' children, racial ghettoes in Peterborough must not be allowed to exist any longer. People of all races, colours and creeds must be inter-mixed and intermingled with city natives to prevent 'second-class citizens' in the next generation. He went on to say that different races should not be allowed to stick together in tight communities but must be scattered about the city. Time so often shows that ideals and realities rarely match. (*Peterborough Evening Telegraph*)

‒ July 14th ‒

1855: The following notice appeared in the *Peterborough Advertiser*:

The MISSES STRICKLAND RESPECTFULLY inform their
Friends and the Public that they intend opening a School after the
Midsummer Vacation, for the instruction of young Ladies. With
hopeful confidence they solicit a share of public patronage, assuring
their friends that every effort will be used for advancement of the
pupils entrusted to their charge. The First Quarter will commence
on Monday July 16th 1855. TERMS – Young Ladies are Boarded
and Instructed in Writing, Arithmetic, Geography, History etc., at
£18 18*s* per annum. Day pupils: 10*s* 6*d* per quarter. French, Music
and Dancing: each 10*s* 6*d* per quarter. Laundress: Two Guineas per
annum. A Quarter's Notice previous to the removal of a young lady.
Each young lady to be provided with a pair of sheets, a fork and
spoon, which will be returned on their leaving. 34 Cowgate Street,
Peterborough.

1988: A leaflet published by the Royal Town Planning Institute,
East of England branch – no, I hadn't heard of them either
– highlighted the Orton Centre as an example of 'positive
planning'. It had been compiled to make people aware of
planning achievements, as controversial proposals often attracted
bad publicity. This leaflet claimed that the Orton Centre had 'now
matured into a pleasant and well laid out centre'. (*Peterborough
Evening Telegraph*; Royal Town Planning Institute)

– JULY 15TH –

1855: On this Sunday, while Mr and Mrs Etherley of Peakirk were at church, two well-known Peterborough delinquents went to their house and asked their young son to give them something. He said he had nothing for them, whereupon the lads went to the cupboard and helped themselves. They then left, but had not got far before an older son of Mr Etherley returned. Hearing what had occurred, he gave chase and caught up with them. Seeing no police nearby, he adopted a very summary way of chastisement and administered a very sound thrashing to one of the party. The other, thinking discretion the better part of valour, took to his heels and fled. (*Peterborough Advertiser*)

1908: For many years, the Robertson family ran a cycle shop at the top of Cowgate. It was on this day that one of the founding family, Arthur (Archie) Robertson, became an Olympic champion when he won gold as part of the winning British 3-mile team race at those games, held in London. He also came second – to another British runner – in the 3,200 metres steeplechase and just missed a third medal when he finished fifth in the 5-mile race. He retired from running in 1909, returning to his first love – competitive cycling. (BBC Scotland; *Peterborough Evening Telegraph*; birchfieldharriers.net)

~ July 16th ~

1958: Many people were instrumental in the growth of the Peterborough Agricultural Society from its foundation in 1797, and everyone involved would surely have been very proud of its successor, the East of England Agricultural Society – by this date, one of the most prestigious in the country. The public face of both was the Peterborough Show, which itself went through many turbulent times before flowering again as the East of England Show. For a great many twentieth-century Peterborians, and the communities around the city, Robert Bibby *was* the Peterborough Show. From 1921 until his sudden death in 1957 he was, without doubt, the man that made the difference. Following his death, an appeal fund for a memorial to him was set up. It raised over £1,200. On this day, one year after his death, Princess Alice, the Duchess of Gloucester – whose husband the Duke of Gloucester had three times been the President of the Agricultural Society – unveiled the Robert Bibby Memorial Clock at the entrance to the Peterborough Eastfield Showground. It has since followed the subtly changing show – proudly telling the time and overseeing the activities – just as Robert would have done. (Liquorice, Mary, *Posh Folk: Notable Personalities (and a Donkey) Associated with Peterborough*, Cambridgeshire Libraries, 1991; Peterborough Memories, available at uk.groups.yahoo. com/neo/groups/peterborough_memories/info)

~ July 17th ~

1854: The diary of George Borrow, rector of East Dereham in Norfolk, tells of his brief visit here:

> So my little family started for Wales in the afternoon of 17th July. We flew through parts of Norfolk and Cambridgeshire in a train which we left at Ely and, getting into another which did not fly quite so fast as the one we had quitted, reached Peterborough station at about 6 o'clock of a delightful evening. We proceeded no further in our journey that day in order that we might have the opportunity of seeing the cathedral. Sallying arm in arm from the Station Hotel we crossed a bridge over the deep quiet Nen, on the southern bank of which stands the station, and soon arrived at the cathedral. Unfortunately we were too late to procure admission into the interior and had to content ourselves with walking round it and surveying the outside. Nothing in architecture can be conceived more beautiful than the principal entrance which fronts the West and which, at the time we saw it, was gilded with the rays of the setting sun. After having strolled about the edifice surveying it until we were weary we returned to our inn, and after taking an excellent supper, retired to rest.

(Russell, John, *Fair Spot and Goodly — Visitors' impressions of Peterborough*, Peterborough Arts Council, 1984)

– July 18th –

1308: On this day, Peterborough Abbey received a licence to crenellate the gate of the abbey and two chambers lying between the gate and the church. It was the exterior of the King's Lodgings and the Knights' Chamber - which Abbot Godfrey had recently erected over the palace gateway – that received the crenellations, which remain to this day. (Mellows, W.T., *The King's Lodging at Peterborough*, Peterborough Natural History Society, 1933)

1966: Peterborough representatives learned few details about what 'new town' status would mean to Peterborough when they met Housing Minister Richard Crossman. After a long wait, they were shown into Crossman's office by his private secretary, who told them not to keep the minister long as he had others waiting to see him. When they asked what sort of offer the minister was prepared to make, he was not specific, responding: 'Gentlemen, you must make up your minds. If you don't want it, please let me know and I shall strike Peterborough off the list. It doesn't worry me, I've got other places.' That wasn't what they wanted to hear, but if they wanted a new town, they needed to accept whatever plan was on offer rather than lose it. Peterborough therefore accepted the offer. (Harper-Tee, John, 'The Peterborough Story', *Peterborough Evening Telegraph*, 1992)

~ JULY 19TH ~

1774: On his classic sailing journey around the Fens, Lord Orford and friends arrived at Peterborough. Thomas Roberts' journal tells us that, after passing through Stanground Sluice into Morton's Leam, they cast anchor to dine. After dining at about 5 p.m., they passed down the new sluice as far as the new bridge, where they anchored for the night. Roberts simply tells us that they 'saw the Races on the course from the bank'. George Farrington's journal is more descriptive: 'after dinner we sailed up Bedford River which runs near the race ground, and anchored at the new bridge. The bank commands a view of the whole course, and, by fixing a telescope, I saw the races with the greatest ease. We then returned to the Fleet.' (*Lord Orford's Voyage round the Fens in 1774: Journal of Mr Thomas Roberts; Journal Mr Geo Farrington*, Cambridgeshire Libraries Publications, 1993)

1919: The First World War had come to an end on 11 November 1918. Today was the day Peterborough celebrated it, with a great Peace Day parade in which every city organisation took part. Thousands from all around had descended on the city to hear the deputy mayor, Alderman Whitsted, read the proclamation of peace declaring the end of the 'War to end all Wars' and to see the parade as it went through Peterborough to the old showground. (*Peterborough Local History Society Magazine Millennium Edition*)

– July 20th –

1774: Thomas Roberts' diary tells us that on this day, Lord Orford and friends had moved nearer the town and 'towed up' at Town Bridge, where a few repairs were made to their rigging.

> Some provisions were brought in and the 'Admiral' purchased a boat. His Lordship, Lord Orford, did not go on shore, having received a hurt on one of his legs a few days earlier. At eight Mr Duggan came on board, and soon after the Revd Mr Jemage, vicar of Peterborough, with the most obliging offers of assistance. In the evening we returned to our former station and saw the Races from the Banks as yesterday.

(*Lord Orford's Voyage round the Fens in 1774: Journal of Mr Thomas Roberts; Journal Mr Geo Farrington*, Cambridgeshire Libraries Publications, 1993)

—

1816: The present museum building occupies the site of a building – Neville Place – that dates back to 1536. The cellars underneath what we see now are part of that original structure – and are home to some very strange ghostly happenings. The steps to the left of the building take you down to those subterranean parts. The original above-ground part was demolished in the early nineteenth century and a new building was constructed for 'Squire Cooke' and his new wife. If you look over the fence around the cellar steps, you will find the date stone 'Tho. A. Cooke 20 July 1816', recording the building of this new house. (Various sources)

– JULY 21ST –

1832: This newspaper advertisement provides an interesting view of Peterborough past.

> TO BE LET at STANGROUND near Peterborough; and may be entered upon immediately; a capital and substantially built genteel house, with parlours, bed-rooms, kitchen and out offices; superior box stalls for six horses, and good granary over the same; together with two acres of LAND, part of which is planted with choice fruit trees and laid out in handsome gardens. Also, EIGHTEEN ACRES of superior LAND, half arable and half grass, very nearly adjoining the above, and all contiguous to the river Nene. It is well adapted for the residence of a respectable family, being a healthy situation, and possessing convenience – distant only two miles from Peterborough. For further particulars apply to Mr R HENERY, on the premises, Stanground aforesaid.

It was obviously considered easy to find. I wonder how much he was asking! (*Huntingdon, Bedford & Peterborough Gazette*)

1913: Was Peterborough being watched by aliens on this Monday evening? A strange light, described as being similar to that from a window, passed quite low and silently over Peterborough from the east. It then rose steadily until the light was no more than that of a small star. Some time later, it was seen to have descended again, travelling back the way it came. Strange – very strange. (*Peterborough Citizen*)

~ JULY 22ND ~

1840: An incident between Mr Marriott, a carpenter and keeper of the Ship Inn on New Road Peterborough, and Mr Stanley, a Peterborough ironmonger, began on 15 October 1839 and went before Northampton Lent Assizes in March 1840. Allegedly Marriott's pony and cart were standing at his door when a dog startled the pony so that it ran away. Marriott chased and caught it, but the cart hit some ploughs laying on the street outside Stanley's shop and Marriott was dragged over them and badly injured. Stanley refused to accept liability, claiming that it was normal Peterborough practice to display goods for sale on the street. The jury could not decide on a verdict, so a retrial was called and the matter finally came to a conclusion on this Wednesday. Among the witnesses called was surgeon Thomas Southam of Peterborough, who objected to being sworn until he had been paid his expenses for this and the last Assizes, pointing out that Gray's 'Practice' stated that he was entitled to 2 guineas a day! In the end, Marriott was awarded 1*s* damages, whereupon the sergeant expressed his exasperation: 'A shilling! This is a trial by jury! I never heard such a verdict. Gentlemen, I hope you will never be tumbled out of a cart yourselves.' (Jenkins, Eric, *Victorian Northamptonshire: The Early Years*, Cordelia, 1993)

‒ July 23rd ‒

1841: John Clare ‒ the Helpston poet ‒ appears to have had little direct involvement with Peterborough, apart from a brief time with the militia at Norman Cross. However, he did make passage through Peterborough on this day. In 1837, he had been admitted to the High Beach Asylum in Epping Forest. On Tuesday 20 July, he left of his own free will to walk the 80 miles home to Northborough. On this morning he left his 'overnight stop' in Stilton and, after seeking directions, headed toward Peterborough. Before he reached Peterborough, a man and woman passed him in a cart. They hailed him as they passed and John recognised them as people from Helpston. He told them his story and received 5*d* in return, although they did not offer him a lift home. John called 'at a small public house near the bridge' and had 'two half-pints of ale and twopenn'oth of bread and cheese'. Feeling quite refreshed but with feet more crippled than ever, he forced himself to keep on the move as he was 'half ashamed to sit down in the street' and 'got through Peterborough better than I expected'. He 'passed Walton and soon reached Werrington'. There he was met by his wife Patty and taken home to their house in Northborough. (Robinson, Eric and Powell, David (eds), *John Clare by Himself*, Fyfield Books, 2002)

~ July 24th ~

1712: On this day, a *Stamford Post* advertisement tells readers that:

> Mr Penn of Peterborough, Bell-Founder, has for many years, with good success and applause, cur'd ruptured people of both sexes, and he continues also to fit Steel Trusses at a reasonable price'. A second advertisement in 1716 records: 'We hereby witness that Henry Penn, Bellfounder of Peterborough in Northamptonshire, fits ruptured people of both sexes and of all ages with Steel Trusses, and has applications internal and external for the cure of even the most desperate cases of that nature. Signed Theop Hill M.B., Sam Pendelton Physicion and Alex Stuart Chiruig.

(The *Stamford Post*, quoted in Lee, Michael, *Northamptonshire Past & Present*, Northamptonshire Record Society, 2004)

1989: A *Peterborough Evening Telegraph* article of this date informs its readers that more than £1.5 million is to be spent on giving a Peterborough arcade a major facelift, which includes changing the name of the 1960s shopping mall to Hereward Cross as the new owners London and Edinburgh Trust plc and Lovell Developments want to give the centre a more eye-catching, brighter image. They plan to transform it into a place where people will meet, and to this end, a glass domed central area with a café will form the focus of the centre. A major part of the plan is to maximise the link to the already pedestrianised Long Causeway by repaving Broadway and Midgate. (Various sources)

– July 25th –

1774: George Lord Orford had set out on his 'tour' of the Fenlands to replicate in his own way the world tour just completed by Lord Anson, and the recent news that Thomas Cook was wintering in New Zealand on his circumnavigation. Today, while moored at Peterborough, where he had come to watch the races, he welcomed on board the Earl of Sandwich – sponsor to Thomas Cook – where they dined on twenty brace of pike and perch. (*Lord Orford's Voyage round the Fens in 1774: Journal of Mr Thomas Roberts; Journal Mr Geo Farrington*, Cambridgeshire Libraries Publications, 1993)

———

1876: Peterborough MP George Hammond Whalley interjected during the committee stage of the Elementary Education Bill, regarding an amendment on removing school boards and passing school management to the clergy. He strongly opposed the Bill and the minutes record that laughter followed his declaration that 'the clerical influence which was exercised over education was responsible for all the ignorance and backwardness which made the country far behind any other nation in Europe in knowledge and culture' and that 'such a position was a disgrace to the richest and most powerful in the country'. The chairman pointed out that the honourable gentleman was deviating from the question. Ignoring the interruption, Whalley declared that 'priests, parsons and preachers, whatever their creed, were the least competent to undertake the education of children'. The Bill became law. (*Leeds Mercury*)

~ JULY 26TH ~

1927: This was the day when Alfred Caleb Taylor, one of Peterborough's unsung heroes, passed away. He started working at the infirmary – now the museum – in 1880 and stayed there to his death. Following the 1895 discovery of X-rays, he knew that he wanted to take that discovery further. Taylor put together his own X-ray machine, made his own batteries that gave him between twenty and thirty hours of power and, later, a six-cell accumulator that needed two people to lift it. He took X-rays of injured feet, hand and arms, and helped the infirmary surgeons work out how best to treat the many injured people they saw. His driving motivation was not investigating science for its own sake, but helping others recover from serious injuries. Continual X-ray exposure cost him three fingers from his left hand and one from his right. Thus debilitated, he was limited as to what he could do and admitted that it hurt him not to be able to use the X-ray equipment in the large, new room that had been built to house the equipment that had been his life. A Carnegie Hero Fund Trust citation in the museum recognises his heroism in endeavouring to save human life. (*'Anne', I lost four fingers working with X-Rays – the story of Alfred Caleb Taylor*, Peterborough Museum/Vivacity, 2010)

~ JULY 27TH ~

1774: After three days on Whittlesey Mere, Lord Orford and friends were back again passing through Stanground sluices, picking flowers from the toll house garden and finally anchoring up at Barnard's Reach, opposite Thorpe Hall. They had their milk supply topped up here. Mr Roberts records that a little beyond is Longthorpe, a small village where there is a large Stone Tower, formerly used as a fortification (we now know better). Here also is a chapel, in the yard of which are many gravestones, as well as some poetical inscriptions. One of these inscriptions, being in a style not usually met with in such obscure places, is here transcribed: 'From human ills remov'd, from every woe; Which Youth or Age is doom'd to undergo; Compos'd, Serene, I've gain'd the happy shore; Where Sickness, Pain, and Sorrow are no more.' I think we can now leave Lord Orford and his friends to look after themselves. (*Lord Orford's Voyage round the Fens in 1774: Journal of Mr Thomas Roberts; Journal of Mr Geo Farrington*, Cambridgeshire Libraries Publications, 1993)

1918: This Saturday saw two US Army teams playing baseball on the Paul Pry ground at Walton. The advertising told Peterborians to 'come in crowds'. First pitch was scheduled for 2.45 p.m. and would be performed by the mayor. Refreshments and programmes would be available and all proceeds would go to the Sailor's Orphan Homes, Newland, Hull. (Gray, David, *Peterborough at War 1914–1918*, David Gray, 2014)

‒ July 28th ‒

1802: William Wordsworth and his sister Dorothy were heading south to visit Calais. Their coach stopped for dinner at Peterborough but the Wordsworths 'went to see the outside of the Minster while the passengers were dining … the West End very grand'. (de Selincourt, E., *The Journals of Dorothy Wordsworth*, MacMillan, 1952)

———

1969: The *Peterborough Evening Telegraph* on this day described the Guildhall as one of the most beautiful buildings in the city, 'a curious blending of medieval Romanesque arches and 17th century Dutch roof and windows'. It is difficult to dispute this. The *Telegraph* goes on to tell us that an earlier, single-story market cross building owned by three feudal guilds of Peterborough was here in 1488. Recent excavations suggest something from the eleventh century pre-dated even that. Until 1842, the Liberty of Peterborough magistrates held their Quarterly Sessions there, and between 1875 and 1933 it saw service as the Town Hall. How did people get to the room over the arches? The two doors at the back give a clue − it was attached to buildings housing a police station and the office of the council clerk. The entry was most certainly *not* via the spiral stairs we see today − they were added in 1966 as a gift from the Boston branch of the Trustee Savings Bank after one of their old buildings had been knocked down.

~ July 29th ~

1630: As we have already seen (February 2nd), children were a problem around the wells of the town. Every well had a winch and bucket, which were often misused. There are many references to a carpenter being paid to do repairs or inserting a pin to prevent them being overwound. Here the record says: 'For putting in of a pin into the wheel of yjr Town Well for keeping the boyes from breaking the same ... 2*d*' (Tebbs, H.F., *Peterborough*, Oleander Press, 1979)

1885: At today's Petty Sessions John Chantry, a railway worker of Deeping Gate, was summoned for not giving notice of swine fever on his premises. Chantry stated that he never knew there was such a thing as swine fever, much less laws concerning it. The bench, believing it was a case of pure ignorance, dismissed the charge. Thomas Hadley of Eastgate in Peterborough was also summoned, for allowing a nuisance to exist on his premises. It was stated that since the summons, Hedley had taken steps to abate the nuisance by connecting the convenience with the main drain, and the case was adjourned for a fortnight. Harry Bryant, a railway labourer of Walton, was charged by J. and T. North of Peterborough with stealing a pennyworth of growing apples on 21 July and was fined 6*d* plus 16*s* 6*d* costs. (*Stamford Mercury*)

— JULY 30TH —

1587: On 8 February 1587, Mary Queen of Scots was executed at Fotheringhay Castle. There her body stayed, embalmed and sealed in a lead coffin, until this day when it was moved, in the dead of night, to Peterborough. On the instructions of Queen Elizabeth I, the burial was a formal affair fit for a queen. The coffin, followed by the royal standard of Scotland, was moved in procession from the Bishop's Palace to the cathedral. As well as the nobility, the Bishop and Dean of Peterborough and the Bishop of Lincoln, 100 poor widows dressed in black walked in procession following the coffin. Following a sermon preached by the Bishop of Lincoln, the dean oversaw Mary's interment. A magnificent funeral banquet, paid for by Queen Elizabeth, followed in the Bishop's Palace. The cost of the whole burial is said to have totalled over £300 – a vast sum. In 1612 Mary's body was exhumed when her son, King James I of England, ordered she be reinterred in Westminster Abbey, in a chapel opposite the tomb of Elizabeth I. (Carnell, Geoffrey, *The Bishops of Peterborough*, RJL Smith & Associates, 1993; Gunton, Symon, *The history of the Church of Peterborough*, ed. Symon Patrick, 1990; *People of Peterborough*, Peterborough Museum Publications, 2009)

— July 31st —

1916: On 30 July, a Red Cross train made an unplanned stop at Peterborough so that a badly wounded and seriously ill soldier – Sergeant Thomas Hunter – could be taken to the Peterborough Infirmary for urgent medical care. Just twenty-four hours later, Thomas died there. Born in County Durham in 1880, Thomas had emigrated to Australia, arriving in Sydney Harbour in 1910. At the start of the conflict in Europe, he enlisted in the Australian Imperial Force. In April 1915, the Australian/New Zealand forces, now known as the ANZAC, were part of the Gallipoli landings. Many died but Thomas came through it intact. The ANZACs now moved on and in July 1916 they were part of the seemingly unending Battle of the Somme. Now a platoon sergeant, Thomas was in the thick of the conflict and, on 25 July 1916, he was badly wounded in the spine. He was moved from the battle zone until he arrived at the General Hospital in Boulogne, crossed the Channel, then travelled by Red Cross train to London. On a northbound Red Cross train his condition worsened and he was taken off the train at Peterborough, dying on this day. He was buried in the Broadway Cemetery with full military honours. (Harvey, John W., *The Lonely Anzac*, Birches Publishing, 2003)

~ AUGUST 1ST ~

1844: Mr Dennison, the Chairman of the London and York Railway Committee (later the Great Northern Railway Committee) came to Peterborough to address a meeting chaired by Earl Fitzwilliam. The meeting had been convened so that the city could consider a resolution in favour of the company's wish to run their railway through Peterborough. Dennison informed them bluntly that the main object of the London and York committee was to shorten the distance between London and Yorkshire – nothing more. If a line through Peterborough was best for the general public, then Peterborough should have it. If not, it should pass outside the town. It is tempting to say he was bluffing because his first choice had been to build the line through Stamford – a shorter and easier route. That plan failed when the Marquess of Exeter said 'No'. Not surprisingly, the meeting passed the resolution that agreed to them seeking such a situation. As it turned out, the GNR decided to consider other options first and it was some six years before their trains reached Peterborough direct. By that time, other railway companies had got to Peterborough first. The London and North Western (1845), Great Eastern (1847) and the Midland (1848) were all ensconced before Dennison's plan became a Peterborough reality. (Tebbs, H.F., *Peterborough*, Oleander Press, 1979)

– AUGUST 2ND –

1932: In June 1927, the Air Ministry asked G.C. Wentworth Fitzwilliam if he would be prepared to sell an area of land to them for an Aircraft Acceptance Park. In May 1928, the Peterborough Town Clerk stated that the Air Ministry would be purchasing just over 30 acres of land at Westwood. Westwood Airfield – or Westwood Farm aerodrome, as it was first called – formally 'opened for business' on this first Tuesday in August. As an airfield, it had pretty basic job – the receipt, storage and delivery of aircraft and equipment for the Home Defence Air Force. In December 1935, the depot moved out to Waddington in Lincolnshire to make way for a newly formed Service Flying Training School. On 1 June 1942, the airfield saw the formation of the RAF 21 Group, 7 (Pilots) Advanced Flying Unit, which taught navigation, amongst other things. During the Second World War it was 'home' to American servicemen, while French airmen were also trained there post-war. Although the base was not used for operational missions, some fifty accidents happened during training, some of which resulted in fatalities, including a serious crash in 1936 when four men were killed. The airfield was also bombed several times during the war. (Osborne, Mike, *A brief history of RAF Peterborough*, Peterborough Educational Development Centre, 1983)

~ AUGUST 3RD ~

1745: It was on this day that Mary Walsham, neé Vokes, died aged 82, leaving bequests 'to feed the hungry, and to clothe the naked'. That was not all she left. On 24 January 1728, she had brought into force a charitable deed, which conveyed 'a messuage in Woodstone with the appurtenances of a full land and one quarter full land lying in the field of Whittlesey'. The land was to be rented out 'in trust', and the income was to be used to provide 'a school and for the habitation of a schoolmaster or mistress'. The deed was also 'yearly to apply the sum of £8 for the support and maintenance of such schoolmaster or mistress for ever to teach 16 poor children of Woodstone in the English tongue and Catechism'. Her will, dated 19 January 1744, bequeathed that 'crops, cattle and farm implements used in connection with farm – Sexton Barns – were to be sold and the money 'put out to interest'. That interest was to help the poor persons of the parish of Woodstone. The 'minister, churchwardens and overseers of the poor' were to look after these interests. Today, the descendants of Mary's school still provide an education to the young of Woodston. (*Bygones of Woodston & District, Woodston & District (St Augustine's Church)*, Local History Group, 1979)

~ August 4th ~

1863: A simple event on this day had repercussions for the Great Northern Railway Hotel, then rented from the railway company for £1,500 a year by a Mr George Wilkins. It began when the Prince of Wales (the future Edward VII) stopped at Peterborough. The next day, the *Daily Telegraph* told of the prince's journey from Leeds to London – commenting that the party had stopped at Peterborough, 'where the Prince alighted and took some refreshment. It is to be hoped that the soup served him was not the horrible puree of horsebeans which is retailed at that station at one shilling a plate to her Majesty's lieges.' Wilkins was understandably upset and wrote to the editor confirming that tea and other articles had been provided for the royal party, but that the prince had asked for something more substantial. He was served a soup retailed at the station and, after partaking of it, asked for seconds. On 8 August, the *Telegraph* responded with a paragraph headed 'Railway Refreshments at Peterborough' that reassured its readers that 'Mr Wilkins, the keeper of the refreshment rooms requests us to state that the soup which he sells at one shilling a plate is not made from horse-beans, as surmised by our reporter, who tasted it on the way from Halifax.' {*Peterborough Local History Society Magazine*)

– AUGUST 5TH –

1850: In November 1846, Thomas Brassey had accepted a contract to build the London–Peterborough Railway, with the date of completion estimated as 1 November 1849 at the latest. He failed on this point, mainly because of the challenge of crossing Whittlesea Mere. When Brassey was trying to resolve this problem, he sought help from Stephen Bollard, the middle level engineer. Bollard showed him a possible solution and was promptly put in charge of that part of the project. The solution was to lay a deep bed of brushwood beneath the track line. Before anything about the solution was noised abroad, the Fenman's cunning of Stephen came into play and he quietly bought up all the brushwood that came to market. The solution was highly effective. The brushwood was weighted so that it sank into the Whittlesea peat and the result was a sound and stable base for the railway. Other delays came from flooding in the Nene valley and the late completion of the viaduct and bridge over the Nene but, by this date, Brassey was able to invite the directors and their friends from the London Terminus at Maiden Lane by special train to lunch with him in Peterborough. (Tebbs, H.F., *Peterborough*, Oleander Press, 1979)

~ AUGUST 6TH ~

1914: Mr Frederick Frank, a long-term resident of Peterborough, was the owner of a pork butcher's double-fronted shop in Westgate. Of German extraction, he had been in Peterborough for many years. On this Thursday evening, two days after war had been declared, trouble began to brew. All sorts of rumours were going around that he, or members of his family, had said uncomplimentary things about the British. One was that a black flag had been shown; another that a member of the family, or a relative staying with them, had 'booed' when a portrait of the king had been exhibited at one of the places of amusement. A third was that invidious comparisons had been made between the British and German soldier. It is impossible to sift the wheat from the chaff on these tales, but it is likely that they were all from a possible verbal altercation, not on Mr Frank's part but someone else's. Be that as it may, public feeling among a certain section of the populace grew very quickly and as night drew in, there was a large crowd outside his shop in Westgate for a long time. They made a lot of noise but nothing of an alarming nature occurred. Tomorrow, however, that would change. (Gray, David, *Peterborough at War 1914–1918*, David Gray, 2014)

~ AUGUST 7TH ~

1914: This evening it was obvious that undercurrents from yesterday's troubles remained. A crowd of between 400 and 500 were in Westgate by 8 p.m. and it was evident that some there were bent on serious mischief. It didn't take long before stones, bottles and other missiles began to be thrown at the plate-glass windows of the shop and, as they crashed through, the crowd cheered, some singing snatches of 'Rule Britannia'. The police were outnumbered and powerless; there was no stopping the crowd. The glass from the shattered shop windows lay over the sausages, pork pies and other goods that were ready for the Saturday shoppers. By 10 p.m., the situation was so menacing that the chief constable went for the assistance of the Northants Yeomanry, who were quartered in the Corn Exchange awaiting orders. Mayor Winfrey read the Riot Act to the assembled mob as upwards of 100 Yeomanry arrived, with a few on horseback. By steady pressure, and what was described as 'great forbearance', the crowd were gradually forced back but it was not until midnight that the streets were really cleared. Meanwhile, a section of the crowd had headed off to Mr Frank's house in Fletton Avenue, which they treated in much the same way. (*Peterborough Citizen and Advertiser; Peterborough Express*)

~ AUGUST 8TH ~

1914: This Saturday saw a third day of troubles in the centre of town. Mr Frank posted bills on the boarded-up shop, announcing that the perishables from the previous day's troubles would be sold by auction at 2.30 p.m. As the purchasers emerged from the shop, sausages, pork pies and joints were filched from them and thrown all over the place. A string of sausages thrown on the overhead tram cable caused the whole system to grind to a halt. In the evening, the Salmon and Compass pub in Long Causeway – owned by Mr Charles Guest, who was also of German extraction – was the target. Anticipating this, and to appease the public, Guest flew the Union Jack from an upper window. Enormous crowds had assembled there, but the police were now reinforced by some fifty special constables sworn in during the afternoon. Nothing of a seriously disordered nature happened until 11.15 p.m., when someone sent a brick through one of the pub's windows. A fusillade of bricks, stones and bottles followed. When the pandemonium was at its height, the police attached a hose to a hydrant but the crowd got control and turned the jet of water on the police. The streets were finally cleared early on Sunday morning. (*Peterborough Express*; *Peterborough Citizen and Advertiser*; Gray, David, *Peterborough at War 1914–1918*, David Gray, 2014).

~ August 9th ~

1802: At the turn of the nineteenth century, Peterborough had two places to hold offenders. Those guilty of petty crimes were held in the Bridewell on Exchange Street, while the more serious offenders were placed in the old Bishops Gaol, on the right as you face the Minster Gate. The trouble was that the gaol was in such a bad state of repair that Lord Burghley, 10th Earl of Exeter, who owned the gaol, had had to pay for repairs. It was on this day that a Dr Lettson visited both the Bridewell and the gaol and reported on his findings. His graphic views on the gaol describe a small courtyard 21 yards by 7 yards with a pump and a 'necessary' in it. There are three dungeons, each about 4 yards square. Two are four steps below ground, and the other two steps down, all with stone floors and no fireplaces. In one, called the gaol-room, the window is stopped up so there is only an iron-grated aperture in the door for light and air, measuring 10in by 7in. Because of these appalling conditions, he considered that 'a term of imprisonment in the old gaol of the Abbott was very likely to lead to the doom of the felon'. (Tebbs, H.F., *Peterborough*, Oleander Press, 1979) & other sources)

‒ August 10th ‒

1942: There is an old saying, as true in wartime as in peace, that 'familiarity breeds contempt'. It can also be dangerous, as a corporal discovered on this evening. On his way home on leave, he had fallen into conversation with another soldier on the train. That soldier gave him an incendiary bomb – a device very familiar to our man – as a souvenir and the corporal put it into his pack and brought it home. When he showed it to his wife she became very upset to say the least so, to keep the peace, he went out into the garden and threw it onto a bonfire that was smouldering there. The incendiary exploded! A police constable walking along Eastfield Road heard the loud bang and saw a piece of burning timber land on a nearby bungalow roof. Fortunately, that went out. On investigating further, the policeman found the soldier laying injured with debris – including three pieces of the exploded bomb – scattered all over the garden. The soldier was taken to the hospital, where he was treated for serious burns on his face and arm. Perhaps another saying for the soldier to consider begins 'Think before you …'! (Gray, David, Peterborough at War 1939–1945, David Gray, 2011)

~ August 11th ~

1873: This Monday marked a bad beginning to the week on Peterborough's railways – or was it quite typical? James Godfrey, a truck labeller employed by coal merchants Gurling & Co., had labelled a truck in the New England goods yards and, crossing the lines, stopped in front of an engine. Without warning the engine started moving and Godfrey was knocked over, sustaining a severe head wound. He was immediately taken to the infirmary where, in the matter-of-fact style of the *Peterborough Standard*, readers were told that every attention was paid to him.

1969: In December 1963, a redevelopment scheme was announced for an area bounded by Star Road, Wellington and St John's Streets and Eastgate, which later came to fruition. On this day, six years later, the *Peterborough Evening Telegraph* declared:

> There's no getting away from it, Eastgate and the streets around it form a blot on Peterborough. Let that not be a slight on the people that live there, but on the awful way this area of the city has been allowed to decay. Residents have shouted long and hard about the appalling conditions under which they live – half demolished houses, waste ground now rubbish tips and bad repairs on houses still standing.

On 20 November, it reported: 'Eastgate is to be demolished and completely rebuilt by the city'!

— AUGUST 12TH —

1914: This Wednesday saw the court sequel to the Westgate riots when twenty-four men were brought before the bench, charged with a variety of offences. The charges included 'causing an affray', 'creating a disturbance of the peace', 'incitement to riot' and 'damaging windows and property'. In most cases the defendants were bound over, but some were fined and others sent to prison. A few were actually recruited in to the army. Mayor Winfrey, one of the magistrates, asked who among the accused was prepared to go to the front. In all, just four said they were prepared to go. Of those who took up the offer of conscription rather than alternative punishment, three would appear to have come through the whole conflict. Just one lost his life when he was killed in action on 3 July 1916. (*Peterborough Advertiser*; *Peterborough & Huntingdon Standard*; Gray, David, *Peterborough at War 1914–1918*, David Gray, 2014).

1919: On this day, five years after the troubles in Westgate and Long Causeway, the War Office and Savings Committee presented a British Army tank to the city as a war trophy. Captain Don Dickens drove it onto a concrete base close to the children's play area in the park. The mayor accepted the tank on behalf of the city and, during the ceremony, the tank was named 'Evelyn' by a Mrs Fitzwilliam. (Perry, Stephen, *Peterborough Vol. 2 – a second portrait in old picture postcards*, S.B. Publications, 1989)

~ AUGUST 13TH ~

1873: On this Wednesday afternoon Thomas Gadsby, an employee of the Birmingham Waggon Co., had been moving a truck in the yard at the Great Eastern Railway Station. In doing so, he got his foot stuck between two points and was unable to get himself free. With the help of colleagues he was finally freed, but his leg and foot were badly injured. As a result he was taken to the infirmary and, after a thorough inspection of the injury, it was considered that the amputation of the damaged limb was necessary. Doctor T.J. Walker performed the operation which, the infirmary advised the *Peterborough Standard*, was a complete success.

1919: One sometimes wonders about the logic of some legal decisions. Among today's *Stamford Mercury* reports, we learn that one Alfred Jinks, a labourer from Murrow, was charged by the Peterborough Guardians for failing to maintain his wife and family. His punishment was one day's imprisonment and a caution. How would one day in prison help his family? At the same court Edward Jenkins, a 31-year-old dealer from City Road, and 51-year-old labourer Joseph Wright from Rogers Street, were summoned for fighting in the public street, fined 5*s* each and let free.

~ August 14th ~

1922: An incident in Peterborough today became headline news across the country. The *Western Morning News* headlined a 'Startling Railway mishap at Peterborough', while the *Dundee Courier* reported 'Engine crashes into cottage: Comes to standstill in kitchen: Fortunate escapes: Invalid woman buried in debris.' It all involved a runaway Midland and Great Northern railway engine, which crashed into a stationary brake van standing at the buffers before carrying on into the old stationmaster's house, then occupied by a railway controller named Ernest Cole, the engine and tender coming to a standstill in the kitchen. Cole's invalid wife was in bed in the room above the kitchen, and fell through the floor among the debris. She was reported as suffering from shock, cuts and bruises – now that is a surprise! Cole's daughter, aged 10, or 17 according to the *Western Morning News*, and named Gladys by local sources, was extricated unhurt from the debris. There are references to her 'emerging from the rubble with a smile on her face'. Cole's 75-year-old mother-in-law was pinned in the pantry and, when rescued, was suffering from severe shock. The engine driver and fireman appear to have jumped from the engine when it was in motion and were unhurt. (Peterborough Pictures; Peterborough Pictures Back in Time; *Aberdeen Journal*)

~ August 15th ~

1559: David Pole, the last Catholic Bishop of Peterborough, was consecrated on this day. He had taken up office following the death of Bishop Chambers in 1556, but his formal consecration had been delayed. He was the personal nominee of Queen Mary Tudor but his actual appointment appears to have been driven by the influence of Pope Paul IV. Un-substantiated claims say he was the illegitimate brother of Cardinal Pole – a papal legate to England! On Mary's death, and the accession of Queen Elizabeth, his days were numbered. Following his refusal to acknowledge Elizabeth's supremacy in the church, he was excluded from the bishopric. (Carnell, Geoffrey, *The Bishops of Peterborough*, RJL Smith & Associates, 1993)

1914: Organised by Lady Winfrey, the mayor's wife, and assisted by Mrs W.T. Mellows and Mrs Felix Bower, War Rose Day was devised to raise money for the Prince's War Fund. They and their lady volunteers hoped to sell 2,000 roses, which had been donated by florist Richard Chapman Brown. Dressed decorously in white, the ladies were obviously persuasive beyond all expectations. Having assembled outside the Guildhall to have their photograph taken, they headed off to sell their roses around the city. By the end of this day, they had actually sold some 8,000 roses and raised £90 for the fund! (Perry, Stephen, *Peterborough Vol. 2 – a second portrait in old picture postcards*, S.B. Publications, 1989)

~ AUGUST 16TH ~

1856: At the Peterborough Petty Sessions today, Barney Hoare was brought up, charged with cutting and wounding Michael White at Werrington. White claimed that between 9 and 10 a.m. on 8 of August, he was reaping with Mr Spencer of Woodcroft, and John Gavan. Gavan went for some beer, and while he was away, the witness drank some, which was offered him by Hoare, and gave him some in return. Hoare then insisted on emptying the bottles and required the prosecutor to fetch some more beer. The prosecutor declined and Hoare struck him in the face. (*Peterborough Advertiser*)

1941: The Peterborough Group of the Home Guard consisted of two battalions – the city and the soke. On this Friday, the largest muster of the city battalion was present when it paraded past a saluting base set up in front to the Town Hall. Brigadier-General Sir Hereward Wake, Commandant of the Northamptonshire Group, was supposed to have taken the salute but he had been called away to see the king, so his deputy, Colonel Hobson, filled in. For some strange reason, the parade was led by a gramophone, with an amplifier mounted on a lorry. This was NOT a good idea, as few could hear the music! (Gray, David, *Peterborough at War 1939–1945*, David Gray, 2011)

~ August 17th ~

1931: Alfred Baker, the son of the owner of a gravel pit at Woodston close by the sugar beet factory, and Harold Cripps were taking the topsoil off to get down to the gravel when a spade struck what proved to be a long bone. Saxon pots and pieces of earthenware had already been found where the two were digging, so it was no real surprise when they found the skeletal upper torso of a man, but no sign of a coffin of any kind. It was a large skeleton - 6ft 4in or thereabout, they claimed – face up with arms by its sides. The skull came away when they were trying to get it out and the face and teeth, which were otherwise perfect, collapsed. One wonders what modern attitudes would have learned from the find. The cameraman for the *Peterborough Advertiser* rushed off in the hope of finding the bones undisturbed. No such luck – they had been collected and placed in a shed. They were retrieved, but the photographer had a better knowledge of taking pictures than he did of anatomy – so what the skeleton actually looked like may never be known. (*Peterborough Advertiser*)

~ August 18th ~

1915: On this, his 80th birthday, Dr Thomas James Walker was granted the Freedom of the city of Peterborough – the first Peterborough-born recipient of this honour. His doctor father – also Thomas – came to Peterborough from Glasgow in 1819, and his son followed in his footsteps. In any study of nineteenth-century Peterborough and beyond, young Doctor Tom's name is likely to appear. He built up and maintained a large practice at No. 35 Westgate. There is a plaque on the wall there marking his presence. In 1862, he was appointed to the post of surgeon at the infirmary and held that post until 1906. A great many people – some of whom are mentioned in this book – owe their lives to his skills and dedication. In his spare time, Walker became interested in both the local and archaeological history of the area. His archaeological finds and acquisitions formed a base for the Peterborough Museum Society collection, and he became their president in 1892. Not far outside was the Napoleonic Prisoner of War camp at Norman Cross and his detailed book of the history of the camp and its people, published in 1913, still remains the keystone to modern-day research on the subject. (Liquorice, Mary, *Posh Folk: Notable Personalities (and a Donkey) Associated with Peterborough*, Cambridgeshire Libraries, 1991)

~ August 19th ~

1651: In 1651 Oliver St John, associate of Oliver Cromwell, Chief Justice of Common Pleas during the Protectorate and the builder of Thorpe Hall between 1653 and 1656, went to seek help from the Dutch for the war against Charles I. His mission failed and led eventually to the First Anglo-Dutch war. On his return, he wrote about his Dutch failure, then turned to more local affairs and wrote that 'the Minster of Peterborough, being an ancient and goodly fabric, was proposed to be sold and demolished but I begged it to be granted to the citizens of Peterborough'. As a result, an Act of Parliament was passed on this day granting the cathedral to the people of Peterborough on the basis that 'the great Church called Minster was to be used, not only for the public worship and service of God, but also for a Work-house to employ the poorer sort of people in manufacture'. After the Restoration of the Monarchy he came back to Thorpe Hall, staying until 1662, then left for Basel in Switzerland, never to return. He left us with the legacy of a cathedral not too badly scarred and Thorpe Hall, close to the heart of many from Peterborough and beyond. (Liquorice, Mary, *Posh Folk: Notable Personalities (and a Donkey) Associated with Peterborough*, Cambridgeshire Libraries, 1991)

– AUGUST 20TH –

1895: Many people in Fletton Recreation Ground watched as a balloon, controlled from the ground by Alfred Norton, rose into the sky. In the balloon's basket was Alfred's partner, 36-year-old Annie Bassett. All were waiting for Annie to jump wearing a form of parachute. Annie came from the East End of London and was an experienced parachutist, having made thirty such jumps before. The plan was for her to ascend in the balloon and jump off wearing the parachute. However, something went wrong and Annie tragically fell to her death. At the inquest that followed, Alfred – who was described as a professional aeronaut – stated that when he gave the order to loosen the balloon, it rose, but not fast enough to clear a tree and telegraph wires. With the balloon entangled, the parachute device worn by Annie became detached from the balloon. Alfred stated that he tried to stop Annie from jumping but that she, it appeared, misunderstood him. She leapt from a height of about 70 yards and 'directly appeared to reach the ground'. The jurymen sitting at this inquest recommended 'that since no useful purpose is served by these senseless exhibitions at which the lives of the performers are risked, they should be made illegal'. (*Family History Magazine*)

~ AUGUST 21ST ~

1911: It is easy for us to forget, when we complain about health and safety rules today, that they are there for a reason. The *Peterborough Standard* of Saturday 26 August reported that on this Monday, the house at No. 36 Clifton Avenue was so damaged that it was estimated that it would need close to £100 to repair it! One of a group of recently completed houses, it had been let to the Noble family. George Noble and Albert, his son, were there in the evening laying carpet by candlelight when they smelled gas and went to investigate. Candle in hand, Albert led the way to the scullery – which was full of gas! The resulting explosion threw Albert backwards, singeing his hair and scorching his face, neck and hands and knocking his father over as well. Albert thankfully received attention at the infirmary. The two were very lucky men; the house, though, was less fortunate. The back walls had been shifted; the roof at the back had lifted and the bay window at the front was 'put out'. The glass in the back and front windows was shattered. The cause of the explosion was identified as a 'gas pipe end being left open. It is feared that the gas pipes were not tested after being put in.' You don't say!

~ AUGUST 22ND ~

1956: One of the major shops at Peterborough at this time was the Robert Sayle store in Cowgate, at the junction with King Street. At about 6.30 p.m. on this Wednesday the caretaker left for home, secure in the knowledge that all was OK. By 7 p.m. the store had caught fire and the flames had reached the second floor or maybe even higher. Many fire brigades attended the blaze and it was basically under control by 8.30 p.m. But 'under control' and 'fire out' are two different descriptions as the store – or what was left of it – burned for a further two days. At its peak, the heat was so fierce that properties on the opposite side of Cowgate were damaged; the woodwork of at least ten of the shops caught fire and one of the streetlamps buckled. There were many 'hidden' stories as well. The Peterborough Volunteer Fire Brigade headquarters was just behind the store and they had to rescue their own fire engines before they were able to attack the blaze! Within an hour of the alarm sounding, both main stores of Robert Sayle had been gutted. The city's most popular shop was no more. (Hillier, Richard, *Ready and Willing: A Centenary History of the Peterborough Volunteer Fire Brigade 1884-1984*, Peterborough Volunteer Fire Brigade, 1984)

1873: When does fact become fiction? Why won't people let the truth get in the way of a good story? I'll leave you, the reader, to decide on this one. The *Peterborough Standard* on this day decided to tell the story of 'The Peterborough Tortoise'. It said that the tortoise had died in 1831, having lived for over 200 years and seen off seven bishops in that lifetime. Therein lies a problem, because seven bishops take us back to 1747 – a mere eighty-four years! A lifespan of 200 years in fact covers sixteen bishops. In 1936, an expert noted that the shell was in a good state of preservation but made no comment on its age. Sometime around 1990, the shell was found in a cupboard and was given to the museum. Experts tell us she – for they say it is a female shell – was a large specimen, some 12in long. Over the years she was often described as a 'little terror'. It appears the tortoise was continually playing havoc with the plants in the bishop's garden. Apparently she loved strawberries and we are told that she followed the gardeners when they were gathering fruit, but was normally kept in check by being tied to a tree! (*Peterborough Local History Society Magazine*)

— AUGUST 24TH —

1911: How accidents happen. At about 7 p.m. on 23 August, 18-year-old Annie Griffin and her friend Lily Woodcock were 'larking about' on the Lincoln Road, where Searjeant Street and Stone Lane join. At the same time, Robert Walker was cycling down the Lincoln Road to the city centre. Annie saw him coming and took a step back to let him pass as he swerved to pass behind her. Annie was knocked down and Robert fell from his bike. He got up and, with Lily and a Mrs Sears, went to Annie's aid. She was unconscious. Annie was taken into a nearby shop, while PC Firmedow sent for a doctor. The doctor was in prompt attendance, diagnosed shock and unconsciousness and called for the ambulance from St Paul's churchyard. Annie was taken to her parents' house at No. 354 Rogers Street. There she died, without regaining consciousness, at 4.30 a.m. on 24 August. The inquest at the New England Workman's Hall two days later recorded accidental death, acknowledging that Robert Walker had done all in his power to avoid the accident and that if Annie had not taken evasive action, all would have been well. Much sympathy was felt for the parents of the deceased – their only child. (*Peterborough Standard*)

~ August 25th ~

1908: Remember reading about the 'disgraceful scenes' in the city centre on 14 March? This day saw the trial of George Dyer. It was revealed that he was not a stranger to the court, being in the habit of assaulting the police and others. He had nineteen previous convictions, all registered within the past five years. After hearing the evidence and witness statements the bench retired to consider the matter. On their return, the chairman is recorded as saying:

> Well, Dyer, the Court feel, and everybody must feel, that the origin of the trouble you got into was because you got too much drink. That is the reason you committed the two assaults in the street and caused the crowd to collect. The origin of it all is you getting too much drink and you will have to suffer for it.

For assaulting labourers Laverack and Clark at the same time and place he was fined 10*s* or seven days' imprisonment for each. Being drunk and disorderly earned him one month with hard labour and for assaulting PC Stevenson, he was sentenced to one month's imprisonment with hard labour – one sentence to follow the other. He would serve three months and fourteen days in total for his behaviour. (*Peterborough Citizen, Peterborough Advertiser*)

~ August 26th ~

1882: The *Peterborough Advertiser* of this date tells us that the Great Northern railway station has been extensively lengthened and is now being repainted. The intention was to light the platform in a very different way, and on Thursday evening, the station had been illuminated for the first time by eight of Calvert's 80 candle-powered lamps. They were a decided improvement, but because the contract for the lamps had been placed before the platform had been lengthened, there were insufficient lamps to light each end of the arcading. However, because the experiment was such a success, three more lamps would be fixed to each platform. Predictably, there was no timescale quoted! What was of interest, though, was that the new lamps had attracted a large number of non-travelling people to the station, and that many were to be seen reading papers by the excellent light provided. (*Peterborough Local History Society Magazine*)

———

1912: The past three weeks had seen frequent and heavy rainfall. By this Monday, conditions were beginning to endanger life and property. Thirteen and a half hours of non-stop rain between 5.30 a.m. and 7 p.m. had effectively closed the Oundle Road under the railway bridge with over 2ft of water. Worse was to follow tomorrow. (Bunch, Allan, *Peterborough in old picture postcards*, European Library, 1996)

~ August 27th ~

1909: As Peterborough's population expanded, the need for new schools – particularly for the very young – increased. This Friday saw the formal opening of the Queen's Drive infant school. It was a council-built school, designed to accommodate 148 children, and had been constructed with primrose-coloured bricks made locally, of course, by the Northam Brick Co. at Eye Green. (Perry, Stephen, *Peterborough Vol. 2, a second portrait in old picture postcards*, S.B. Publications, 1989)

1912: By this Tuesday, the incessant rains had caused the River Nene near the Town Bridge to rise to a height of 17ft 6in, about 8ft above normal, with virtually no space between the water level and the top of the arches. The green at Stanground had 1ft of standing water on it while the road from Stanground High Street to Peterborough was under some 4ft of water in places. People were now becoming worried about their livestock and more than one family had taken their pigs upstairs. There were many cottages in Bodgers Yard – where Rivergate Centre is now – at the rear of William Bodger's shop in Broad Bridge Street. Every family had vacated their downstairs rooms and rigged up a temporary outside walkway that they could access by ladder from their bedroom windows. It was not until Thursday that the water levels began to subside. (Bunch, Allan, *Peterborough in old picture postcards*, European Library, 1996)

~ August 28th ~

1900: Founded by John Sturton in 1833, and based in Bridge Street, 'Sturton & Sons – Wholesale & Retail manufacturing and dispensing chemists' were, to many Peterborians, the Boots of their day. On this day, disaster struck when their oil store caught fire, with estimated damage costs of £1,200. (Mellows, W.I., 'Peterborough's Municipal Jubilee', *Peterborough Standard*, 1924)

1940: Throughout the Second World War, there was much support from the non-combatant population. In Peterborough in the early days of the war, there was a well-supported 'Spitfire Fund' – the aim being to raise enough money to build a Spitfire. By the end of August, the total fund stood at £1,236 11*s* 6*d*. This August, as in other months, contributions came from many sources. The families in Norfolk Street between the Lincoln and Cromwell Roads had raised £18 4*s* 3*d*; Beryl Dale had given her birthday money of 5*s*; ten three-penny pieces had come from 18-month-old Malcolm Thorpe; and Graham Aubry, aged 11, had raised 5*s* by the sale of old newspapers he had collected in Lime Tree Avenue which also linked the Lincoln and Cromwell roads. On this Wednesday, the fund also received two guineas (£2 2*s*) from Mrs Heath and 'Jimmy', a donkey whose story is told here on May 10th. (Gray, David, *Peterborough at War 1939–1945*, David Gray, 2011)

~ AUGUST 29TH ~

1870: The *Peterborough Times* of 3 September reports on a Foot Race at Stanground on this August Bank Holiday Monday:

On Monday last Mr Bannister of the Blue Bell contributed to the amusement of the residents in this place by getting up a foot race (open to all England) for a valuable timepiece. The distance was 150 yards and Mr R Blades officiated as starter. There were only six entries, but the racing throughout was exceedingly good. The first heat was between Strickson of Yaxley and Warwick of Whittlesea, the first named being declared the winner. Second heat was won by J Clay of Peterborough, Warwick of Stanground being his opponent. W Blake of Peterborough had a walk over in the third heart, as the sixth man did not put in an appearance. The heats were then run off, J Clay taking four yards start of Strickson, and winning by a foot only, after a very exciting race. Clay and Blake next made their appearance, which caused some little excitement, the latter being considered one of the best runners in this part of the country. Blake gave his opponent 14 yards start and lost the race by about five yards. Everything passed off satisfactorily, notwithstanding the number of persons present.

– August 30th –

1654: John Evelyn records in his diary:

> Taking leave of my friends who had now feasted me more than a month I, with my wife, set our faces toward home and got this evening to Peterborow, passing by a stately palace of St John (one deepe in ye bloud of our good king) built out of the ruines of the Bishop's Palace and Cloyster: The Church of this city is exceeding faire, full of monuments of greate antiquity.... On the steeple we viewed the fenns of Lincolnshire ... Peterborow is an handsome Towne, and hath another well build church to it.

(De la Bédoyère, Guy, *The diary of John Evelyn*, Boydell Press, 1995)

—

1855: The ceremony of laying the foundation stone of St Mark's church by Bishop George Davys was anticipated with great interest. Programmes in circulation promised something inviting for the lover of novelty, the harmless pleasure seeker and the devout. Such a prospect could not fail to attract a large assembly of people and an autumnal sun without a cloud in sight was the perfect supporting act. The day began with a full choral service in the cathedral nave, followed by a procession to the site of the new building. After the laying of the stone, the schoolchildren had their usual treat – food, what else would a child want? (*Peterborough Advertiser*)

– August 31st –

1895: It is very easy to forget that in the nineteenth century, Peterborough had one of the most successful corn exchange markets in the country; their business levels were reported nationwide. However, as now, prices had their ups and downs. The *Lincoln, Rutland and Stamford Mercury* of 6 September reported that on this Saturday the corn market was quiet, with produce scarce and the price of wheat about 6*d* a quarter below the previous Saturday's level. There were a few samples of barley on show, but insufficient to set a price, and the price of oats was rather lower than previous. One of the prime reasons for this slack trade was that all the farmers were too busy bringing in the harvest to attend the market.

1940: Peterborough was rocked by a second bombing raid on this Saturday morning, with an estimated 100 incendiary bombs being dropped in a V formation from the city to Milton Park. The police and air-raid wardens put out small fires in the meadows by the river and the gardens of some private houses, while fires from four large bombs were extinguished by the Auxiliary Fire Service. Records say that a frog that was burned to death and the partial destruction of a wasp's nest were, miraculously, the only casualties! (Gray, David, *Peterborough at War 1939–1945*, David Gray, 2011)

– September 1st –

1857: By the mid-nineteenth century, the growing population of Peterborough needed more churches for worship. There had been significant new housing built around the New Road so, on this first day of September, a new parish of St Mary was created by Order-in-Council. This parish included the communities of Eastfield and Boongate as well as Newark, which was then an outlying village. Two years later, a church was commissioned to serve the parish, with the foundation stone being laid on 30 September 1859. The church, built of relatively cheap local stone and consisting of a nave and south aisle, was consecrated on 7 August 1860 by the Bishop of Peterborough. During the twentieth century, the church began to fall into a state of disrepair and the upkeep of the bricks and mortar, together with the problems of heating and leaks, led the congregation to consider building a modern church in its place. A plan was put forward to sell the old church and surrounding prime land to the new town developers, in return for a new church for the parish. This was eventually agreed and the last service to be held at the old church was on 22 October 1989. (*Peterborough Advertiser*)

— September 2nd —

1464: In medieval England, the major power brokers were the 'Gilds' (or Guilds) – associations for both religious and social purposes. By the fifteenth century they were at the peak of their influence as merchant organisations controlling trade and land ownership within town boundaries. In Peterborough, this could result in conflict between the monastery and the town. During the War of the Roses the monastery supported the Lancastrian side, while the town supported the Yorkists. It paid off, because on this day Yorkist King Edward IV granted to 'the brethren and sisters of the gilds of St Mary, St George and St John, in the church of St. John within the King's Town of Peterborough, in consideration of their good and faithful service, licence to acquire in mortmain [church land not liable to feudal dues] lands and possessions to the annual value of £20' for the maintenance of the guilds and for the relief of the guild chaplains. The town's folk often supported the guilds through bequests – Thomas Mason in June 1495 bequeathed 'to the three gilds in the parish church of St. John the Baptist viz: St Mary, St John the Baptist and St George and St James two tenements lying in Retenrowe' (Rotten Row?), later Highgate, then Broad Bridge Street. (Peterborough Churchwardens' Accounts)

~ September 3rd ~

1856: J. Carritt, baker of Fletton, summoned T. Skellet, labourer of Yaxley, seeking sureties against further harassment. It appears that Carritt was in his cart near Yaxley when Skellet attempted to get in without asking his permission. Carritt refused to let him ride so, it was alleged, Skellet took up some stones and threatened to 'smash the brains' out of Carritt. Skellet admitted that he had been drinking but claimed he had merely touched the cart when the complainant struck at him with a whip. Skellet was found guilty of a breach of the peace and bound in his own recognisances of £5 to keep the peace for three months. He was also to pay 18s 6d to the court for expenses incurred. As he had no money with him, Skellet was held in custody until the money arrived. The bench also advised him to reduce the quantity of his beer intake until he had worked out the expenses. (*Peterborough Advertiser*)

1900: On this Thursday, the Theatre Royal opened on Peterborough Broadway. In April 1916, it was renamed The Grand, reverting to the Theatre Royal in 1919. It later became The Empire before finally, in 1940, becoming the Theatre Royal & Empire. The 600-seat theatre eventually closed in November 1959. (Tebbs, H.F., *Peterborough*, Oleander Press, 1979)

– September 4th –

1541: By letters patent, Henry VIII declared that 'His Vill of Peterborough', thenceforth and forever, should be a city to be known, called and named the city of Peterborough. This royal grant meant that Peterborough citizens acquired the right to send two members to represent them in Parliament. The letters patent also stated that 'trusting in the wisdom, character, probity and virtue of our beloved chaplain John Chambers, clerk, bachelor in holy theology, late abbot of the late monastery of Peterborough I elect, nominate, make and credit the same John, Bishop of Peterborough'. (Carnell, Geoffrey, *The Bishops of Peterborough*, RJL Smith & Associates, 1993)

1933: A letter from Baker Perkins Ltd to the secretary of the Willesden Works Shop Committee dated 9 August said that:

> We are advised that 48 Houses in Peterborough will be available for occupation on Monday September 4th and the remainder on Friday September 15th. With regard to the allocation of these houses – it is suggested that the names of Willesden applicants, plus those from Peterborough employees to make up the number, be drawn and the houses 1 to 96 allocated according to the draw.

A copy of this letter was also sent to the secretary of the Peterborough Shop Committee. True to this promise, Baker Perkins workers from Willesden began moving into Willesden Avenue, Walton on this day. (Mitchell, Neil, *The Streets of Peterborough*, Neil Mitchell, 2007)

~ SEPTEMBER 5TH ~

1877: This day marked the twenty-fifth year of Revd Thomas Barrass' position as pastor of the Baptist church in Peterborough. When he had accepted the position, Peterborough's Baptist church had just thirty-six members. On his twenty-fifth anniversary, there were 409. There were special services held in his honour through the day. Revd Robinson of Wisbech preached a sermon 'to a large congregation, which contained a most graceful compliment to the Pastor. At half-past five a public tea was held in the school room which was crowded, about 500 being present, the tables being tastefully adorned with a choice selection of flowers.' At 7 p.m. a public meeting was held in a crowded chapel. After many speeches and recognitions of Revd Barrass' achievements, a presentation was made of a clock – described as 'a timepiece of handsome workmanship in a black marble case' – and inscribed 'Presented to Mr and Mrs Barrass, accompanied by a purse containing 120l (£120) as a token of affectionate esteem to commemorate the completion of his twenty-five years Pastorate of the Baptist Church.' Members of nearly all the denominations in the town had kindly and generously contributed to the testimonial, many of them unsolicited. (Jones, B.R., *Thomas Barrass – an Evangelical Individualist*, TalkingHistory, 2001; *Peterborough Advertiser*)

1855: The newspapers reported a brief stop on this Thursday morning by Queen Victoria, Prince Albert and their children on their way to Scotland by train. On the bookstall immediately opposite where the royal saloon stopped, several children had been placed, that elevated spot affording them the opportunity of getting a good sight of the royal party. As soon as Her Majesty had received the bishop and dean, and was at liberty to cast her eyes where she pleased, she gave a hasty glance up and down the crowded platform, bowing graciously in reply to the hearty cheers that arose from all points. Her eye caught sight of the row of children and was evidently much delighted with their appearance. She touched the prince and drew his attention to them and appeared to say to him 'Look at those dear little children.' (*Peterborough Advertiser*)

1856: Two newspaper advertisements on this day catch the eye: 'BREAD! BREAD!! BREAD!!! – Is regularly supplied to Families in any part of the city by J ELLABY, Albert Place, Peterboro: warranted free from Rice, Alum, or Potatoes.' Immediately below that was another notice concerning food: 'CHEAP FOOD FOR PIGS. A LARGE Consignment of GROUND RICE for Feeding Pigs, in bags containing 14 stones, at 16*s* 6*d* per bag, bag included.' (*Peterborough Advertiser*)

⸻ SEPTEMBER 7TH ⸻

1855: The entry for 6 September records Queen Victoria's Peterborough stop through the eyes of a local newspaper. Written after the royal party's arrival in Scotland, the following day's *Bristol Mercury* tells a very different story. It reports that, as usual, the royal train had been thoroughly checked before leaving London but, not long after leaving the capital, an axle problem was identified on the last brake van. The train stopped at Peterborough, the axles were checked and one or two of the axle boxes were washed out. The train then set off, but at Grantham, the matter was found to be worse and a man was stationed on the footboards of the train in order to grease the axles as it was running! Further stops at Retford and Bawtry were necessary. On reaching Doncaster, the brake van was changed and all was well. Now, if this story is true, Peterborough should be applauded for arranging the involvement of the bishop and the children at short notice. But what if Peterborough was a planned stop – as were all the others – and the *Mercury* had it totally wrong and there were no axle problems? We'll never know, but both make good stories!

— September 8th —

1856: A regular advertisement at this time was being placed by J.S. Clarke, bookseller of Market Place, Peterborough, offering 'CURTIS ON MANHOOD – SHILLING EDITION; a Medical Essay on Nervous and Generative Diseases by J L Curtis, a surgeon of 15 Albermarle Street, Piccadilly who is at home for consultation daily from 10 to 3 and 6 to 8; Sundays from 10 to 1.' The book supposedly contained:

> plain directions for perfect restoration of health and vigour; being a medical review of the various forms and modern treatment of nervous debility, impotency, loss of mental and physical capacity, whether resulting from youthful abuse, the follies of maturity, the effect of climate or infection &c; with observations on a new and successful mode of directing spermatorrhoea, and other Urethral Discharges &c. to which are added Curious and Interesting Cases with the Author's Recipe of a Preventative Lotion.

It is claimed to be 'Just published - the 77th Thousand, with numerous plates, in a sealed envelope, price 1s, or sent, post-paid, by the Author, for 14 stamps.' A 'testimonial' from the *Sunday Times* tells us this 'is a truly valuable book that should be in the hands of young and old'. (*Peterborough Advertiser*)

– September 9th –

1901: This was the day that James 'Jimmy' Blades was born in Peterborough. He was to become one of the most distinguished percussionists in Western music, with a long and varied career. For many years he was the Professor of Percussion at the Royal Academy of Music. In 1970, he wrote a book entitled 'Percussion Instruments and Their History', which remains a standard reference work on the subject. Always in demand as one of England's finest percussionists, he played under the most prestigious conductors in the world – often as a chamber musician with the English Chamber Orchestra. As a tutor, his students ranged from rock drummer Carl Palmer to percussionist Evelyn Glennie. Probably his most widely heard performance was the sound of an African drum playing 'V for Victory' in Morse code, introducing the BBC broadcasts made to the European Resistance during the Second World War. He provided the sound of the gong seen at the start of films produced by the Rank Organisation. For many years he collaborated with Benjamin Britten as percussion advisor, often acting as Britten's personal percussionist. Together they created the background music for the Post Office's 'Night Mail' promotional film. Jimmy died on 19 May 1999 in London. *(Jones, B.R., Interesting People – Fascinating Lives*, TalkingHistory; 2006)

— SEPTEMBER 10TH —

1856: According to the *Peterborough Advertiser* of Friday 12 September, this Wednesday night saw 'a burglarious entrance effected on the premises of the Rev'd Mr Chamberlain of Woodstone'. It reported that there had been a previous attempted break-in last year, so additional precautions were now in place. One such precaution was a bell hung on a hook, fixed to a door leading from the dairy to the kitchen. In the course of Wednesday night the housekeeper had been awakened by a noise and, on descending the stairs, she found that an attempt had been made to force the kitchen door. She stated that the bell had been dislodged and thrown to the floor. The situation was reported to the police who 'on examining the neighbourhood found traces of the thieves in a hovel where they had apparently lain, and also the remains of hay bands which they had twisted and evidentially worn on their feet to prevent noise'. The *Advertiser* reassured its readers that the officer had 'other clues, which may possibly lead to the detection of the marauders'. There appears to be no trace of anyone being arrested in regard to this failed intrusion, though.

~ September 11th ~

1897: This day's *Peterborough Advertiser* carried an interview given by William Bailey, landlord of The Swan in Midgate. He was not talking about the pub, though; his subject was the Peterborough Omnibus and Carriage Co., of which he was general manager and a member of the board. Starting last year with a fleet of four or five vehicles and twenty-nine horses, he explained that it had expanded and now ran twelve buses, three cabs and fifty-four horses. Operating seven days a week from 8 a.m. to 10.30 p.m., the passenger numbers were between 500 and 600 a day. One bus was taking up to £4 10s a day, made up mainly of penny and two penny fares. During the day, the busiest route was that from Stanground to New England. The busiest day was Saturday, with additional traffic on bank holidays and Peterborough Show week. Some twenty men were employed, with drivers earning £1 a week and conductors 17s. It wasn't to last, though: the British Electric Traction Co. had eyes on growing Peterborough. By 1904, William Bailey knew that it was a lost cause; by 1905 all was indeed lost, and in August of that year the Peterborough Omnibus and Carriage Co. was no more.

— September 12th —

1635: In 1634, Lieutenant Hammond of the Military Co. in Norwich set out to visit all the English cathedrals. On this day, he reached Peterborough and noted in his journal:

> Againe then I mounted and troop'd through a little Nooke of Huntingdonshire by the same pleasant River Nenn to the old Mother Church and ancient Fen city of this Shire: The Buildings and her Inhabitants much alike poore and meane; I found in her not anything remarkable, that was worth observing or travelling to, but her Cathedrall, which is an ancient lofty, strong and fayre compacted Building of 1000 yeeres standing; Her west entrance is somewhat differing from others which I have seene with a lofty fayre Arch that makes a fayre walking Ile before you enter thereinto.' Ascending the roof he notes: 'I did behold about me a little Kingdome of Marishes and Fens...and her 2 old neighbouring, watry and phlegmaticke Sisters, Crowland and Ely, with their tatter'sd and Ragg'd blew Azure Mantles about them... Heere I was satisfy'd enough with their sight, without marching to them.

Through his journeys, he thought the music in churches and cathedrals was great, except Carlisle – really disappointing, apparently – and Peterborough, which he classed as 'indifferent'. (Russell, John, *Fair Spot and Goodly – Visitors' impressions of Peterborough*, Peterborough Arts Council, 1984)

— September 13th —

1908: Elsewhere in this book, the story has been told of Peterborian Arthur 'Archie' Robertson's gold medal-winning performance in the 1908 Olympics. What is rarely written about, though, is what Archie did next. He closed off his Olympic season with a highly successful tour of Scandinavia. On this day, running on a banked concrete cycle track in Stockholm, he set a new 5,000-metre world record of 15 minutes 1.2 seconds. The next day, he attempted to break Walter George's world record 1-hour time. The records show that he failed to beat it by just 83 yards! In 1910 Archie, at the age of 30 and after a track and cross-country career lasting only four years, returned to his original love – cycling. (bbc.co.uk)

1914: At the outbreak of the First World War, many Belgians were made homeless and became refugees. Sir Richard Winfrey, Peterborough's mayor, launched a public appeal for money, furniture and clothing to help them. The appeal fund ultimately raised some £2,000. The corporation took over untenanted housing and turned it into hostels. This Sunday saw the first refugees arrive. Many more arrived in the following months and soon a dozen or so houses were providing them shelter. (Perry, Stephen, *Peterborough Vol. 2, a second portrait in old picture postcards*, S.B. Publications, 1989; Tebbs, H.F., *Peterborough*, Oleander Press, 1979)

⁓ September 14th ⁓

1972: In 1968, Newell Engineering did the 'industrial double', winning the Queen's Award for Industry and the one for Technical Achievement. In 1969, it had been appointed by the government to be one of just eight companies approved to test equipment made by other firms. That was all in the past as, on this day, it was announced that Newell Engineering – one of Peterborough's 'blue chip' companies – was to close two of its factories in the city by the end of the year. It was estimated that up to 200 jobs would be lost. The announcement came after top-level talks between the joint managing directors of Newell's, senior executives, heads of department, union representatives and shop stewards. The decision to close and sell the two factories and axe the jobs came less than a month after the company had announced a loss of over £750,000 in the previous financial year. Five years later, Newell Engineering was taken over by B. Elliott Ltd and, at the end of June 1984, the closedown was complete when all the manufacturing equipment and office furniture was sold at auction. One of the region's best-known engineering firms was no more. (*Peterborough Advertiser*; *Peterborough Evening Telegraph*; Harper-Tee, John, 'The Peterborough Story', *Peterborough Evening Telegraph*, 1992)

~ September 15th ~

1886: Under the subheading 'MISCHIEVOUS BOYS – FLOGGING OR PAYING', today's *Peterborough Express* tells the story of John William Brown and John Lightfoot, two little boys about 8 or 9 years of age, being charged by Mr Bodger of Peakirk with cruelty to certain sheep at Paston. With both boys accompanied by their fathers, Brown pleaded guilty, while Lightfoot pleaded not guilty. The prosecutor said that he had some lambs in a field, and that he saw some boys running them about and riding on their backs. The lambs were also beaten with sticks. He saw the defendants running away from the field. A lad named John Gardiner, who saw the defendants in the field stated that they were simply running after the sheep and that he saw no ill treatment. The bench, however, had no doubt that the defendants did abuse the sheep. Both were fined 5*s* 6*d* plus costs. The chairman added that if the parents would allow the boys to receive six strokes of the birch rod, to be inflicted by an officer of the court, the magistrates would remit the fines and costs. Brown preferred to pay the fine; Lightfoot was willing to allow his boy to be flogged rather than paying the fine.

~ September 16th ~

1907: It is not just people that create Peterborough's history – buildings have had a major part to play as well. One such building was the Hippodrome music hall on Broadway. Initially owned by a London syndicate, it opened its doors for business on this Monday. That was the beginning of a chequered history. Very quickly it discovered the problems of a tin roof when it was raining hard! In 1908, it was acquired by the famous Fred Karno and over the next fifteen or so years, leading stars such as Marie Lloyd, Charlie Chaplin and Thorney-born H. Vernon Watson, better known as his character Nosmo King, appeared there. With the coming of the cinema, the music hall's popularity declined. In February 1922, the theatre was modified to accommodate cinematic film and renamed the Palladium. It became the Palace in December 1924. As Karno's business had sunk into bankruptcy the lease, and then outright ownership, was acquired by Jack Bancroft who, in 1937, built the Embassy Cinema next door. Surprise surprise – soon after, the Palace was demolished. The last films shown there were *Clarence* and *Trouble in Morocco*. Peterborians, though, had little trouble in remembering the glory days of the Hippodrome/Palladium/Palace between the wars. (Harper-Tee, John, 'The Peterborough Story', *Peterborough Evening Telegraph*, 1992)

1838: Mary Gretham appeared before Peterborough magistrates on this Monday dressed as a man. In late spring, she had been discharged from Northampton asylum and, finding that it was impossible to gain employment as a female, had begun to wear the male clothing in which she appeared in court. During harvest time, she had earned 12*s* an acre as a reaper. She had then worked as a rick-maker and thatcher, earning half a crown a day until a few weeks previous, when she had fallen off a rick stack. On trying to stand up, she realised that she had injured her hip. It was when her master and mistress went to her aid that, to their surprise and horror, they discovered her sex. Although they did not broadcast their discovery, it soon became public knowledge. As a result, Mary had attracted the notice of idle boys and people of the city, who followed her in crowds as she sought some relief. She stated to the magistrates that there was still some money owing to her for the work she had done for her late master. Mary was sent to the workhouse until inquiry could be made. (*Stamford Herald*)

— SEPTEMBER 18TH —

1816: The war with France was over and all the prisoners held at the Norman Cross prison camp had long gone. Everything that was left had to be sold, and this day was the first of a scheduled four days of selling activity. The buyers were at hand – most clutching their copy of the Government Sale Catalogue. The catalogue cover tells the story:

> Government Sale. Norman-Cross Barracks. A catalogue of the lots into which the coals, candles, furniture, utensils, and fixtures at Norman-Cross Barracks are divided for Sale by Auction – without reserve – by Wm. Edwards under the authority of the Commissioners for the Affairs of Barracks – on Wednesday the 18th of September 1816 and three following days: the sale to commence each day at Eleven o'clock punctually.

Due to the volume of items to be sold, the sale went on for a total of thirteen days. It is arguable that the sale was not the success the government expected. The whole paving area of the depot market went for just £20, for example. At the end of the auction the total takings added up to £11,060 4s 4d. Much of the wood from the dismantled buildings was used in the erection of houses and outbuildings in Peterborough and the surrounding communities. (Walker, T.J., *The Depôt for Prisoners of War at Norman Cross, Huntingdonshire 1796 to 1816*; Lloyd Clive L., *A History of Napoleonic & American Prisoners of War 1756-1816*, Antique Collectors' Club, 2007)

– September 19th –

1928: 'Milk Slightly Dearer' reads a headline in today's *Stamford Mercury*.

> The new retail terms announced by the distributor's representatives will mean that the public will pay an increased price for two months during the coming year. The present retail price is sixpence a quart (two pints) during the six month's summer period and seven pence during the six month winter period. The new retail prices are to be seven pence per quart for eight months and six pence per quart for four months. The result will be that a household using a quart of milk daily will pay five shillings more during the next year than the twelve months now expiring.

In the area now known as Greater Peterborough, this could be a benefit for some and a challenge for others. Where you lived, where you worked and the size of your family affected whether this was good or bad news. Average wages for factory workers was just over £4 a week; agricultural wages were lower. Dairy farmers would be pleased with the increase, while factory workers with large families would be unhappy as milk was considered an important part of a child's diet.

— September 20th —

1907: The *Stamford Mercury* of 25 October records the court appearance of Joseph Hodierne of Coventry. Joseph had been summoned for driving a motorcar at a dangerous speed at Wansford on this day. PC Kind told the court that Hodierne had been driving at the rate of 18mph. The defendant retorted that he had in fact been driving at 8mph! The court believed PC King and Joseph was fined £7 10*s* plus 3*s* costs.

1934: The first bridge over the Nene in Peterborough was constructed by Abbot Godfrey in 1308. It was not until December 1872 that this oft-repaired crossing was finally replaced by an iron bridge. By the early twentieth century, with road traffic increasing, and the Great Eastern Railway crossing to the south of the bridge in the way – sometimes holding up road traffic for four or more hours a day in total – things moved on another step. In 1931, L.J. Speight & Co. had begun the construction of a reinforced concrete replacement and traffic had begun flowing over the bridge in October 1933. But it was not until this Thursday that the 5th Marquess of Exeter performed the formal opening ceremony for the bridge, which had cost some £140,000 to build. (*Peterborough Advertiser*; Mitchell, Neil, *The Streets of Peterborough*, Neil Mitchell, 2007)

1439: No one is sure whether the king was here or not but, on this day, King Henry VI gave Abbot Richard Ashton permission to hold an annual fair on St Matthew's Day and the two following days 'at the bridge of Peterborough by the River Nene, as well in the County of Huntingdon as in the County of Northampton, on all sides of the bridge'. Thus, the Peterborough Bridge Fair was born. After morning prayers, the notables of the city formed a procession and the town crier read the proclamation at the fairground. The modern proclamation dates back from 1878, and it asks all persons to 'behave soberly and civilly, and to pay their just dues and demands'. Since this foundation, the fair has always been opened by proclamation. Exactly 572 years later, the Peterborough press reported that 'fun lovers flocked to the official opening of the Bridge Fun Fair last night. The Mayor of Peterborough, councillor Paula Thacker, led a procession from the Town Hall, in Bridge Street, to the entrance of the fair. After the official opening, the mayor returned to the Town Hall to host the traditional sausage supper.' (Tebbs, H.F., *Peterborough*, Oleander Press, 1979)

— September 22nd —

1939: The *Peterborough Advertiser* carried a graphic story of the sinking of the light cruiser-destroyer HMS *Courageous*, which had been torpedoed and sunk on 17 September while on anti-submarine duty off the coast of Ireland. Struck by two torpedoes, it capsized and sank in fifteen minutes, with the loss of 518 lives. It was the first British warship to be lost in the Second World War. Able seaman William Hill of Woodston was one of the lucky survivors and he provided the *Advertiser* with a graphic account of his ordeal. Covered in fuel oil, he had swum some 200 yards toward a raft. He said that he would have failed to reach it if he had not been able to cling to a drifting spar 'heading that way'. There were several others on the raft, all of whom were picked up by the lifeboat of one of the convoy's merchant ships some twenty minutes later. Once on board, they had been 'rubbed down, given a slug of hot rum, and put to bed'. William and the others had arrived safely in port on Tuesday 19 September and had arrived home in Woodston on Thursday lunchtime. He told the *Advertiser* that he was now on fourteen days' 'survivors leave' before returning to active service.

~ SEPTEMBER 23RD ~

1966: The *Peterborough Advertiser* carried a story which, when taken out of context, may baffle a modern reader. It was highlighting the fact that the council was worried about being able to let the new houses being built at Westwood because they felt that few potential tenants would be able to afford the weekly rent of £5 7s. The question they posed was: 'Who will live in them at such high rents?' They asked that 'If the London overspill does come in time, who is to say whether they will, or will not, be able to pay this much a week for such accommodation?' It was considered that if tenants did not have a net income of at least £16 or £17 a week – an above-average wage for the time – they could be very hard pushed to meet such rents. The paper also pointed out that Westwood, like much of Peterborough and other parts of the country, had been hit by rising costs and the 'squeeze'. One should add that this was accommodation that had previously attracted criticism: the buildings were apparently too close together and the gardens were too small. They had been described as being more like rabbit hutches!

— September 24th —

1883: During the second half of the nineteenth century, there had been a change in the attitude of many people with regard to alcohol consumption. Abstinence and teetotalism increased. To meet the need (or was it to cash in on the changing attitude?), on this Monday, the Fitzwilliam Coffee House at the corner junction of New Road and City Road was opened. In 1911, the Labour Exchange took over part of the building – now you could have a coffee while seeking a job. In the heart of town, on the corner of Exchange Street and Queen Street – now an entrance to Queensgate – was the Bedford Temperance Hotel. In 1906, that was offering beds for between 9*d* and 1*s* 9*d* per night. On the corner of Bridge Street and Bishops Road, meanwhile, was the City Temperance Hotel – originally built as a private house but by 1906 doing a steady trade for the traveller who did not require alcohol. So where are they now? The Fitzwilliam closed in the 1920s. It later became the Ex-Servicemen's Club and this plot of land is now covered by the modern Peterborough Passport Office. The Bedford vanished into Queensgate, and you will read about the city Temperance in the entry for 19 November. (Jones, B.R., *Peterborough's Inns & Taverns - a guided walk*, TalkingHistory, 2003)

~ September 25th ~

1876: The *Liverpool Echo* reported that Mr Whalley, the MP for Peterborough, was today present at the laying of a memorial stone in connection with the construction of a new United Methodist Free Church at Cefn Mawr near Wrexham. In the course of his address he referred to the present condition of the affairs in the East – saying that England should not drift into war without the consent and full knowledge of the people, and that he rejoiced that the great question of the Bulgarian atrocities had agitated the country. He went on for quite a time but one wonders quite what Peterborough's MP was seeking to achieve. Certainly no local Peterborough paper reported the speech.

———

1970: The *Peterborough Advertiser* reported that the town – with a population in 1970 of 80,000 – was to become Greater Peterborough by 1985, with a population of 188,000. It would be a new regional city, offering a wide range of employment opportunities, shopping and recreation plus four new, distinct townships – Bretton, Paston, Orton and Castor, each housing 20,000 people. The plan would produce 51,000 more jobs and five times as many cars, as well as shops and services within pram-pushing distance in the townships. The cathedral, precincts and Cathedral Square would be designated conservation areas. (Harper-Tee, John, 'The Peterborough Story', *Peterborough Evening Telegraph*, 1992)

— September 26th —

1807: Begun in late 1796, the Norman Cross Depot was 'home' for many thousands of predominately French prisoners during the Napoleonic conflict. Many prisoners attempted escape – and some succeeded – but they were all small-scale plans, with no more than three or four prisoners involved in the affair. The escape attempted today was different. Now almost ten years old, the depot was still protected by the original outer wooden fencing with the inner area divided into four stockades, also surrounded by wooden fencing. It was in the early hours of this Saturday that 500 or so prisoners in one stockade made a concerted attempt to escape. As a body they charged one side of the quadrangle, smashing it all on to the ground. As they rushed toward the outer wooden fence, they were confronted by soldiers, militia and guards. These were too well organised and the potential escapees were driven back into their own quadrangle. It is reported that up to fifty of the prisoners suffered bayonet thrust wounds, but not one shot was fired and not a single person died. One outcome, though, was that the camp now built an outer brick wall. (Walker, T.J., *The Depôt for Prisoners of War at Norman Cross, Huntingdonshire 1796 to 1816*; Lloyd Clive L., *A History of Napoleonic & American Prisoners of War 1756-1816*, Antique Collectors' Club, 2007)

− September 27th −

1816: Following the end of the Napoleonic War in 1814, the prisoner of war camp was soon emptied but it took the powers that be two years before they felt comfortable disposing of it. On this Friday, according to an annotated copy of the sale catalogue, William Richards, a blacksmith of Cumbergate in the city centre, bought lots 255 and 256 − '2 staff sergeant's rooms, 2 ends and a stack of chimneys, with paving in front together with the Regimental store adjoining'. He made good use of these pieces, constructing a cottage - which he called Norman Cross Cottage − on the corner of Milton Street and St Leonard's Street. That was finally demolished in 1950. (*Peterborough Local History Society Magazine Millennium Edition*)

—

1875: For centuries, Whittlesea Mere had been a place of fun, adventure and relaxation for the people on its 'shores'. By this day the Mere had long been drained. E.W. Cooke summed up people's feelings:

> Whittlesea Mere was a scene of interest to the visitor both to the painter, sportsman and naturalist. One now looks in vain for that broad expanse of water, reflecting the grey passing clouds and margined with vast masses of reed and sedge. How fine were those bright, broad-leafed and cup-like flowers through which we poled our little punt.

(*Bygones of Woodston & District, Woodston & District (St Augustine's Church)*, Local History Group, 1979)

— September 28th —

1460: On this day, Richard Harlton handed over a book to his successor, William Leicester. As the abbot's seneschal, he was officially responsible for the daily functioning and discipline within the abbot's household. Among many other things, the book tells us that in the Abbot's House there were four new 'fedybedds' and 'much other bedding'. Just in case there is trouble, it records that there are also 'three bows and six sheaves of arrows'! Also there is 'one brasen busshell' – a brass container capable of holding 8 gallons of liquid or a significant quantity of grain. Perhaps it was used to store some nice, strong, ale. (*Peterborough, Dean and Chapter manuscripts*; *Cartularies and Registers of Peterborough Abbey*, Northants Record Society, 1978)

———

1963: This Saturday was a day so many people did not want to happen – it was the last day the market would be held in the city centre. A weekly event since the twelfth century, it was now to be no more. Peterborians lamented that it was just not the same. A common comment was that 'they' – the council – had 'transplanted the heart of the city and dumped it in Cattle Market Road'. Predictably, the younger generation had a different view: they thought it was a good move. There were all mod cons and, best of all, it was covered and therefore dry. (Harper-Tee, John, 'The Peterborough Story', *Peterborough Evening Telegraph*, 1992)

– September 29th –

1820: Peterborough's Michaelmas Sessions record book for this year contains a sketch of a promissory bank note of the Wisbech Bank. The note, 'No. 50000 Great Britain', dated 'March 10th 1804', is ornamented with a drawing of a military cannon. It is apparently the reason why one John Gambell of St John the Baptist, Peterborough, appeared before the court charged with fraud, it being claimed that he 'did pretend and affirm to one Sarah Hurdlestone that a certain false and counterfeit Note in the Possession of him, the said John Gambell, was a true promissory Note of the Wisbech Bank for the payment of the sum of one pound of lawful money of Great Britain'. The note bears the declaration that 'I promise to pay Mr Buonaparte or order a Pill Five Pounds weight being in full of all demands for the Insolence he has given us Shop Keepers.' It is signed 'I Volunteer'. (*Peterborough's Past Vol. 1*, Journal of Peterborough Museum Society; *Stamford Mercury*)

1855: Miss Brown had much pleasure announcing to the 'Ladies of Peterborough and Neighbourhood' that she had returned from London with 'all the latest Novelties from Paris, in Embroidery, Collarets, Sleeves, Bugle and other Head-dresses with the Eugenie Falls and Barbes', promising that 'the new Selection will be arranged for inspection on Tuesday 2nd October, and during the forthcoming Fair'. (*Peterborough Advertiser*)

— September 30th —

1975: In November 1972, the city's Engineers' Department had released proposals to radically transform the general Gladstone Street area that was home to some 8,000 residents. Nothing happened! Finally, in April 1975, following repeated complaints by residents about the state of the district, council leader Charles Swift ordered a massive clean-up of the area. In mid-June it was reported that 268 houses in the area stood empty, derelict and vermin-ridden – 12 per cent of the total and an increase of 150 over the previous year. The *Evening Telegraph* could finally report on this day that something was to be done. It had been promised, it reported, that by the end of 1975 work would be underway to refurbish and redevelop the whole of the Gladstone Street area. It would not be instant, though. The whole scheme was forecast to take around eleven years and cost something in the order of £4.25 million, with much of that money going in grants to existing tenants to do some of the work themselves. By the end of May 1981, the *Peterborough Evening Telegraph* was able to inform its readers that the work was almost complete, the council having agreed on 26 May to spend a further £428,000 to complete the neighbourhood improvements.

~ OCTOBER 1ST ~

1838: At the Peterborough Fair on this Monday, Mr Vergette was hustled and robbed of his gold watch, 15 sovereigns and a cheque for £60. A few minutes after the robbery one of the thieves, accosting him with great civility, gave him back the cheque, saying that he feared it would prove useless to his friends, and might be of service to him. The thief most politely thanked Mr Vergette, and then darted into the crowd. (*Lincolnshire Chronicle*)

1912: In 1876, the 'October Fair' was renamed the Bridge Fair. Traditionally it was opened by the mayor reading a proclamation asking all persons to 'behave soberly and civilly, and to pay their just dues and demands according to the laws of the realm and the rights of the city of Peterborough'. Over the years, the *Peterborough Advertiser* had printed many complaints about the 'amount of evil and drunkenness' during fair week. In its report on this year, the *Advertiser* almost gloated reporting that 'Aquarius, in a Puritanical fit, summoned all his forces to put down the fair, which comprised of drinking booths; canvas arcades housing hardware; gingerbread and coconut stalls; wax museums and numerous oyster and shellfish dealers.' In other words, it rained.

⚊ October 2nd ⚊

1855: The *Peterborough Advertiser* of 22 September had carried an intriguing front page advertisement targeting today's – and tomorrow's – fair-goers:

> Peterborough Bridge Fair. 2nd and 3rd of Oct., 1855: JOHN ELLIS, Wentworth Hotel, takes this opportunity of thanking those Ladies and Gentlemen who have honored (sic) him with their Patronage, and begs to inform them that REFRESHMENTS will be provided in the Large Assembly Room, Wentworth St., on the above days, at Moderate Charges, when he again hopes to receive those favors (sic) so liberally bestowed upon him. N.B. – Private Rooms for Ladies. Hot, Cold, and Vapour Baths. Well-aired Beds.

1907: The *Peterborough Express* editorial on this day addressed the question of Greater Peterborough, claiming that: 'It almost seems as if another movement to expand the Borough is impending. This time it is not a question of uniting brickopolis to Peterborough but one of absorbing the opposite rapidly growing extremity.' What was being discussed at this time was the framing of uniform by-laws – particularly those relating to house sizes and the widths of the new streets needed. Walton was the immediate consideration, as it hadn't yet committed to a new drainage scheme and other works that would inevitably follow. (*Peterborough Local History Society Magazine*)

~ October 3rd ~

1824: John Clare records in his journal that he began to read the *Garden of Florence* by John Hamilton Reynolds. 'It is a beautiful simple tale with a few conceits.' It begins prettily: In the fair city of Florence there did dwell etc: and ends sweetly. (Robinson, Eric and Powell, David (eds), *John Clare by Himself*, Fyfield Books, 2002)

1897: This day's sitting of the Peterborough Petty Sessions had some interesting 'little' cases. Arthur Steels, a labourer from Eye, was summoned for an offence against the by-laws – although the actual offence is not stated – and was fined 7*s* 6*d*. Newborough labourer William Clarke was fined 2*s* for neglecting to send his son John William to school. Also from Newborough, we find farmer Frederick Williams in trouble. After pleading guilty, he was fined 10*s*, including costs. What was his crime? He had employed 13-year-old John William Clarke! In a 'man and wife' case, Hensman Pridmore, an innkeeper of Eye, was bound over for twelve months to keep the peace towards his wife. Also at the sessions, we find John Manning, a groom of King's Newnham – a village between Coventry and Rugby – being ordered to pay Sarah Coulson of 211 New England 2*s* 6*d* per week. Now I wonder what that could be about! (*Peterborough Advertiser*)

~ OCTOBER 4TH ~

1747: On this day John Thomas 'popped into' the Bishopric of Peterborough when he was consecrated at Lambeth by the Bishops of Rochester, Bristol and St Asaph. The 'popped into' comment stemmed from the fact that he had become the chaplain to King George II, with whom he had contact when George was the Prince of Wales. In 1752, he became tutor to the future King George III. In 1757 – ten years after coming to Peterborough – he moved a step higher, becoming Bishop of Salisbury. As has so often been the case through the centuries, Peterborough was not a quiet backwater but a stepping stone to something greater. (Carnell, Geoffrey, *The Bishops of Peterborough*, RJL Smith & Associates, 1993)

1796: As the eighteenth century came to an end, Peterborough was still, in many ways, a medieval market town – watched and regulated as of old. 'Forestalling' (the buying or selling of goods on the way to market or before the market opened) and 'Regrating' (buying things such as corn on the way to or at the market and then selling them at the same market) were still commercial crimes. This day's *Stamford Mercury* reports that 'at the late Peterborough sessions a cow-jobber was fined for regrating by buying beasts and selling them at Peterborough market the same day' (Tebbs, H.F., *Peterborough*, Oleander Press, 1979)

– OCTOBER 5TH –

1856: Until the mid-nineteenth century, Peterborough had had no formal place for Roman Catholics to worship since King Henry VIII's decisions over 300 years previous. This had meant that practising Catholics had to travel many miles to follow their faith. The Religious Census of March 1851 had recorded seventy persons attending morning service, and forty in the afternoon, in a chapel in Cumbergate described as 'a portion of an old building opened as a Catholic place of worship in 1850'. Following false starts and frustrated hopes, it was on this day that their efforts were rewarded as Bishop Wareing dedicated Peterborough's Holy Family chapel. The *Peterborough Advertiser* described the new building as being of white brick and Bathstone dressings; plain in style yet substantial in presence. The worshippers were delighted but other Peterborians were less so. During the night following the opening, some stoned the building and broke windows and anti-Catholic letters appeared in local newspapers in the following weeks. When Bishop Wareing returned on a formal visit in May 1859, he found that for the previous year there were 365 Catholics of all ages on the register. Twenty years later, the church was in a position to prepare plans for its successor – the church we see to this day. (*Peterborough's Past Vol. 3*, Journal of Peterborough Museum Society, 1988)

~ OCTOBER 6TH ~

1909: Under the headline 'Football on the recreation ground', the *Peterborough Express* reported on a letter to the council from the Secretary of the Peterborough and District Football Association that offered his council's thanks to the corporation for rescinding a resolution prohibiting football being played on various recreation grounds and expressed the hope that, in the near future, they would see their way clear to allow goalposts to be erected and the opportunity to play matches; the same as was done in various other towns. The mayor asked, incredulously, 'they want us to provide goal-posts?' Mr Lamplugh explained that it was not a request for the present but a constructive look into the future. Alderman Batten asked what the actual request was. Mr Lamplugh explained that there was none at all - they were merely thanking the council for what we have done, and expressing a hope that in the near future we may permit the 'what you may call 'ems' to be erected. After the laughter subsided, Alderman Batten supposed that the town clerk would advise the council if they had the power to set apart public recreation grounds for the purpose of football matches. Mr. Lamplugh said that would come on when they asked and that 'we shall fight it then'!

~ October 7th ~

1998: On this day, the local paper carried a headline about an unnamed family in Westwood being terrified by the irregular appearances of a ghostly airman in their home over a two-year period. The father, speaking to the *Evening Telegraph*, described how had 'woken up one night to see a figure standing by the window. I thought I was dreaming,' he said.

> I could not make him out clearly but he seemed about 30 years old, and he was wearing a blue-black airman's uniform. He walked straight by me. I don't know why but I followed him. I watched as he walked down the stairs and then, when he got to the front door, he disappeared. I wasn't scared, but it worried my wife.

He went on to describe strange noises and other occurrences, and how, when they continued, they called in an exorcist. In fact, the family tried two exorcisms, to no avail – the airman still loiters and strange noises continue. The houses in the area are built on the site of RAF Westwood, a Second World War airfield mainly given over to training. A great many airmen who passed through there quite probably did not live to see the end of the war. (Orme, Stuart, *Haunted Peterborough*, The History Press, 2012)

~ October 8th ~

1723: Today the Peterborough Feoffees established that the cost of building the new workhouse had totalled £426. Following discussion, they agreed to pay £300 if the parish inhabitants consented to pay the balance of £126 via an assessment upon themselves. It was also agreed that the Feoffees grant a lease to the Overseers for twenty-one years at an annual rent of 3s 4d. Meanwhile, in the vestry the vicar of St John's, two churchwardens, three overseers and eleven parishioners certified that:

> Matthew Marriott has put our parish to such regulations touching the poor by erecting a house of maintenance for feeding, lodging and clothing of all the poor in the parish that should want relief from the parishioners whereby the parish rates are likely to come to less than one half of what they formally were, which for the last 8 years one with another (on average) was £499 18s 6¼d. In the half year since the erecting of the house of maintenance, buying of furniture, brewing vessels, clothing and repairs amounted to £220 13s 5¼d. However, the last half year since Lady Day amounts only to £113 14s 6¾d.

The poor do cost a lot of time and money, you know. (Mellows, W.I., 'Peterborough's Municipal Jubilee', *Peterborough Standard*, 1924)

~ OCTOBER 9TH ~

1845: It was on this Thursday that the *Morning Post* reported the results of a Tuesday meeting of the directors of the Midland Railway, at which several deputations from different newly projected railways were in attendance, but no publicity was given to their proceedings. A great number of tenders were made for the different lines advertised to be let. Among those to be accepted was a bid of £47,000 for the line from Stamford to Peterborough – estimated to be a distance of some 12 miles – some £100 million at the time of writing! The works were required to be commenced immediately and to be completed in eight months. The subject of a proposed Norfolk and Midland Counties railway linking Kings Lynn, Wisbech and Peterborough, which appeared to have multiple companies seeking rights, was raised. It was hoped that the plans being discussed would not interfere with these plans already in place. The benefit of this link would be to provide cheap, direct and expeditious communication with Birmingham, Manchester, Liverpool and other great manufacturing towns in the north of England. This was not a scheme propounded by mere speculators, but by men of capital and influence. Peterborough would be a key hub of this network. (Various sources)

~ October 10th ~

1884: Stained glass windows are the pride of any church, and St John's church is no different to the rest in this regard. On this day, a faculty was proposed to remove stained glass from the central east window and replace it with glass representing Messrs Butler & Bayne. It also records the church's intent to place stained glass in the east windows of the north and south aisles. These windows were to represent the 'Resurrection and Descent of the Holy Ghost at Pentecost' and the cost of £780 was to be met by James Pears Esq of No. 1, The Crescent, Peterborough. Once done, the stonework of the east windows of the north and south aisles was to be restored in accordance with plans agreed on 19 January 1882. Based in Covent Garden, London, Butler & Bayne were one of the leading firms of Gothic revival stained-glass manufacturers, whose work was commissioned by the principal Victorian architects. During a long career, the firm produced stained glass for numerous churches throughout the Britain, the Empire and even the United States. Their work was to be found in Westminster Abbey, Wimborne Minster and Peterborough Cathedral (1864). St John's was aiming high. (Bull, J & V., *A history of Peterborough Parish Church – St John the Baptist 1407–2007*)

— OCTOBER 11TH —

1878: Whittlesea farmer Jonathan Truman hired James Green
for twelve months as foreman on his farm. An agreement was
signed for a term commencing 11 October 1877. Green was to be
paid 21s per week, 15s to be paid weekly, the remainder (£15 12s)
to be paid on 11 October 1878, when the engagement ceased.
One months' notice by either party was agreed. In mid-February,
Green gave a month's notice. On leaving, he asked for his weekly
wages arrears and the proportionate part of the 6s per week left
in hand. Truman refused to pay. At the May Assizes, Truman
claimed that as Green had not remained the year, he couldn't
claim any portion of the £15 12s – just the weekly 15s due.
Green claimed the agreement clearly intended that if either party
terminated the agreement by a month's notice, £1 1s a week must
be paid up to the time of leaving. His Honour disagreed, stating
that agreement required the man could not liberate himself
until the end of the twelve months. As Truman had accepted the
months' notice in the middle of the year, he would give judgement
of 15s a week to the time of leaving but no more. (*Stamford Mercury*)

∼ October 12th ∼

1864: The *Peterborough News Magazine* on this day records that robbery with violence is not an uncommon event. It also records that the Income Tax Commissioners had fined William Hedeswell £10 for submitting false returns. (Tebbs, H.F., *Peterborough*, Oleander Press, 1979))

———

1910: Peterborough was, and still is, unusual in having a corporation/City fire brigade and an active Volunteer fire service operating in both competition and unison. As Peterborough grew, a contentious matter arose – 'should the Corporation Fire Brigade be attending out of town fires?' Mr Herbert declared that it didn't appear right that the public of Peterborough should find the money for the purposes of a fire engine, pay the firemen, yet be left unprotected while the engine and brigade went off to a fire in, say, Yaxley. He acknowledged that the surrounding parishes contributed to the costs on an annual basis but, he asked, what would happen if they 'forgot' to pay? He then tabled a motion that 'the Corporation Fire Brigade shall only attend fires within the Municipal Borough, and the Parishes of Peterborough Without and Longthorpe, so long as those Parishes continue their annual payments under the agreement'. The proposition was carried unanimously. Mr Herbert then reminded people that the Volunteer Fire Brigade, with an engine, were willing and eager to take fires out of town or anywhere else! (*Peterborough Express*)

~ October 13th ~

1870: The *Peterborough Times* of 15 October carries in its correspondence column the following letter:

> HMS 'CAPTAIN'; Sir: I shall be glad if you will again allow me to acknowledge through the medium of your column the receipts of the following sums towards the fund for the relief of the sufferers by the loss of the above ship. I am thankful to those who have already made me the agent of their munificence, and hope that many more will yet do the same. I am proud to say the movement is becoming more widely spread each day. I am, sir, yours faithfully E Waller, M.D. Surgeon R.N., Bridge Street, (Peterborough) 1870. Rev: Coney 10*s* 6*d*; J Edgar 2*s* 6*d*; J M Vipan Esq £1; A Thank Offering £2; S.J.D. 2*s* 6*d*.

HMS *Captain* was an unsuccessful warship built for the Royal Navy due to public pressure. A masted turret ship, she was designed and built by a private contractor against the wishes of the Controller's department. The *Captain* was completed in April 1870 and capsized off Cape Finisterre on 6th September 1870 with the loss of nearly 500 lives because of design and construction errors that led to inadequate stability. (*Salisbury and Winchester Journal*)

~ OCTOBER 14TH ~

1887: Wallace Wells asked if he might have the use of the Town Hall – the elevated room overlooking the modern Cathedral Square - for a singing class. He was informed that the use of the Town Hall was reserved expressly for matters of public interest. (Mellows, W.I., 'Peterborough's Municipal Jubilee', *Peterborough Standard*, 1924)

1909: A notice affixed in the Minster Precincts – about 25 yards from the West Front doorway – said simply: 'Motorists visiting the cathedral are asked not to bring their motors beyond this point.' It was nothing to do with parking restrictions. The problem was simply that the noise of throbbing engines just outside the door was annoying to the worshippers! (*Stamford Mercury*)

1941: As the war continued, Peterborough systematically informed and trained the populace. On this Tuesday evening, Sergeant Beal, an Air Raid Precaution officer, gave a detailed talk in the Town Hall describing, discussing and demonstrating how to deal with incendiary devices. He advised that if one came through the roof, one should deal with it promptly and throw it out of, or through, the window if possible. He told his listeners that an incendiary bomb would probably burn for around seven minutes and that a stirrup pump had proved its worth many times. However, he stressed that one should not throw a bucket of water over the bomb, as it would cause the device to explode! (Gray, David, *Peterborough at War 1939–1945*, David Gray, 2011)

– October 15th –

1926: It's in the early sixteenth century, while Peterborough still had monastic 'rulers', that the expression 'putting the cart before the horse' is first recorded. It's a figure of speech about confusing cause and effect, or doing things the wrong way round. That fits the story of the present Town Hall perfectly. A proposal for a new Town Hall to replace the Guildhall in the Market Square was first aired in 1874. Nothing materialised. In the early 1920s, a decision – in principle – was made to widen what was then called 'Narrow' Bridge Street. 'What about building a new Town Hall?' also seems to have reared its head because, on this October day, the city council decided to put wheels in motion for one. It was decided that the fairest – and probably cheapest, if truth were known – way to address this would be to hold an open design competition for the new building. Sixty-one design submissions were received. In March 1928, it was announced that a design had been agreed and in March 1929, John Thompson & Sons' tender to build was accepted. Of course, the old Narrow Bridge Street buildings were still standing – and were very much in the way! Their demolition began on Tuesday 30 April 1929. (Jones, B.R., *A Monumental & Memorial walk around central Peterborough*, TalkingHistory, 2004)

~ OCTOBER 16TH ~

1905: In 1904, the Barrass Memorial Hall – named after the Baptist pastor in Peterborough for fifty years – had been opened, adjoining the large chapel he had built on Queen Street in 1870. On this Monday morning, one of the largest fires experienced by Peterborough until that time totally destroyed the chapel and badly damaged the Memorial Hall. The cost of the damages was estimated at some £5,500 – around £500,000 at time of writing. The hall was restored and only vanished with the building of Queensgate, but the chapel was never rebuilt. Instead, a new one was built in Park Road. (Jones, B.R., *Thomas Barrass – an Evangelical Individualist*, TalkingHistory, 2001)

———

1948: After a day's shooting, city councillor and former Mayor of Peterborough, Arthur Mellows was driving home with his faithful Labrador and his friend Mr Percival. It was about 5.30 p.m. when they reached the Conington railway crossing – a crossing where road users had to open and shut the gates. Mr Percival got out and opened the gates and Mr Mellows began to drive his large black Chrysler across. He appears to have been concentrating on driving – and, perhaps, keeping an eye on a stationary train to the south, and therefore failed to notice an express coming from the north. It ploughed into the car, killing both him and his dog. (Orme, Stuart, *Haunted Peterborough*, The History Press, 2012)

– OCTOBER 17TH –

1857: An advertisement in all the local papers reads:

> OMNIBUS from New England and Mill Field to Peterborough.
> SIX times every Saturday. J Chamberlain, Black Boy Inn, Long
> Causeway begs to inform the inhabitants of New England, Mill Field
> and the public in general that he has made arrangements to run an
> Omnibus between the above places at the following times and prices,
> commencing on Saturday October 17th 1857.

There then followed a timetable showing the first journey,
from Peterborough to New England leaving the Black Boy at
10.00 a.m., and returning from New England at 11.00 a.m.
The next out from Long Causeway was at 1.00 p.m., returning
an hour later. The departures were then every two hours, with
the last 'bus' from New England leaving at 10.00 p.m. Single fares
cost 6*d*, and return or double journeys 9*d*, with no extra charge
for market baskets or luggage. These early omnibuses were often
simply carts modified for the Saturday business by the addition of
seating on both sides. Although the fares seem quite reasonable
now, they were quite expensive for the working man of the time.
Chamberlain was the first to introduce this service, but within
fifteen years, there were over three dozen such services connecting
Peterborough centre with the communities and villages over a
significant area. (Mitchell, Neil, *The Streets of Peterborough*, Neil
Mitchell, 2007)

~ OCTOBER 18TH ~

1879: Page 628 of Whellan's 1874 History – Topography and Directory of Northamptonshire – records that the Peterborough Billiards and Chess Rooms were situated in Cumbergate having been established at a cost of £1,000 raised in 200 £5 shares. That project appears to have collapsed as the *Peterborough Standard* noted that, following a meeting at the Greyhound hotel, the formation of the Peterborough Town Club by subscription was agreed. It would be for billiards, chess and other activities and would have a newsroom. It was proposed that £1,000 be raised via the sale of £2 shares. Immediately, 237 shares were subscribed to, with 100 more in the short space between the meeting and this published report. In December 1879, the club had moved to new purpose-built premises in Priestgate. This club seems to have fared no better than its predecessor, as the *Peterborough Advertiser* of 26 April 1884 records the club as in liquidation, with fixtures and fittings to be sold by auction on 1 May 1884. (*Peterborough Local History Society Magazine*)

1895: An agreement was made this day between William Joseph Moser of Peterborough (clerk in Holy Orders) and Henry Hammond of Padholme Road Peterborough (builder and contractor) to build a Roman Catholic church in Peterborough – the first such building since Henry VIII's split with Rome. (*Peterborough Local History Society Magazine*)

~ OCTOBER 19TH ~

1859: Charles Dickens visited Peterborough a few times. Although he didn't seem to like it too much, it didn't stop him weaving Peterborough into some of his stories. For instance, the workhouse where a meagre amount of gruel was doled out to the unfortunate urchins under its roof, where Oliver Twist asked if he could have some more and where Mr Bumble, the beadle, ruled the roost, was based on one in Peterborough – the Wortley Almshouses pub on Westgate. Nor did the dislike stop him being in the town on this Wednesday to give a reading, recreating scenes from *The Pickwick Papers* and *Dombey and Son*. The *Peterborough Advertiser* described the event in glowing terms, paying tribute to Dickens' 'essentially dramatic genius' and continuing that 'our emotions seem to be at the command of a potent magician, who, at will shakes us with laughter or moves us to tears'. Dickens appears to have been delighted with this reading, saying in a letter to a friend about the Peterborough event that 'we had a splendid rush last night; I think the finest I have ever read to. It was as fine an instance of thorough absorption in a fiction as any of us are likely to see again.'

– OCTOBER 20TH

1870: On this day 52-year-old William Gibson – a man with a respectable reputation – allegedly stole money to the total of £2 and a wooden bowl – the property of Mr Thomas Pritchard, refreshment shopkeeper of Peterborough. The case finally came to court on 6 January 1871 when the court was told that at about 6.30 a.m. on the day in question Gibson had put his head round the door and told Pritchard that a dog was 'worrying' the meat in the window. He then left. No dog was seen and no meat had been touched but when Pritchard returned to his counter, he found £2 and the tray containing it missing. The empty bowl was later found and, on apprehension, Gibson was found to have money on him 'corresponding in great measure with the money missing'. Gibson stated that the money was a gift from Mr Clarabut, who confirmed the fact. The session chairman noted that the accuser's weak point was that the source of the money could not be identified and advised the jury that if they had any doubts about the accusation, they must give the accused the benefit of the doubt. This they did and the accused left the court an innocent man. (*Peterborough Standard*)

~ October 21st ~

1908: The *Peterborough Express* of this date reports on a discussion initiated by Alderman Batten. He had pointed out that the council generally considered the matter of tree planting at this time of year, and that he wanted to propose that they plant some trees on the Broadway continuation of Long Causeway. Mr Vergette asserted that he would support the suggestion, provided they did not plant Plane and other useless trees that did damage to paths. He preferred apple and pear trees, which would be of some use to later generations. Mr Rowe said they should think carefully because, recently, they had spent a considerable sum to lay tarmacadam 4 or 5in thick there. Various other points for and against the proposal were discussed, with the proposition finally being lost 9 votes to 5. (Peterborough Express; *Peterborough Local History Society Magazine*)

2005: To celebrate the 200th anniversary of the Battle of Trafalgar, a granite plaque was unveiled today in the Broadway Cemetery at the grave of Robert Base. He had survived the battle while serving on HMS *Bellerophon*. He later settled in Peterborough and married Elizabeth Barrett of Barnack at St John's church – the records telling us that he was in the Royal Marines at the time. He died on 28 February 1878. (*Peterborough Herald and Post*)

~ OCTOBER 22ND ~

1818: For many, the spire of a church reaching up towards the sky is a symbol of faith, of reaching for strength and support. In other instances it is not just showing piety – it is a symbol of the wealth and prestige of the building or the patron who funded it. So what do you do when it's damaged, or becomes dangerous? This was the challenge confronting the vicar, churchwardens and church representatives of St John's church. The lead-covered spire had been condemned as 'defective' on the east and west sides toward the base. It was also becoming too heavy for the tower; something needed to be done. Approval had been sought under church building regulations for the total removal of the spire – and it was on this day that approval was finally granted. But it didn't end there. The removal of the spire also needed approval via an Act of Parliament. Approval of such an application takes time – eight months in this case – so there was considerable relief amongst all parties when the twenty-three-page Royal Assent to its demolition was received on 14 June 1819. While removing the spire they also took the opportunity to strengthen the tower. Two birds, one stone? (Bull, J & V., *A history of Peterborough Parish Church – St John the Baptist 1407–2007*)

– OCTOBER 23RD –

1917: Having opened as the New England Workmen's Hall Co. in November 1905, times appear to have been tough, as it hit financial problems and was formally wound up. It reappeared as the Brotherhoods Club and eventually the New England cinema, which opened on this night with a programme described as 'Fragments from France'. In later years, the cinema was referred to as 'The Bug Hutch'. I wonder why! It continued as a public cinema until Saturday 21 May 1966 – the last film shown being *The Guns of Navarone* with David Niven, Gregory Peck and Anthony Quinn. Not a bad exit, don't you think? (*Peterborough Local History Society Magazine*)

1950: Runaway loco engines are dangerous, and the New England depot had recently experienced two runaway incidents. As a result, stringent security measures had been put into force at the depot. The *Western Morning News* reported on this day that a third such incident had nearly occurred there when a Green Arrow-type express locomotive, in the process of raising steam, was found to have the regulator open, the reversing lever in gear, and the cylinder waste-cock shut. The new measures brought the situation to light. Without this check, when a sufficient head of steam had been raised, the engine would probably have moved off with danger to life and limb.

~ October 24th ~

1906: Without entering into the debateable question of the desirability of two fire services in the city – one official, one volunteer – the *Peterborough Express* believed that it had become important to get a second steam fire engine in the city. It also pointed out that the volunteer team needed to become 'practically acquainted with the handling of a steamer'. Praising the volunteer service for their determination to raise sufficient money, it commented that they already had around £50 put aside for a steam engine. The *Express* also suggested that 'all citizens should show their gratitude for the Volunteer Fire Brigade by liberal donations to their fund'.

———

1976: Today saw the last service by the Wesleyan Methodists in the chapel that had been built 110 years earlier to serve the non-conformist worshippers of New England. Afterwards, both this and the chapel at Werrington were closed – the replacement being the Brookside Chapel in Gunthorpe Road. The old chapel was taken over by the council and, over a four-year period, it was converted into a community centre – opening in November 1979 as the Asian Cultural and Community Centre. As such, it was the first centre of its type in Britain, and represented a unique experiment in relationships between the different communities of Peterborough. (*Peterborough Local History Society Magazine*)

‒ OCTOBER 25TH ‒

1883: This Thursday saw the reopening of St John's church following the extensive repairs that had proved necessary following the great gale of 1881. That gale had blown down the north-east pinnacle of the tower, which crashed down through the aisle roof. As it fell, it had smashed one of the gallery staircases to the balcony pews, which provided the extra seating often needed. During the period of closure, services had been held in the adjacent Corn Exchange (now the grassed area near the tower). However, that proved far from ideal as, on sunny summer days, the glass roof made the interior too hot! When this happened, the congregation had temporarily relocated to Broad Bridge Street school. Throughout this time, however, the bells still rang out from the tower of St John's. The repairs to the church had been carried out under the watchful eye of John Pearson, who was the architect of Lincoln Cathedral. It was therefore perhaps appropriate that it was Christopher Wordsworth, the Bishop of Lincoln (and nephew of the poet William Wordsworth) that saw in the reopening in place of the unfortunately ill Bishop of Peterborough, William Conner Magee. (Bull, J & V., *A history of Peterborough Parish Church – St John the Baptist 1407–2007*)

~ OCTOBER 26TH ~

1910: The *Peterborough Express* reported that, at the Saturday evening council meeting, a letter from the Post Office authorities had been read out. It stated that the Post Office desired to close the Percival Street post office at 1.00 p.m. on Thursdays instead of 2.00 p.m., and asked if the council had any objections. As other post offices already closed at 1.00 p.m. on Thursdays, the council had no objections to this change. (*Peterborough Local History Society Magazine*)

1949: City administrative life had begun to return to normal at the end of the war. One of the early steps taken recognised the need for improved education facilities. This led to the amalgamation of the Soke and City Education Committees into the Joint Education Board. Arthur Mellows was appointed its first chairman, a post he enhanced with a mixture of high ideals and practical common sense. He later became a member of the Association of Municipal Corporations Education Committee. His accidental death on 16 October 1948 was a great loss to Peterborough and education. His name and ideals live on at the Village College at Glinton, which opened its doors for the first time in September 1949 and was formally named in his honour as Arthur Mellows Village College on this day in October 1949. (*People of Peterborough*, Peterborough Museum Publications, 2009)

~ October 27th ~

1814: At 3.00 a.m. on Sunday 16 October, Robert Butler, James Penniston, Emmanuel Marton, William Hitchcock, Robert Wass and others had broken into the house of Mrs Plum at Maxey and made off with 90 guineas in gold, a watch and two silver spoons. Within a week, only Wass remained free. Today this notice was published:

> FORTY POUNDS REWARD: Notice is hereby given that Robert Wass, who has been concerned in divers Burglaries and Robberies in Lincolnshire and Northamptonshire is still at large. He is by trade a carpenter, 5 feet 9 or 10 inches high, fair complexion, good looking, rather thin, has a clean, neat appearance. His voice is squeaking and broken and he has a sore leg. He had on when he absconded a light fustian frock coat, a swansdown waistcoat, with spots, dark corduroy breeches and dark speckled stockings. He is supposed to have about 60 guineas in his possession.

Any person apprehending the said Robert Wass would receive the above award on his conviction by applying to Mr William Hopkinson, clerk to the magistrates in Bourn. The hunt was on and that squeaking voice – he was often called 'Squeeky' Wass – must have made his identification and arrest easy. (*Drakard's Stamford News*)

~ OCTOBER 28TH ~

1889: The Victorian era saw the appearance of many itinerant 'quack doctors' travelling the country, offering amazing cures for all sorts of complaints. One such quack was Yorkshireman William Henry Hartley. Starting in Portsmouth in 1887, he soon built up an almost cult-like following, giving shows and selling miraculous 'cures' and affordable 'medicines'. It was all done under the name of Doctor Sequah, with a lot of Wild West-style entertainment. He claimed his products, such as Sequah's Prairie Flower and Sequah's Oil, were made to traditional Native American recipes. He also offered 'painless' dentistry. Following serious discussions, Peterborough councillors agreed to allow him to hire the Market Place from Saturday 28 October to 1 November at 10*s* per day. A crowd, claimed to be in excess of 5,000 people, greeted him with a large bouquet and loud cheers. However, he had become so successful that he needed to be in at two places at once. He solved his problem by recruiting some more 'Dr Sequahs' to cover different areas of the country. Soon there were twenty-three of them across the country, and Sequah grew to be a big-business brand name throughout Britain and Ireland. We have no idea which of the twenty-four Dr Sequahs Peterborians saw! (*Peterborough Advertiser*)

1802: The *Lincoln, Rutland and Stamford Mercury* carried the following notice:

> I, Sarah Robinson wife of John ROBINSON, baker, Spalding, Lincolnshire, did on October the 1st 1802 insult Mrs BRIDGES of Peterborough, wife of Mr Bridges Dancing Master, without the least provocation: I hereby declare that the assertions frequently made against the character of Mrs Bridges representing her being connected with my husband, are totally false; and I do hereby publicly ask Pardon, and hope she will not proceed in the Spiritual Court or any other Court against me; those false and injurious Reports having been propagated in the Heat of Passion, for which I am very sorry.

It is signed with the mark of Sarah Robinson, Spalding, 22 October 1802. (*Peterborough Local History Society Magazine*)

———

1917: On this day, the Grand Theatre advertised an 'extraordinary attraction'. For six nights, W.W. Kelly's London Co. presented 'The play of two centuries – A ROYAL DIVORCE' with Miss Mabel Scudamore as Josephine and Mr George Hudson as Napoleon. Offering 'popular prices', theatregoers are advised to 'book your seats early', either at the box office, or by telephoning 223. The performances were advertised as beginning at 7.15 p.m., with the doors opening at 6.30 p.m. There were NO Early Doors and it was 'First Come – First Served with seats.' (Bull, J. and V., *Peterborough – a portrait in old picture postcards*, S.B. Publications, 1988)

~ October 30th ~

1314: King Edward II had 'called in' at the monastery on his way north to confront and subdue the Scots. Following his disastrous defeat at Bannockburn in June, he was making his slow way back to London and again stayed at the monastery. This time he was more subdued – but still, I suspect, expensive! (Jones, B.R., *A personal view of Mediaeval Peterborough*; TalkingHistory, 2003)

1722: This day saw a vestry order signed by two churchwardens, three overseers and seventeen parishioners, agreeing that Matthew Marriott should undertake the care of the poor of the parish of St John the Baptist and hamlets 'to take care to feed, lodge, cloath (sic) and keep to work all the poor of the parish that should be sent to the house of maintenance by order of the parishioners and at the charge of the parish'. It was also agreed that they should pay him £50 and provide one new coat, not to exceed 30*s* for one year. Perhaps they were too generous, because one year later – on 12 September 1723 – Thomas Tinkerton, the Feoffees' Town Bailiff, was appointed 'to officiate and manage, as master of the house of maintenance'. He was to be paid just £20 per year but still with 30*s* for a blue coat! (Mellows, W.I., 'Peterborough's Municipal Jubilee', *Peterborough Standard*, 1924)

~ October 31st ~

1872: It's often said that Peterborough is 'sometimes the first to do things and often the last to do something'. The idea of Peterborough applying for a Charter of Incorporation – the right to self-manage was in the Municipal Corporations Act of 1835 – is a case in point. It had been discussed many times over the years, but never taken any further by the powers that be. An 1867 letter in the *Peterborough Advertiser* had raised the subject again, calling for a committee to make arrangements for a town meeting. Nothing happened. This day finally saw a public meeting held in the Drill Hall to 'consider whether or not a corporation should be obtained'. It resolved, by a majority estimated at 600 to 29, that 'in the opinion of this meeting it is desirable that a Charter of Incorporation be obtained for the city and borough'. Following the meeting, the proponents took to the road to obtain wider support. A July 1873 public enquiry to determine whether it would be 'advantageous for the city to be administered by a municipal corporation' gave a positive response and the city council, originally called the Peterborough Corporation, was founded by Charter of Incorporation dated 17 March 1874 – just under forty years after the discussion began! (Tebbs, H.F., *Peterborough*, Oleander Press, 1979; Mellows, W.I., 'Peterborough's Municipal Jubilee', *Peterborough Standard*, 1924)

– NOVEMBER 1ST –

1898: Today's municipal elections created a challenging situation in the Peterborough west ward. Following the count Mr C.H.J. Butterfield, the editor of the *Peterborough Standard*, was declared the winner by one vote. The narrowness of this vote prompted the losing candidate, Mr H.B. Hartley, to petition for a recount. Carried out in the High Courts of Justice, the recount confirmed that Harley's votes totalled 755 – the same as in the first count – and that Butterfield had been credited with one vote too many. The situation was now a tie! A further examination then established that one of the votes for Butterfield did not have the official mark and was therefore invalid. This reduced his total valid votes to 754. As a final result, therefore, Mr H.B. Hartley was duly elected to represent residents in west ward by one vote. (Mellows, W.I., 'Peterborough's Municipal Jubilee', *Peterborough Standard*, 1924)

1937: This Monday was the day when the new Embassy Theatre opened for business amid 'unprecedented scenes'. The coloured neon lighting was described as 'emphasising the bold lines of its noble outline', and it was said that they 'projected a glow which could be seen for miles around against the banks of low clouds'. (*Peterborough Advertiser*)

— NOVEMBER 2ND —

1926: On this Tuesday, John William Topley of Stone Lane, Millfield, Peterborough, brought a case at Peterborough County Court against the London, Midland and Scottish Railway Co.. Before his Honour Judge Farrant, John Topley was suing the company for £6 7s 1d because of damage to his goods, a sifting and mixing machine, while in their care and in transit. He claimed that everything pointed toward the machine being put on a truck without sufficient other goods to prevent it moving about. Mr Yates, for the company, pointed out that the consignment note, clearly signed by the plaintiff, laid down that as the machine was not properly packed in a crate, the owner's risk rate applied. In this situation the company was relieved of responsibility, except upon proof that 'loss or injury arose from wilful misconduct on the company's servants'. There was no loss involved and no injury had occurred. When Topley stated that he had no witnesses, the *Mercury* tells us that 'His Honour non-suited the plaintiff with costs.' In other words, His Honour decided that there was no evidence which could prove the claim, so 'pay up and go home'. (*Stamford Mercury*)

– NOVEMBER 3RD –

1769: When Bishop Robert Lamb passed away on this day, he left behind a strange legacy. He was appointed Dean of Peterborough in 1744 and, from 1747 to 1763, was also Rector of Peakirk with Glinton. In 1758 he became a Fellow of the Royal Society and, in 1763, accepted the post of Rector of Hatfield in Hertfordshire. This would appear to be his favourite place because, though he was elected Bishop of Peterborough in 1764, he died at Hatfield rectory and was buried there. He is one of the few British bishops who does not have a biography in the Dictionary of National Biography, and *The Gentleman's Magazine* for 1769 records his death, but omits any biographical notes. (Carnell, Geoffrey, *The Bishops of Peterborough*, RJL Smith & Associates, 1993)

1885: It was on this day that Isaac Carter of Wellington Lane asked Thomas Jackson to cart a useless horse to the Milton kennels for him. Jackson was to receive money from the kennels and return it to Carter, less his expenses of carting. Carter neither saw the money or the horse again. When he heard Jackson had sold it elsewhere, and kept the money, he instituted a prosecution. At the Peterborough Petty Sessions of 28 April 1886, Jackson was committed for trial at the next assizes. (*Stamford Mercury*)

~ NOVEMBER 4TH ~

1864: The St Peter's Masonic Lodge had been founded at the Angel Inn on Narrow Bridge Street in 1802. Over the next fifty years, the lodge found a variety of 'homes', eventually settling in 1854 in the newly built Wentworth Hotel in Wentworth Street, where one of their members was taking over as manager. However, in 1859 they decided that it would be to their advantage to have their own, purpose-built, Masonic Hall. That idea finally began to be reality in September 1863 when a plot, once occupied by Squires Brewery, was purchased for £100. There, on the corner of Lincoln Road and North Street, they built a new two-story hall at the cost of £323. It was consecrated on this Friday. The lodge only occupied the first floor, letting the ground floor to brewers and wine & spirit merchants Elijah Eyre & Co. of Kings Lynn. Eyre & Co. also owned The Ostrich Inn next door to the new lodge, the Wheatsheaf in Eastfield Road and the Smithfield Arms in Midgate. While their meetings were now held in their new Masonic Hall, the lodge's Festive Boards and Ladies' Festivals continued to be held at the Wentworth Hotel. Makes sense to me. (*Peterborough Local History Society Magazine*)

– November 5th –

1926: Today's *Stamford Mercury* gives us a snapshot of Peterborough in the week just gone. The west ward house-to-house collection in aid of the ward's quota for the New War Memorial Hospital amounted to £64 10*s* 10*d*. At a Labour meeting Mr J.F. Horrabin, the prospective Labour candidate for Peterborough, addressed a large gathering of women at the Temperance Hall in Lincoln Road. The Knights of the Willow dined at the Great Northern Hotel on Saturday for the presentation of League cups and medals. The Westwood Works Concert Party contributed musical items during the evening. Also dining the previous Saturday at the Grand Hotel on Wentworth Street was the Peterborough Rugby Football Club when eighty members, under the presidency of Doctor L.C. Burrell. Mr Bert King's first boxing tournament for the season was held on Monday evening at the Corn Exchange. In addition to a splendid programme of contests, there was a special lightweight novices competition. At Wednesday's police court, Edward J. Allen of no fixed abode was charged with breaking into the dwelling house of Mrs Willoughby and stealing a lady's gold wristlet, ten £1 treasury notes and 22*s* in silver. In court he apologised to Mr and Mrs Willoughby and was committed to Quarter Sessions. (*Stamford Mercury*)

~ November 6th ~

1884: This Thursday in New England saw the completion of a project that had been initiated almost a year before for a drinking fountain to be erected on a triangle of wasteland within the junction of Lincoln Road and Walpole Street. The 21ft-high fountain was dedicated to the parents of the Revd Charles Ball, the first vicar of New England. A plaque was fixed to the east side facing the Lincoln Road. The plaque reads, in Latin, 'In pious memory of their well-beloved parents Joseph and Rebecca Ball, a son, the survivor of four, and daughters, dedicated this fountain.' Mr W. Barford, Mayor of Peterborough, with the Revd Ball, five aldermen and eleven councillors in attendance, was there to celebrate the occasion. The mayor was the first to drink from the newly installed fountain, followed by the Ball family, then the councillors. The junior inhabitants were next to sample the delights but such was the rush that the police were required to control each of the four taps. Those present – somewhere around 1,000 people – then sang the national anthem and dispersed at 2.00 p.m. Subsequently the council added some posts around the fountain, followed later still by thirteen trees. (Perry, Stephen, *Peterborough Vol. 2, a second portrait in old picture postcards*, S.B. Publications, 1989; *Peterborough Local History Society Magazine*)

— November 7th —

1828: The *Stamford Mercury* makes one of the early references to resurrection men, or body snatchers, operating in Peterborough. It describes how, during the past week: 'these wretches have forced their way to the neighbourhood of Peterborough, and, one night last week, succeeded in taking the body of a young man recently buried from the churchyard in Stanground. A fellow is now in custody at Peterborough on suspicion of involvement in the foul deed.' Two others, supposed to be his companions, had made a rapid getaway by horse and cart, heading full tilt toward Yaxley and the Great North Road. They had been followed by many of the local men, with more joining in the pursuit as it went on. The two suspects did make good their escape – but on foot, vanishing into the countryside. Their horse and cart appears to have ended up in the ditch. The cart was described as 'containing the various instruments used in this horrid traffic'. The items in question were 'taken into custody' by the Peterborough constables at Norman Cross. There is no record of these grave robbers ever being caught but quite a few more such situations would arise in Peterborough and its locale over the next four years or so. (*Lincoln, Rutland and Stamford Mercury*)

– November 8th –

1886: This Wednesday's *Peterborough Express* provided a comprehensive description of the laying of the foundation stone for the new church of All Saints on Park Road that had taken place two days previous on All Saints Day. The laying of the stone had been performed by the bishop of the diocese – William Connor Magee – in the presence of a large number of the clergy of the neighbourhood, the mayor and corporation and about 1,000 of the general public. A spacious marquee had been provided but the whole event benefitted from very fine weather. The foundation stone had a cavity, into which was placed an urn containing current copies of the *Peterborough Standard* and the *Peterborough Express*, along with 'numerous current coins of the realm'. Inscribed on the stone were the words 'this corner stone of All Saints Church was laid by the Right Rev. the Lord Bishop of Peterborough on All Saint's Day, 1886'. The church was being built on land given by the Peterborough Land Co. and the immediate plan was to build a portion of the church, in fourteenth-century style, to seat some 300 worshippers, at a cost estimated to be approximately £2,000. This first element of the church was in use before the end of 1887. (Tebbs, H.F., *Peterborough*, Oleander Press, 1979)

~ November 9th ~

1934: On this Thursday, the Fletton United football ground was the venue for a match between ladies representing Peterborough Cinemas and Marks & Spencer. Admission for adults was 6*d* and for children 3*d*. Profits were in aid of Mayor A.E. Fletcher's Unemployment Fund. I wonder who won? (Bull, J & V., Perry, S. and Sturgess, R., *Peterborough – a third portrait in old picture postcards*, S.B. Publications, 1990)

1962: 'How will Peterborough grow in the future?' was the question posed by the *Peterborough Advertiser* on this day. It deduced that two options appeared to be on offer. One would see the city continue its steady, natural, expansion that was, in itself, impressive at three times the national average. The other would be a government-sponsored 'overspill' expansion, which would involve a doubling of the population in the next twenty years. This latter option had come to the fore with the announcement by Sir Keith Joseph, the Minister of Housing and Local Government, that Peterborough was one of three large towns selected for consideration – the others being Ipswich and Worcester. A study would be placed in the hands of 'experts', led by Sir Henry Wells, who were to draw up a report on the feasibility of building a new town on an existing town. The *Advertiser* noted that the scales of expansion to be studied were 50 per cent or 100 per cent growth. The report was finally published on 10 March 1964. (Harper-Tee, John, 'The Peterborough Story', *Peterborough Evening Telegraph*, 1992)

~ November 10th ~

1943: At the Magistrate's Court on this Wednesday a sad – but far from unusual – case unfolded when 18-year-old Beryl Constance Grindley of no fixed address pleaded guilty to a charge of sleeping out on this day and not being able to give a good account of herself. The magistrates were told that she had travelled from London to March, where she found work. However, she had absconded with some money and had later been fined 10s for travelling from March to Peterborough without a railway ticket. She had been found sleeping in an air-raid shelter at 1.30 a.m. and, having said she lived in a caravan in Westwood, was told to go home or risk being arrested as a disorderly and idle person. Two hours later she was still in the same shelter, now saying she lived in Wansford, which was too far to walk. Having reason to believe she had been sleeping rough in shelters for some weeks, she was arrested. Medical examination showed sores all over her arms and legs. Sentencing her to two months in prison, the chairman of the magistrates told her that while in custody she would be properly looked after. (Gray, David, *Peterborough at War 1939–1945*, David Gray, 2011)

~ NOVEMBER 11TH ~

1926: On this, her 90th birthday, Miss Margaret Gibson was made an Honorary Freeman of the city of Peterborough – the first woman to be awarded this honour – 'in recognition of her long and distinguished services to the city in the cause of education of girls'. It is said that, while on a visit to Peterborough, she heard Bishop William Connor Magee speak and felt that this was the place for her to stay. With her friend Miss Annette Van Dissel, she opened a school. In the spring of 1870, they moved their school to Laurel Court, where it stayed until her death in 1928. An advertisement in the 1884 Peterborough directory states that:

> The aim of this school is to give a high moral training, offering to the pupils the advantages of home life. French and German are the language of the house. Especial attention is paid to the culture of Music. Pupils are prepared for the Cambridge and Oxford examinations. Fees are 60 Guineas per Annum, paid in advance and a term's notice is required before the removal of a pupil.

One of her pupil-teachers was a Miss Edith Cavell. Miss Gibson died on 12 April 1928, aged 91. (People of Peterborough, Peterborough Museum Publications, 2009; *Peterborough & Huntingdon Standard*; *Peterborough Advertiser*; Liquorice, Mary, *Posh Folk: Notable Personalities (and a Donkey) Associated with Peterborough*, Cambridgeshire Libraries, 1991)

~ November 12th ~

1864: Whittlesea Mere was famous and popular with locals and the upper classes alike for its fishing and shooting opportunities. The summer months saw many 'leisured gentlemen' and students from Cambridge making it a regular fixture in their social calendar. As winter set in, they could call back and share memories of those relaxing and fun summer days. By the 1860s the Mere had effectively vanished; drained to aid farming and to carry the railway tracks for the expanding network. Writing in his diary on this day, Thomas Rooper recalled those days gone by, never to return: 'My friend Hopkins and I always spent a week in August with Berry who rented the Mere. We paid him 7 shillings each per day for Board and Lodging and spent our time in shooting Flappers, Moorhens and Halfers.' So what are these elements of joy he recalls? Moorhens I can understand but 'flappers?' Well they are not quite what came first to my mind – young ladies of the 1920s – though the word is descriptive. They are 'young birds just enabled to try their wings before flight'. Come to think of it, the 1920s term now makes sense. A 'halfer' is defined as a 'gelded male fallow deer'. (Various sources)

― November 13th ―

1844: Today was a very special – and stressful – day for George Davys, the Bishop of Peterborough. In 1827, he had taken up residence at Kensington Palace with the position of principal master to Princess Victoria, a situation he held until she became queen in 1837. He was advanced to the bishopric of Peterborough in 1839. At his burial, the queen sent one of her carriages with servants in state livery to attend the funeral as a mark of her affection and esteem. But back to this day: the day of the baptism of the daughter of Brownlow Cecil, the 2nd Marquess of Exeter at Burghley House. On a four-day stay there were Queen Victoria and Prince Albert. Albert was to stand sponsor for the baby, who was to be christened Victoria by the Revd George Davys. Lady Victoria Leatham, a descendant of the 2nd Marquess, described the event:

> The Bishop of Peterborough took the service, but he arrived rather under the influence of sherry which he had taken to calm his nerves. In addition he had forgotten his glasses, which meant he had to guess how the wording went. He began the christening first of all without the Queen, then without the baby. Finally the deed was done.

(Leatham, Lady Victoria, *Burghley*, Herbert Press, 1992)

– November 14th –

1768: John Morton in his 1712 work *The Natural History of Northamptonshire* commented that the recently drained Borough Fen was 'justly accounted one of the richest Parcels of Feeding Land in the Kingdom'. Among the crops grown there were flax and hemp, which, of course, needed people to store it and sell it. One such person was Robert Muggleston, who ran a flax and hemp dressing business in Peterborough. This day's *Northamptonshire Mercury* carried the following prominent advertisement:

> To all Dealers of HEMP and FLAX: ROBERT MUGLISTON (sic) & Co. beg leave to acquaint them that they have lay'd in a large Assortment of HEMP and FLAX, both of Foreign and Home Growths, and the Produce of Lincolnshire and the Isle of Ely, at their Warehouse in Bridge Street, Peterborough; where all Dealers therein may be served wholesale, upon the lowest Terms.'

An addendum reminded the dealers that the company could acquire tools for dressing hemp and flax of any size to any degree of fineness and 'as such as are allowed by experienced Judges to be as complete-made Tools as any in England, and at moderate Prices'. The business was still flourishing in 1784. (*Northamptonshire Mercury* quoted in 'A Northampton Miscellany', Northampton Record Society, 1983)

— November 15th —

1814: Having started in late October, and been seen in Long Sutton within the past week, the search for the notorious housebreaker Robert 'Squeeky' Wass came to an end today when he was discovered at a small public house in South Witham. He had about 40 guineas in gold and £2 in silver in his possession. He was promptly committed to Peterborough Gaol. It was hoped that the atrocities of a desperate set that had kept Bourn and the neighbourhood in constant alarm would now cease. Well that's what the papers said, and people hoped! (*Drakard's Stamford News*)

1930: The Peterborough Electric Traction Co. (PETC) had replaced the horse buses with their electric trams in 1903, and today they themselves were being replaced as the last tram made its final trip from Long Causeway to the depot. It carried just ten passengers. Since 1925, the local passengers had preferred to travel on the petrol driven buses, and in 1926 the company had purchased its first two double-decker buses. The tramlines were all taken up and the roads resurfaced. The electric tram standards were sold off to the city council and they, in time, converted many of them to street lighting standards. In 1931, the PETC merged with the newly formed Eastern Counties Bus Co.. (Tebbs, H.F., *Peterborough*, Oleander Press, 1979; Mitchell, Neil, *The Streets of Peterborough*, Neil Mitchell, 2007)

— November 16th —

1940: In the fourth — and (so far) most destructive — bombing raid on Peterborough, six high-explosive bombs were dropped in Fletton. Thirty-one houses were damaged and two totally demolished. Fortunately, just two people were injured. The house at No. 37 Queen's Walk was one of those demolished. When the ambulance officer arrived, he found that a bedroom floor had collapsed and the daughter of the house had fallen, still in bed, into the room below. She was rescued through the dining room window. Her parents, meanwhile, were stranded in their bedroom upstairs and in danger from falling masonry. The ARP rescue squad got them out via the upstairs window. In another of the wrecked rooms they found an unbroken electric light bulb still hanging from the badly damaged ceiling while a single bottle of milk stood surrounded by a pile of bricks. Next door was equally damaged. There, the family of two adults and six children had found that their stairs had vanished. There was also a smell of escaping gas. One lad shinned down the drainpipe, falling the last bit of the way. Their cat came to the front bedroom window but refused to leave! (Gray, David, *Peterborough at War 1939–1945*, David Gray, 2011)

— November 17th —

1939: It was in September 1935 that the British prime minister, Stanley Baldwin, published a circular entitled Air Raid Precautions (ARPs), inviting local authorities to make plans to protect their people in event of a war. Although notorious for so often being last to do things, Peterborough appears to have been on the ball here and began to implement ARP soon after the outbreak of the conflict. It was on this day that the London Brick Co. at Fletton stated that all of its precautions were completed and, in all the works at Fletton, some form of protection was available. A number of old tunnels with 15ft to 20ft of earth above them had been turned into shelters with 'baffle walls' at the ends to make them safe from blasts and flying debris. Where there were no convenient tunnels they had built brick-lined trenches, covered them with sheets of corrugated iron and then piled quite a few feet of earth on top. All protective places had seating, a water supply, toilet facilities and emergency lighting. At the museum in Priestgate, the old cellars – dating back to the sixteenth century – were brought into use as very effective air-raid shelters. (Gray, David, *Peterborough at War 1939–1945*, David Gray, 2011) .

– November 18th –

1897: On this Monday Herbert Gray, a 23-year-old platelayer working on the Great Eastern Railway line near Manea, was knocked down by the 10.27 express to London, sustaining a severe compound fracture of the thigh. It appears he didn't notice the approach of the express due to fog. He was taken to Peterborough Infirmary, where the injured limb was set. The *Peterborough Citizen* notes that 'thanks to prompt surgical treatment' Gray was improving, but that the nature of the accident would cause 'incapacitation for a protracted period'. It was considered a miracle that the man was not killed.

1939: Starting from their headquarters in the Bishop's Road car park on this Saturday, 150 men of the Peterborough Auxiliary Fire Service paraded in full uniform through the streets of Peterborough. As they paraded, they showed off some of the equipment at their disposal. These included four large trailer pumps, each with eight men to operate them and fourteen smaller, six-man pumps. They also showed off 500- and 1,000-gallon water containers – just in case people wondered where the pumps would get their water. By 24 November, some much-needed gas helmets for use by children under two had arrived and were soon being made available from various centres around the city. (Gray, David, *Peterborough at War 1939–1945*, David Gray, 2011)

1870: The Quarter Sessions of 6 January 1871 saw Robert Newstead indicted for stealing a pony and cart, the property of William Duffill, a Yarmouth fishmonger. At the Bridge Fair in November, they had made arrangements for Newstead to sell Duffill's herrings. The use of a pony and cart was also agreed on a deposit of £5, the pony and cart being kept at the Talbot at Duffill's expense. Duffill claimed that on 19 November, Newstead stole the pony and cart – worth £16 or £18 – and sold them to a Mr Dolby at Wisbech. Thomas Blackman of the Talbot confirmed the taking of the cart. James Treliving confirmed going with Newstead to Wisbech, where the pony and cart were sold for £6 5s; Dolby confirmed this. In his defence, Newstead proved the trade between himself and Duffill had lost money. Having paid the greater amount of the expenses, he considered Duffill was indebted to him about £2 3s 9d. He stated – and proved – that he, not Duffill, advanced the £5 security. Newstead maintained the prosecutor had forfeited any rights, so sold the pony and cart and called upon the jury to consider the evidence carefully. The jury's verdict of 'not guilty' was received with applause and the prisoner was discharged. (*Peterborough Standard*)

1969: For many years, the council had been under pressure to do something about the housing in Eastgate. 'Disgrace' and 'slums' had been words often used to describe the area, so many readers would have been relieved when they read in this day's *Peterborough Evening Telegraph* reports that Eastgate was to be demolished and completely rebuilt by the city council at a cost of at least £2.25 million. It also reported the council promise that it should not cost the ratepayers anything! In all, 200 houses in what it called 'this twilight area' would be demolished and replaced by 300 new homes. The council, it said, hoped to make a start on the project in about eighteen months and have it completed within five years. Less than two months later, the *Peterborough Advertiser* was reporting that a survey regarding this development scheme had revealed that many elderly residents were unwilling to leave their homes. Eighteen months later, the government approved the scheme and the Minister of the Environment confirmed compulsory purchase orders for various properties in the area. On 4 September 1972, the mayor of Peterborough, Mr Roy Topley, finally 'lifted the first sod' of the redevelopment plan.

– NOVEMBER 21ST –

1897: Many ladies of Peterborough would have given careful attention to a small piece in this weekend's *Advertiser*.

FASHIONS IN SLEEVES: we learn from Myra's Journal (of dress and fashion) that the Spring sleeves promise to be very pretty. The new sleeves are tight, with a slight fullness or a small drapery at the shoulder. The best dressmakers try as much as possible to cut drapery and sleeve together, as the effect is always better. Ruffled sleeves remain fashionable, and tucked sleeve is daily becoming more prevalent. There is little doubt that the tucks will play an important part in Spring modes, just as they are doing with Winter evening dresses.

1924: A report in today's *Peterborough Advertiser* lamented the loss of another link with the past industries of the city. It was talking about the imminent demolition of John Gregory's – or 'Gentleman Jack's' – an old wooden nail maker's shop in Albert Place. But this, it must be said, was nostalgia as nails and the like had not been made there since the mid-1880s and 'Jack' himself had not made it to the 1901 census. It made a good little story though. (Liquorice, Mary, *Posh Folk: Notable Personalities (and a Donkey) Associated with Peterborough*, Cambridgeshire Libraries, 1991)

~ NOVEMBER 22ND ~

1897: The *Peterborough Citizen* of 27 November carried the following story which highlights the inherent dangers of the nineteenth-century railways and their passengers:

MUTILATED ON THE RAILWAY – A shocking accident occurred on Monday night (22nd) on the Great Eastern line between March and Black Bank. A labourer named Aaron Hobbs, aged 27, of Black Bank, was travelling by the six o'clock train from his work at March to his home, a dense fog prevailing at the time. Subsequently, the officials at Black Bank found him on the line with both feet terribly mangled, and with a sever contusion over the right eye. According to the unfortunate man's statement, it appears that he was in a confused state at the time, and alleges that he alighted from the train on the wrong side, though he is unable to assign any exact cause for the accident. He does not remember being run over. He was removed to Peterborough Infirmary in the evening, when it was found necessary to amputate both feet. The man was in a state of collapse when found after the accident, but has now rallied, and is progressing very satisfactorily. He was not an employee of the company, but worked as a labourer at March.

~ NOVEMBER 23RD ~

1830: On this Tuesday evening, a drunken Richard Weston entered a hut outside the city and fell asleep on a convenient pile of hay. He woke up the next morning on a suspiciously hard and uncomfortable bed. Beneath the hay, he found a sack containing the dead body of a young woman, believed to be Elizabeth Billings, who had recently died and been buried. She was promptly reburied with due reverence. On Thursday, magistrates heard a man named Ladds state that he had assisted in the removal of many bodies from the graveyard, the 'customers' taking them to London. There was proof that the gravedigger had done well out of the trade, it being reported that he had, at various times, placed considerable sums of money in one of the Peterborough banks, although before he held the office he was in abject poverty. He was dismissed. Later, it was discovered that the raided grave was not that of Elizabeth Billings – she had actually been buried in the wrong plot first time around! This led to the exhumation of the first body, the interment of Elizabeth in her correct plot, and the body of the unknown woman being buried in a new, unmarked, grave. (*Stamford Mercury*)

1884: A fascinating spat between William Connor Magee, the Bishop of Peterborough, and his dean, John Perowne, was reported both in the local press and nationally. The *Birmingham Daily Post* and the *London Daily News* recorded that the restoration work on Peterborough Cathedral had come to a standstill, with workmen being withdrawn. They reported the bishop's disapproval of the Restoration Committee's change to the plans, while the dean stated that little had changed. The *Ipswich Journal*, however, repeated the bishop's antagonism. It also reported the dean's claim that all the committee wanted was to raise the tower 15ft; if it was not done now, it would not be possible to do it later. The dean also sought to vindicate the Restoration Committee's action by stating that the raising of the tower was in the original contract. He said Mr Pearson, the architect, had furnished a design for a noble tower, and proposal to restore the discovered fragments of the Norman lantern and a large portion of the Norman arcading. The bishop, emphatically against the proposal, threatened to withdraw his promised subscription. The dean responded that subscriptions already promised would more than cover the cost of the tower and urged the speedy removal of the misunderstanding.

— November 25th —

1879: Today's council meeting was considering schemes by Speight & Sons of Leeds and Mr Winby of Nottingham for providing Peterborough with a system of tramways. John Addy, the council's consulting engineer, supported the Speight scheme; Councillor Gaches, meanwhile, preferred the Winby plans. Councillor Redhead's motion, seconded by Mr Barrett, agreed that tramways should be allowed in Peterborough. The town clerk read the applications and presented testimonials supporting both schemes. After an extended council discussion on both schemes, the town clerk stated that he had just had a letter handed to him from Mr Speight, who was in an adjoining room. It stated that he was willing to withdraw his scheme and felt the town would be well served by Mr Winby. That annoyed John Addy, who claimed that this withdrawal could not be countenanced without his consent – and that if Speight was withdrawing, he wished to go on with the scheme himself! The mayor argued that it was not Speight's signature on the letter – it had been written for him, at which point the clerk claimed he was being called a liar. Speight confirmed it was his signature and that he had written and signed it of his own free will. Over twenty years were to pass before Peterborough got trams! (*Stamford Mercury*)

— November 26th —

1870: This Saturday's *Peterborough Times* carried a small piece that will mean absolutely nothing to 99.9 per cent or better of Peterborians. It read:

> The Peterborough Jockey – a table has just been published, which shows the performances of the principal winning jockeys in 1870, up to the conclusion of the Shrewsbury meeting. In the list Custance is placed as having 45 mounts, out of which he won 12 races and was second in 8, and third in 8 others. This is better than any other jockey with the same number of mounts. Custance, the celebrated jockey, made his first appearance in the pigskin after his marriage, at Shrewsbury races last week.

Henry Custance was born in Peterborough on 27 February 1842. As a jockey, he won the Cesarewich in 1858 and 1861; the 1,000 Guineas in 1867; the Derby in 1860, 1866 and 1874 and the St Leger, also in 1866. He is one of a very small number to have ridden the winner of the Derby and the St Leger in the same year. He retired from riding at the end of the 1879 season, when he was no longer able to beat 8 stone 10lbs and became proprietor of the George Inn in Oakham. He died in 1908. (jockeypedia. co.uk)

1926: The fracture of the gas main in Westwood Street had a fatal sequel this weekend. On this Saturday Thomas Ladds, the licensee of the Three Tuns in Westwood Street, noticed a strong smell of gas apparently coming from the street. During the morning, his customers complained of the odour. One came over faint in the taproom and was taken home in Ladds' car. At evening opening, he again noticed a strong smell of gas. During the evening his assistant Mr Sam Bray and the maid were both taken ill, and a customer, Mr William Ball, was so overcome by the fumes that he fell down in the yard and cut his head. Still nothing was done about it. On Sunday morning, corporation employee Julius Kebball came on duty. About two hours later, he heard people knocking at a door; they were concerned about the occupant, as they could get no reply. Kebball smashed the door open with a pickaxe and found the elderly lady lying dead on her chair-bed. Witnesses at Monday's inquest reported noticing the smell for a fortnight. Dr H. Clapham said indications were quite consistent with death from coal gas poisoning and the jury returned a verdict of 'accidental death due to gas poisoning'. (*Stamford Mercury*)

1873: The *Northamptonshire Mercury* of this date reported the erection in the nave of Peterborough, near the organ screen, of an extremely handsome pulpit. It was said that it would cost £700 and that it was being raised to the memory of the late John James D.D., formally a canon of the cathedral, by the deceased gentleman's family. It is certainly a magnificent structure, a great ornament to the interior of the sacred edifice, and would supply a want long felt at the Sunday evening services. The materials of which the pulpit is built are red Mansfield stone and Devonshire and Greek green marble. The Revd James was a prolific writer on the many strands of Christian belief and worship. His 1842 work on *The Mother's Help Towards Instructing Her Children in the Excellences of the Catechism, and of the Services Appointed by the Church of England for the More Special Occasions which Mark Christian Life* and his 1853 book *A harmonized summary of the Four Gospels, comprising every chapter and verse therein* are typical of his ability to cover complex subjects in a way that the families of the time could understand and use.

— November 29th —

1539: On this day the Benedictine monastery of St Peter bowed to the will of King Henry VIII and was formally no more. However, the Peterborough abbey church – and its last abbot, John Chambers – can claim to be unique in the whole countrywide dissolution of the monastic communities of these islands. The magnificent building remains to impress visitors to this day, as do some other abbey churches – it is one of just six new bishoprics centred on monastic land and buildings following the Dissolution (Oxford, Gloucester, Chester, Bristol and Westminster are the others). Following the Dissolution, Abbot John Chambers became Warden of the College of Peterborough before, in 1541, he was consecrated as the first Bishop of the See of Peterborough – the only abbot to make such a transition to bishop in the whole country. (Tebbs, H.F., *Peterborough*, Oleander Press, 1979)

1941: On 10 May Mr Frank Kingston, his wife and their daughter Edna had been injured when a bomb demolished their cottage in Cross Street. Neither he nor Edna had ever really recovered from the incident; Edna had spent a number of months in hospital afterwards. Almost immediately after her release, her father was admitted to hospital. Edna died on 14 November, and her father on 26 November. He was buried at Gedney Hill on this day. (Tebbs, H.F., *Peterborough*, Oleander Press, 1979)

– November 30th –

1872: The *Peterborough & Huntingdon Standard* commented on one aspect of the 'problem with servants'. Complaints, it said, were frequently made about the short time domestic servants were now staying in one place, and of the inconvenience of the frequent changes which mistresses were compelled to make in their households. It commented that its readers would not be surprised to learn that girls would become unsettled in their situations when they saw the promises that were now held out to them. The paper quoted a note addressed simply to 'the domestic' from the Registry Office, All Saints Street, Stamford which had been delivered on the previous Sunday to the house of a lady not many miles from Peterborough. It read: 'I take the liberty to inform you that if you require a situation as general servant or cook, I am in want of several immediately, and will obtain one for you if you will call, or forward by post my fee, which is 14 stamps.' The *Standard* hoped that when missives of this description were received by servants they would, as in this case, hand them promptly to their mistress. Of course – they may not do that.

— December 1st —

1814: The 'Squeaky' Wass story continues, as on this date, he and James Penniston almost escaped from Peterborough gaol. They are reported to have made large excavations in the walls of their cells. The news report paints the picture: 'It may appear incredible, but true it is that they had taken down upwards of two cartloads of stone and mortar during the night. Guards, both on the outside and inside the prison, with loaded firearms are now placed, and every possible precaution has been adopted to keep the prisoners secure.' In early January 1815 they made another escape attempt, and this time they were successful. They were 'seen' at the Dog & Doublet and in Wisbech, where one of them – Wass it was supposed – was disguised in women's apparel. His squeaky voice would help there. The final assumption was that they had headed to the Norfolk coast and could now be anywhere! (*Drakard's Stamford News*)

1875: The National Municipal Accounts were published today for the year ending August 1874. Only two of the 256 municipal boroughs are omitted from the list: London, which claimed exemption from making a return under the Act, and Peterborough, which had not been incorporated as a municipal borough a sufficient time to render any account. (*Birmingham Daily Post*)

‒ December 2nd ‒

1905: In 1891, Peterborough had finally adopted the 1850 Public Libraries Act and, in 1892, set up a library in the Fitzwilliam Hall in Park Road. By 1900, that library had outgrown its space. An approach made to the Andrew Carnegie Foundation for funding to build a new one was successful, with a sum of £6,000 for the new resource being agreed. The new Central Library opened for business on this Saturday (*People of Peterborough*, Peterborough Museum Publications, 2009)

‒‒‒

1929: An inquest held on this Monday concerned the death of 55-year-old George Bateman, a fitter of Balham Road, Peterborough. George had died the previous Saturday as a result of scalds received whilst at work at the Central Sugar Factory on the Thursday. Evidence presented stated that he was engaged at the time in making a connection to a pump which led to an existing 'juice line' that carried a hot sugar solution. The loosening of the bolts on the vertical pipe caused hot juice to escape. It appears that it was not unusual for small quantities to escape, but in this instance 'too great a volume' escaped with the result that George Bateman was extensively scalded. A verdict of accidental death was returned. (*Stamford Mercury*)

⁓ December 3rd ⁓

1926: Under the headline 'Farm Insurance – Peterborough Farmers Pleased', the 10 December issue of the *Stamford Mercury* harked back to the meeting of the Executive Committee of the Peterborough and District County Branch of the National Farmers' Union the previous week. Whilst for city dwellers the story may have appeared to be trivial, for the agricultural farmers and their employees, it had significant reassurances. The union members were reminded that they came within the provision of the Milk and Dairies Order if they only sold milk to farm workers and their families – a perk that workers enjoyed – and also if they produced butter. The chairman, Mr F.W. Griffin, said that they would all be pleased at the announcement of the government, in which it was definitely decided not to adopt the recommendations of the majority report of the Interdepartmental Committees on agricultural unemployment insurance. The opinion of the meeting was expressed that agriculture had more than enough difficulties thrown upon it in recent times, and that the arrangements made within the industry to deal with slack periods worked so satisfactorily that it would not have been advantageous to have imposed yet another burden on the employers and workers.

— DECEMBER 4TH —

1895: By the end of the nineteenth century, Peterborough city had over 100 different places where one could buy and drink alcohol; walking round what is now Cathedral Square offered you the choice of ten or more such places. This day's *Peterborough Advertiser* newspaper gave significant space to reporting on a sequence of meetings organised by the Women's Total Abstinence Union. They had begun on Tuesday evening at the Temperance Hall on the Lincoln Road, when Revd Thomas Barrass had presided over a good attendance that had come to listen to Mr F. Hinde, barrister at law, give an address on 'The Genius of Teetotalism'. He claimed that the great influence of drink on the present-day society could be attributed to much of the poverty and crime extant to the intemperance which prevailed. Citing statistics, and quoting from testimonies of several eminent men 'past and present', he set out to prove that achieving the greatest mental capacity was associated with the practice of total abstinence. In summing up, he claimed that 'a moderate drinker was a vast improvement on a drunkard, but a teetotaller was a great deal better than even a moderate drinker, physically and morally.' (*Peterborough Advertiser*)

~ December 5th ~

1585: On this day, at the age of 89, Robert Scarlett – the famous gravedigger of Peterborough – married Maud Gosling, following the death of his first wife. (*People of Peterborough*, Peterborough Museum Publications, 2009)

———

1884: The infirmary fire of 9 May 1884 had prompted a change in the attitude to firefighting in the city. The council reorganised the city brigade and a number of the prominent businessmen of the city set about forming a supporting brigade. In a meeting at the Angel in Narrow Bridge Street, they formed the Peterborough Volunteer Fire Brigade. The city by this time had a reasonably reliable piped water supply. Mr J.C. Gill was the waterworks engineer and the council asked him to provide advice and to recommend new rules for the firefighters. On this day, just short of seven months after the infirmary fire, Gill took over as Honorary Captain of a fire brigade consisting of a chief engineer, a superintendent, a captain, a lieutenant, the corporation water-turners, the borough police and ten firemen. The volunteers' structure comprised three trustees, a captain, two lieutenants and twelve firemen. The city was now equipped and ready to face any fire hazard. (Tebbs, H.F., *Peterborough*, Oleander Press, 1979)

~ DECEMBER 6TH ~

1852: At this time, general elections were still a public event. Only one man in seven across the country had the vote and that was cast in public; furthermore, the majority of the men who had a vote were often told or bribed as to whom to vote for. In Peterborough, this was the Fitzwilliams' candidate, and not voting as instructed could cost a man and family their home and jobs. For this election George Hammond Whalley – the Fitzwilliams' opposition – employed some 500 men to 'arrange' voter's choice of candidate. Based in a number of city-centre beer shops, they were successful in their 'suggestions' and Whalley won a seat in parliament. He was later unseated following a petition for illegal conduct. At the election of 25 June 1853, there was a similar success and disqualification. It was not until 30 April 1859 that Whalley finally succeeded in winning a place in parliament. (Review of 1900, *Peterborough Advertiser*)

1914: Today men from the 5th Essex Regiment, the East Anglians, the Norfolk & Suffolk Army Service Corps, the Norfolk Regiment and the East Anglian Field Ambulance attended a church service in St John's. With over 3,000 troops in winter training quarters locally, many people commented that Peterborough had become a 'city of khaki'. (Bull, J & V., Perry, S. and Sturgess, R., *Peterborough – a third portrait in old picture postcards*, S.B. Publications, 1990)

~ December 7th ~

1870: The Peterborough Quarter Sessions of the late nineteenth century provide interesting insights into the day-to-day life and attitudes of people in the city. In the sessions of 6 January 1871, Edward Perrin had stood accused of stealing a bread tin and a strainer, the property of his employer Mr John Thurstun, ironmonger, of No. 9 Narrow Street, on 7 December 1870. Perrin pleaded not guilty of the offence, but Thurstun had found a bread bin secreted in his workshop. Having advised the police of his find, he marked the tin and left it where it had been found. These items were subsequently found as having been sold by the accused, but not accounted for. For the defence, Thos Lamplugh, Ed Spriggs and Thos Baker, workmen also in the employ of Mr Thurstun, stated that it was understood they might make articles for sale in their own right. The chairman, in summing up, remarked that the system that had originated in Mr Thurstun's shop could not be too severely reprobated. They, however, had to decide whether the prisoner had acted feloniously or under a mistaken right. The jury returned a verdict of 'not guilty' and the prisoner was discharged. (*Peterborough Standard*)

~ DECEMBER 8TH ~

1828: The *Huntingdon, Bedford and Peterborough Gazette* of Saturday 13 December carried a letter recording an incident on this day. It reads:

> Sir: Hull, the coachman, and Dyer, the guard, of the Lincoln Mail through Peterborough, will state the particulars to the authorities and officers of that city, of an accident which nearly occurred to them and the passengers travelling by the down Mail this morning in a street called Westgate, in consequence of some rubbish and mortar left in the public thoroughfare. If the inhabitants will not light their town with the best light that can be had, they ought not to endanger the lives of travellers suffering nuisances to remain in the public streets. I am, Sir, Yours etc. 'One of the Passengers'. Sleaford, Monday December 8th 1828.

One week later, the newspaper reported a similar incident with the Boston 'Perseverance' coach when some manure being barrowed out in Narrow Street in the night caused the horses to be 'thrown down'. They could not be extricated without 'cutting and doing much damage to the harness'. It was providential that the coach was not overturned. The newspaper condemned the Commissioners of Pavements for not lighting the town with gas as many other towns had done.

~ DECEMBER 9TH ~

1916: Edith Cavell spent only a short part of her life here in Peterborough – working in a pupil/teacher capacity at Miss Gibson's school in Laurel Court. It was there that she learned and mastered the French language that proved so useful to her in Belgium. She was not forgotten in Peterborough, and was rapidly accepted as a Peterborian following her death. It was on this day in 1916 that an Irish blue marble plaque in her memory was unveiled by Dean Page in Peterborough Cathedral. This is widely believed to be the first commemoration stone/plaque in the country dedicated to her. It reads:

> Right dear in the sight of the Lord is the death of His Saints. In thankful remembrance of the Christian example of Edith Louisa Cavell who devoted her life to nursing the sick and for helping Belgian French and British soldiers to escape was on October 12th 1915 put to death by the Germans at Brussels where she had nursed their wounded this Tablet was placed here by the Teachers Pupils and Friends of her old School in Laurel Court.

As well as this plaque, Edith is remembered in the name of Peterborough's modern hospital complex and a city-centre car park. (Liquorice, Mary, *Posh Folk: Notable Personalities (and a Donkey) Associated with Peterborough*, Cambridgeshire Libraries, 1991; People of Peterborough, Peterborough Museum Publications, 2009)

~ December 10th ~

1916: It was on this day that William Cliffe – at 82 the oldest person ever to be elected Mayor of Peterborough when he took office in 1910 – passed away aged 88 years. The highlight of his year in office was probably when, on 11 May 1910, he proclaimed King George V's accession to the throne of Britain. In many ways he was a classic Peterborian businessman. Starting his working life as a groom, he moved on to being a porter and warehouse man at Griffin's Ironmongers in Narrow Street. His next move was to become foreman for Joseph Thompson in his general store next to the Bull in Westgate. In 1854, he left Peterborough to open his own general store in the Deepings. He didn't stay long because in 1860, together with a partner, he bought out his old boss in Westgate. Not long after, he moved across the road, where his general store was two individual shops with a large yard between them. He stayed totally involved with his business until his death. The next time you walk through the Westgate end of the Westgate Arcade, just pause and think of William Cliffe – Peterborough's oldest mayor and dedicated shopkeeper. (Mellows, W.I., 'Peterborough's Municipal Jubilee', *Peterborough Standard*, 1924)

~ DECEMBER 11TH ~

1895: The annual Christmas Fat Stock Show was held at the cattle market on this Wednesday. Around £70 in cash prizes were available, plus various special cups and trophies. Whilst there were just 'an average number of entries', with cattle forming the main feature, the show was considered to compare favourably with any previous exhibition. What really counted was the quality of the animals exhibited – and this was considered 'exceptionally fine'. The battle for the championship in the cattle category was recorded as very close, with the rosette being awarded to Mr T. Nixon of Abbots Ripton. Among the other trophies on offer was one for the 'Best pair of Steers' – excluding the champion steer. This was a cup offered by Mr John Smith of Farcet. Guess who won – Mr John Smith of Park House, Farcet! Not only did he get his own cup back but he received the £5 prize, awarded by the show organisers. (*Lincoln, Rutland and Stamford Mercury*)

1915: With the rate of military recruitment in Peterborough almost at a standstill, the Peterborough Parliamentary Recruiting Committee sent a letter to each unmarried, eligible man in the city who had not put his name down in early recruitment drives. It stated that after 11 December, they would 'find themselves in a very undesirable position'! (Gray, David, *Peterborough at War 1914–1918*, David Gray, 2014)

— DECEMBER 12TH —

1920: Joseph Batten was a founding partner in solicitors 'Batten and Whitsed' and Mayor of Peterborough in 1907. His son, also Joseph, had entered the practice in 1909, articled to his father. At the declaration of war in 1914, the young Joseph was within a few months of obtaining his qualification as a practising solicitor. He was a Territorial officer in the Bedfordshire Regiment and received the one-word telegram, ' MOBILISE', on 4 August 1914. From that time onwards, he performed special duties across Britain before, in April 1918, he went to France as a senior captain and company commander. 'Going over the top' on 27 September, he was hit and died almost instantaneously. When the sad news reached Peterborough the mayor, rising before the commencement of Council business, said he was sure members would desire him, in their name, to refer to the death of Captain Keith Batten, eldest son of their colleague, Alderman Batten, and to express their deep sympathy and condolence in his great loss, and sorrow, his son having fallen in the great conflict now raging. The members of the council sorrowfully rose to signify their assent. On this day two years later, Joseph Sr passed away, aged just 62. (Mayors of Peterborough; huntscycles.co.uk)

– December 13th –

1872: The bridge over the Nene had been in use – and repaired many times – since Abbot Godfrey had first built it in 1308. Now, as Peterborough grew, it was time for a more substantial one to take its place. After many discussions and predictable delays, a contract was placed with Handyside & Co. of Derby for a new bridge at the cost of £5,426. It was on this Friday that the new iron bridge was opened for traffic – but even the opening did not go smoothly. 'On reaching the foot of the bridge the road was found to be blocked and the approaches occupied by a mob. The consequence was that the procession was disorganised and broke up. Very few heard Mr Ward Hunt declare the bridge open.' It could, in fact, be said that the bridge was opened by a rag and bone merchant, because he and his wagon were actually the first to cross the bridge! The bridge was now safe to cross, but on the south side was the Great Eastern Railway crossing, and in the twentieth century, that would pose problems. These issues would not get addressed and resolved until the 1930s. (Mitchell, Neil, *The Streets of Peterborough*, Neil Mitchell, 2007; Tebbs, H.F., *Peterborough*, Oleander Press, 1979)

~ December 14th ~

1690: In Volume 11 of the House of Commons and Command Parliamentary Papers 1831, it is recorded that every year, on this date, Dr Thomas White, Bishop of Peterborough, by will dated in 1690, gave to the poor of the parish of Peterborough £240 which he directed to be laid out in land; and he allotted £10 a year of the produce thereof to the poor of the parish, and the surplusage (sic), whatever it should be, to the rector, vicar or incumbent, of the parish, as a reward for his pains in the distribution of the £10 to the poor, which he appointed should be made by him in the presence of the churchwardens and overseers of the poor, in the church porch, on the 14th December yearly, to 20 poor families or persons, by equal shares, reckoning husband and wife for one, who should, before receipt, distinctly repeat the Lord's Prayer, Apostle's Creed, and the Ten Commandments; and he desired, that whatever persons should be relieved by his charity, might be continued still in the poor roll, and receive the same allowance from the parish as they did before. You may recall that we came across Bishop White in very different circumstances on June 8th above. (*Herapath's Journal* reported in the *Chelmsford Chronicle*)

– DECEMBER 15TH –

1700: In this year, John Sparkes gave £50 to be laid out in lands, the product thereof to be yearly given by the minister and some of the better sort of inhabitants of the parish of Peterborough, to the poor not receiving alms of the parish in sums of 2s 6d a piece. At the same time Elizabeth Sparkes bequeathed the same sum – that to be equally divided amongst such 20 poor widows of Peterborough not receiving collection, as the minister and church wardens there for the time being should direct. (Robinson, Eric and Powell, David (eds), *John Clare by Himself*, Fyfield Books, 2002)

———

1904: The annual Peterborough Christmas Fat Stock Show was held in the Cattle Market off the New Road in this week. Reports describe a very wet day – all day – but, in the true spirit of things, the show went on as usual. However, the show was not as large as previously, which was disappointing. The upside was that prices were consequently better than normal. Beef prices were singled out as being particularly good and contrasting very favourably with the low prices achieved just a few weeks previous. The champion bullock weighed in at 17.5cwt and fetched the very attractive price of £38 10s. (*Northampton Mercury*)

– DECEMBER 16TH –

1872: The Peterborough Union today published a notice advising interested parties that 'the Guardians of the Poor at this Union would, at their meeting to be held on 28th December, be prepared to receive tenders for supplying good Elm coffins for the workhouse for twelve months commencing 1st January 1873'. The coffins were to be delivered free of charge to various parishes and places within the union, and at such times as the guardians or their receiving officers may order in writing. There then followed a long list of these areas. Each coffin was to be well pitched inside and of good workmanship as well as initialled with the names and ages of the deceased. The tenderers were to specify a separate price according to the item supplied. There were three sizes for children: those under 2, those under 5 and those under 10. These coffins were to be made of ³⁄₄in board. Also supplied were coffins for persons under 16 and for persons aged 16 and upwards. These were to be constructed in 1in boarding. All tenders were required to be sealed and presented to the boardroom before 10 a.m. on Saturday 28 December. Not much time to do a good quote! (*Peterborough Standard*)

– December 17th –

1898: On this day, Paten and Co. of No. 19 Long Causeway, and also Nos 32 and 34 Broad Bridge Street, took a full front-page advertisement in the *Peterborough Advertiser* and *South Midland Times* listing beers, wines and spirits that were now available from them as the successors to Nichols & Co. – the company founded by Alderman Nichols, three times mayor of Peterborough. That acquisition also included the Bull and Dolphin pub at No. 94 Broad Bridge Street. This was the beginning of a company that over the following 100 years would be a major player in hotels and beers, wines and spirits across East Anglia and the East Midlands. (Padley, Priscilla, *Paten's Centenary – history of Paten & Co. Ltd 1898–1998*, Paton & Co, 2000)

1910: Opening on this day was the Broadway Electric Theatre, Peterborough's first purpose-built cinema, with seating for 700 people. It closed during 1912, while alterations were being made, and reopened in 1913 as the Broadway Kinema with 1,000 seats. It showed its first talkie in September 1929, when the Movietone Follies headlined. In November 1961, the Kinema became the Gaumont and, two years later, hosted the final movies to be shown at the venue – *It's All Happening* and *Watch It, Sailor!* After a further two decades as a bingo hall, the old theatre building was demolished in late 1983. (Bull, J. and V., *Peterborough – a portrait in old picture postcards*, S.B. Publications, 1988)

~ December 18th ~

1855: On this Tuesday, Charles Dickens visited Peterborough to do one of his famous public readings. In September he had written to Mrs Watson of Rockingham Castle – a very good friend who he visited whenever he was able – telling her 'I have appointed to read at Peterborough on Tuesday 18th December. I have told the Dean that I cannot accept his hospitality and that I am going with Mr Wells to the inn, therefore I shall be absolutely at your disposal.' In January 1856 he wrote again to the family, describing an incident at Peterborough railway station. There is some doubt as to the actual date of this stop, but the message was crystal clear:

> At two or three o'clock in the morning I stopped at Peterborough again and thought of you all disconsolately. The lady in the refreshment room was very hard on me, harder even than those fair enslavers usually are. She gave me a cup of tea, as if I were a hyena and she my cruel keeper with a strong dislike to me. I mingled my tears with it, and had a petrified bun of enormous antiquity in miserable meekness.

(Russell, John, *Fair Spot and Goodly – Visitors' impressions of Peterborough*, Peterborough Arts Council, 1984)

~ December 19th ~

1866: The last third of the nineteenth century was a time of major change in Peterborough. New businesses were developing – and beer, in its many forms, was still a drink of choice. 'Supper to Workpeople': this was the heading in the *Cambridge Independent Press* of Saturday 22 December. It reported:

> Mr Henry Nicholson, maltster of New-road, gave a supper to the workmen employed in the erection of his premises on the New-road on Wednesday evening last, the repast being provided by Mr House, of the Vine Hotel, Church-street. Seventy sat down, Mr Nicholson in the chair. The health of Mr Nicholson was drunk with three cheers. Mr Nicholson responded and proposed the health of the visitors, coupled with the name of Mr Leeds who, he remarked, had decorated the room with evergreens. Mr Leeds responded, and proposed Mrs Nicholson's health, which was drunk with much enthusiasm. Mr Nicholson acknowledged the compliment, and concluded by calling upon the Rev. W Hill to address a few seasonal words to them. The rev. gentleman made a very appropriate speech and concluded by invoking God's blessing on the building and all present. The malting – standing on an acre of ground - is the largest building of the sort within many miles of Peterborough.

~ December 20th ~

1576: On this day, Bishop Scambler surrendered a significant portion of the bishopric's revenue-producing estates and all his judicial rights to Queen Elizabeth I, making the Bishopric of Peterborough the poorest in the kingdom. She passed them to William Cecil, Lord Burghley, making him Lord Paramount of the Liberty of Peterborough. That authority and the benefits remain with Cecil's direct bloodline to this day. (Carnell, Geoffrey, *The Bishops of Peterborough*, RJL Smith & Associates, 1993; Gunton; Tebbs, H.F., *Peterborough*, Oleander Press, 1979)

1856: To the Editor of the *Peterborough Advertiser*:

Sir, - May I suggest through the medium of your paper that an effort be made to obtain an additional day's holiday to our usual one on Christmas day. Our employers have kindly granted it on former occasions, and I think they only require to be solicited to again comply! If so, many of those confined in places of business will be enabled to visit their friends, who would be prevented from so doing by the distance, if only one day is theirs. And I would venture to add that such a favour will not be thrown away upon those it would benefit. Many tradesmen have already expressed their willingness to forward the movement if started. Trusting that it will be taken up in the right quarter and with a good spirit, I remain, Sir, ONE WHO STANDS BEHIND A COUNTER.

- December 21st -

1837: St Thomas has long been considered the patron saint of the elderly. Today was traditionally the day when old people of the parish were allowed to go round to their fellow parishioners to ask for food or money. Many will remember the pre-Christmas rhyme 'Christmas is coming, the geese are getting fat, please spare a penny for an old man's hat. If you haven't got a penny, a ha'penny will do; If you haven't got a ha'penny, well God bless you.' This was called 'Going Thomasing'. The *Northamptonshire Mercury* reports this tradition being kept alive in 1827: 'This being Saint Thomas's Day the Earl Fitzwilliam, with his usual consideration, caused upwards of 500 stones of beef to be distributed among the poor of his neighbourhood in Christmas week; and on St Thomas's Day his lordship distributed bread to 1,800 poor persons.'

1858: William Prockter Stanley died on this day. In his will, he left the Queen Street Stanley Iron Works in the trusteeship of his brother-in-law George Maples and John Warren. They leased the property to Thomas Amies and William Barford. In March 1865, one Thomas Perkins became part of the company in a deed of co-partnership. The seeds of what would become Perkins Engineering were thus sown. (Hillier, Richard, *Northamptonshire Past & Present Vol. VI*, Northamptonshire Record Society, 1983)

1712: In the Stanground Parish records for today's date is the cryptic entry: 'Joseph Jenning stole Mrs Margaret Bellamy. At night.' Was it a theft or did they elope? At this time 'Mrs' did not necessarily mean a married lady – it could be short for 'mistress', an unmarried woman of good family. While it was not legal to sell your wife, such transactions often happened. If the lover could not afford the purchase price, then he could steal her – often with the tacit agreement of the husband! On 23 December 1712, a Joseph Jenning married a Margaret Bellamy at Great Gidding. Later there appears a Joseph Jennings with a wife named Margaret living in 'Farcett'. They have children baptised between 1714 and 1722. I wonder ... (Maureen Nicholls; Peterborough Family History Society)

1839: 'The Charter' reports on this day that in just ten years, three respectable natives of Peterborough have taken conspicuous situations attracting the notice of their own townsmen and the public generally. Eminent mechanic Francis Ruddle came to London to put a new organ case in Westminster Abbey; Sir Chapman Marshall had been elected to become the Lord Mayor of London; and Mr Robert West arrived from Peterborough to execute the duties of his office on Lord Mayor's day, being regularly appointed hairdresser to the Lord Mayor of London! (The Charter)

~ DECEMBER 23RD ~

1862: A cautionary tale appears in the *Northampton Mercury* of this date:

Caution to railway travellers – an extraordinary case of robbery on the Great Northern Railway has just been brought to our notice. A lady, residing in the neighbourhood of Stamford, left London by the 5 o'clock express on Tuesday evening. Her fellow passengers, in a second class carriage, were a well-dressed man and woman, whom she took to be a newly married couple. They were very polite in their demeanour; and on the journey the man offered the lady a copy of an illustrated newspaper, which he produced from a travelling bag. An overpowering odour proceeded from the paper on its being opened, and the lady immediately became unconscious, in which state she remained until the arrival of the train at Peterborough, where she had to change carriages. Directly after the express had left the station on its northward journey, she discovered, on being applied to for her railway ticket, that she had been robbed, not only of that but of her purse and its contents. On entering the carriage she had placed the ticket in her purse in the presence of her fellow passengers. The lady's idea was that the newspaper had been saturated with chloroform, the scent of which was disguised with lavender.

~ DECEMBER 24TH ~

1673: The Dean and Chapter accounts record a new deal bookcase being built for the library. Material and labour cost £2 0s 2d. Bringing Mr Halle's books from Leicester and Mr Gunton's from Lincoln along with books from Mr Wingfield the Earl of Westmorland, Mr Gray and Lord Fitzwilliam cost another 6s 10d. With a craftsman typically earning 5s a week, this expenditure of almost 50s on just one bookcase shows just how much a library was valued in the cathedral. (Mellows, W.T. and Gifford, Daphne H., *Elizabethan Peterborough*, Northampton Record Society, 1956)

1847: Edmund Artis – an archaeologist and geologist well known and highly regarded in Peterborough and the Nene Valley – passed away in Doncaster. He had discovered and excavated the extensive Roman remains at Castor – something that still ranks among the most illuminating of such discoveries. What is far less well known is his support for John Clare, the Helpston Poet. It was Edmund that persuaded John to allow him to take a cast of his face so that he could make a plaster bust of the poet. John was given the completed bust, which unfortunately fell apart a couple of years later! In his journal of 1 October 1824, John noted that Edmund Artis was to be one of the executors of his will. (*Durobrivae – a review of Nene Valley Archaeology Vol. 6, 1978 and Vol. 9, 1984*)

~ DECEMBER 25TH ~

1901: On this Christmas Day, the occupants of the Peterborough Workhouse had a special – or maybe unusual – treat. They were all served beer with their Christmas meal. To the outside world this would not be anything unusual – beer was still the safest drink for many and the norm for even more. It was under the headline 'BEER FOR PETERBOROUGH INMATES' that the world at large was 'advised' of this treat. The Peterborough Board of Guardians, by the casting vote of the chairman, had decided to allow the inmates of the workhouse to have beer with their Christmas dinner. The National United Temperance Council had asked that the use of beer might be discontinued, on the grounds that it was due to excessive drinking that many inmates found themselves obliged to come on the rates. After a detailed discussion, a proposition was moved that the beer be discontinued, various members suggesting that instead of beers there should be extra allowances of tobacco, milk or cocoas. On a division, in which the chairman exercised his vote, the result was a tie – 17 votes each way. Amid laughter, the chairman said, 'the beer is allowed'. I wonder if they noticed that the chairman had actually voted twice. Happy Christmas, inmates. (*Northampton Evening Post*)

~ DECEMBER 26TH ~

1939: On this, the first Christmas period of the Second World War, people appear to have decided to make the most of what might be the last one they'd celebrate for some time to come. The Posh had lost 2–1 away to Boston in their Christmas Day Midland League match. For this return Boxing Day match, poor weather was blamed for only 1,765 supporters turning out to watch Peterborough get their revenge with a 3–1 victory. That poor weather, though, didn't dampen the joy of Lance Corporal R.W. Caswell, of the staff of Barclays Bank Church Street branch, and Miss Mary Keene, who got married at All Saints church on this Boxing Day. This was just one of some forty weddings in the city and close vicinity over the Christmas period. At least ten of the bridegrooms were in service uniform for their ceremony. Over the whole Christmas period, the Embassy Theatre reported that it had been packed at both performances, while the Empire claimed a 'full house' three times. Between 18 December and Christmas Day, 615,000 postal packages had been handled by Peterborough post office – up 15,000 on 1938. There were also 50,000 more letters handled. Peterborough was making the most of this 'last hurrah' before wartime stress took hold. (Gray, David, *Peterborough at War 1939–1945*, David Gray, 2011)

1856: 'Etiquette for evening parties':

> Punctuality is the soul of evening parties. Be careful, therefore, always to arrive to a moment at the time you are invited for. If the hour be not specified, as is occasionally the case, it is considered good breeding to call the day before and make inquiry of the servant. Your conduct in the supper-room must depend on circumstances. If it is to be a half-stand-up affair, ladies' business first and gentlemen's pleasure afterwards, you will be expected during the first part to do duty of course as an amateur waiter; when, unless you practice well beforehand, you will no doubt contrive to cover yourself with jelly and confusion. But if the repast be a sit-down-all-together one, you may eat and drink in comfort, if you only take care not to have a lady next you; otherwise, of course you'll have to minister to her wants instead of satisfying your own. In taking your departure, don't forget to make an offer of your thanks for the pleasant evening you have spent; and if you then proceed to shake hands all round with such of the guests as still remain, you will do much to confirm the favourable impression which your previous behaviour will doubtless have produced.

(*Peterborough Advertiser*)

– DECEMBER 28TH –

1626: Following his arrest, blacksmith John Walton, late of Castor, made the following confession:

> … he came to the house of Vincent Finamore of Castor about ten of the clock in the day time upon this day and, seeing the door open in the servants lodging, he went in and searching the pocket of a pair of breeches that lay upon a bed he thence took a purse and 10*d* in money in the purse which was the goods of Robert Bate servant to Vincent Finamore and saith he took it of necessity to buy bread for him, his brothers and sisters.

(*Peterborough's Past*, Peterborough Museum Society, 1983)

———

1940: On this Saturday, the *Peterborough Standard* held a party at the Salvation Army Citadel for children of men from Peterborough who were away serving in the armed forces. Their 400 'guests' between the ages of 5 and 14 had what was described as 'rollicking entertainment' before they sat down to a 'grand tea'. With crockery in short supply, and broken pieces hard to replace, all children were asked to bring their own cups or mugs. After all was done, every child received a present from Father Christmas, who appeared to have arrived safe and sound, despite the conflict all around. (Gray, David, *Peterborough at War 1939–1945*, David Gray, 2011)

~ DECEMBER 29TH ~

1866: Today's *Cambridge Independent Press* praises Peterborough's annual show of meat at this festive season. It continues:

> ... for some years past the show as to quality, and indeed quantity, proportionate to the size of the town, has been considered second to none in the country, and the butchers appear to be determined to vie with each other in retaining for the city its good name in this respect. Never has been better meat seen in Peterborough than that sold last week; fatter meat there may have been, but certainly not more useful. In former years we have noticed that much of the beef was too fat to be eaten and have wondered what became of all the fat, and how it could pay the butcher to retail it; but this year no one need wonder at the large quantity of meat sold when we look at the quality. Poultry appeared to be plentiful, both in the shops and in market, and good prices were obtained. The confectioners' and grocers' show of their respective edibles was very good, and for the most part tastefully arranged; but the shop windows generally were not so well dressed for the season as we have seen in other years.

1912: Dealer Alfred Thompson of Fletton pleaded 'not guilty' today for receiving forty-one bags and six sacks, the property of Farrow & Co., well knowing them to have been stolen. George Clark of New Fletton, previously convicted for the theft of the bags, said the prisoner had asked him if he could get some and he took several lots, for which the prisoner paid him at the rate of 1s 3d per dozen. John Graham, works manager for Farrow & Co., identified the sacks and said that 1s 3d was no price at all for the sacks. Harold Carter, manager to Cliff & Co., marine store dealers in Peterborough, gave details of the purchase of several lots of bags from the prisoner at 5s a dozen. He claimed that the prisoner told him that he had got them from a friend in the coconut trade in London. Lydia Clark, wife of George Clark, said she heard the prisoner ask her husband if he had captured anything. PC Varley gave evidence of arrest, with the prisoner, on oath, saying he knew nothing about the sacks. He had never bought any from Clark and he had never sold any to Carter. Thompson was found guilty and sentenced to three months' hard labour. (*Stamford Mercury*)

― December 31st ―

1889: While reconstructing a coal cellar at the end of the cathedral's south transept, workmen came across the carved cap of a Barnack stone pillar of the decorated period. The design represented the cowled head of a monk with his neck resting on the belly of a dragon, the repulsive head of which, with its prominent fangs, turned toward the head of the monk, the lips touching the left ear. On the right side, the twisted tail of the body is seen. The dragon is no doubt intended to represent the devil, whispering in the ear of the cowled inhabitant of the cloister. Unfortunately, the monk's face was damaged by the workman's pick before it was ascertained that the stone had any carvings upon it. (*Western Daily Press*)

1927: By conceding a single goal, Peterborough United lost two valuable Southern League points on this day, the defeat lowering them to the unlucky 13th position. The experiment of including Beck and Saunders in the forward line was a failure. Though United were as good as the victors in midfield exchanges, the attack lacked forcefulness in front of goal. The deputies tried hard, but just did not fit into the scheme of things. Millwall paid Peterborough the compliment of fielding a strong side, fresh from the hot seawater bath treatment at Southend. (*Peterborough & Huntingdon Standard*)